the Death of Economics

PAUL ORMEROD

JOHN WILEY & SONS, INC.

New York • Chichester • Weinheim • Brisbane • Singapore • Toronto

Library of Congress Cataloging-in-Publication Data:
Ormerod, Paul
    The death of economics / Paul Ormerod.
      p. cm.
    Includes bibliographical references and index.
    ISBN 0-471-18000-9 (paper)
      1. Economics—History—20th century. I. Title.
  HB75.076 1997
330'.09—dc21   97-6434

Contents

List of Figures

Preface to the North American Edition

This book is mainly addressed to members of the general public. Economics has assumed a dominant position in the political life of the West, and orthodox economic theory has exercised great influence on the conduct of public policy over the past ten to fifteen years.

Even to the intelligent member of the public, economics is often intimidating. Its practitioners pronounce with great confidence in the media, and have erected around the discipline a barrier of jargon and mathematics which makes the subject difficult to penetrate for the non-initiated.

Yet orthodox economics is in many way an empty box. Its understanding of the world is similar to that of the physical sciences in the Middle Ages. A few insights have been obtained which will stand the test of time, but they are very few indeed, and the whole basis of conventional economics is deeply flawed.

An important purpose of this book is to try to convey this message in a way which is accessible to the general public. This does not mean that the arguments are in some sense diluted, for the book addresses difficult issues which are at the very heart of orthodox economic theory. But the style of the book is designed as an aid to the comprehension of a wider audience. Deliberately, there are relatively few footnotes, and the text is not cluttered with a large number of references to articles in academic journals.

A new introduction to the North American edition is needed for two reasons. First, to take account of developments since the book was written. The text was finalized during 1993, and was published in Europe in 1994. Second, to acknowledge more fully some important differences between economics in Europe and America.

The book received a mixed response in Europe. Non-economists greeted the book favorably, since one of its main purposes was to convey to the non-specialist reader the highly tenuous nature of modern economic orthodoxy.

The reception by conventional economists was in many cases hostile, some to the point of abuse. The very title of the book seems to have enraged many economists. Yet their fury only served to expose the futility of much of their endeavors. Economics is supposed to be, uncontroversially, about how economies work. In particular, the discipline should be about how the Western economies operate, for they are by far the most successful form of economic organization which has ever been invented.

An important aspect of business activity in the West is the marketing function, and the title of the book was chosen with this in mind. A equally valid designation might have been something along the lines of 'A theoretical critique of neo-classical economics from a non-linear systems perspective', but somehow one feels it would not have had the same impact. The failure of many economists to appreciate this speaks volumes for their true understanding of capitalism.

But the title serves a more general function. The study of human societies and economies is of great importance, and it is not the purpose of the book to suggest otherwise. Rather, it is to argue that conventional economics offers a very misleading view of how the world actually operates, and that it needs to be replaced.

Criticisms of the book by economists have been twofold. First, that they are already aware of the problems which I raise for the discipline, and indeed the reviewers themselves know far more about it than I do. Second, that the book is plain wrong. Despite the contradictory nature of these arguments, some economists appear to subscribe to both at the same time.

Taking the reaction to the book of economists as a whole, I cannot help but notice with amusement the clear correlation between the degree of hostility shown and the amount of taxpayers' money which the economist concerned and his or her institution receive to carry out conventional economic research (although, as any economist will tell you, correlation does not necessarily prove causation).

Economic research in most of Europe is carried out along lines which the state planning institution, Gosplan, in the old Soviet Union could only envy. A central committee decrees which lines of research, which methodologies are to be pursued. The diktat is sent out to the factories—the economics faculties—around the country, and enormous piles of articles are produced exactly in accordance with the rules in order to qualify for further state subsidies. The only problem is that very little of what is produced is of the slightest interest to anyone else, and the papers simply gather dust in the offices of the central committee.

Such problems are far from unknown in the United States. Indeed, the discipline with which orthodoxy is enforced in many American universities is truly awesome.

But economics in America operates on curiously schizophrenic lines. For the most part, conventional approaches dominate, and set the tone for work throughout the rest of the world. Yet a great deal of the innovative work which is being done, and which needs to be done to restore the sanity of the discipline, is accomplished in the United States. The financial organization of the best American universities undoubtedly helps. Support from successful alumni, far-sighted industrial investment and the pride that Americans have in their successful institutions produces a climate which can be quite different from that in Europe. The opportunity exists for the best minds to think original thoughts, to behave as scholars and not as researchers, and not to cower before the exigencies of the next grant application.

Criticisms of economics are by no means new, though many of them can be dismissed readily by the profession. As chapter 4 in particular shows, the most devastating critiques have come from within economics itself, from those equipped with the formal modeling and mathematical skills to expose the limitations of orthodoxy on its own terms. I studied economics as an undergraduate at Cambridge, England, whose leading lights had for decades locked horns in a theoretical tussle with those of Cambridge, MA. Yet these debates now lie largely forgotten, for the British of those days made the fundamental mistake of trying to link criticism of free market economic theory with ideological criticism of the Western market economic system as it exists in practice.

It is the very success of Western capitalism which makes it so important to comprehend its workings better, and to consider how some of the problems to which it gives rise can best be resolved. This was the motivation of Keynes, a liberal gentleman scholar writing in the 1930s at a time of massive unemployment, who saw himself working to save the capitalist system.

Orthodox economic theory simply does not offer a proper account of the workings of the economies of the West. Indeed, since this book was written, Kenneth Arrow, the American Nobel prizewinner who has done more than anyone to create a modern mathematic basis for conventional theory, has stated that he regards the high levels of unemployment which are frequently observed to exist for long periods of time in Western countries as an 'empirical refutation' of free market theory. Arrow's recent criticisms extend far wider, but it is this which he regards as the single most decisive piece of evidence.

Reflecting on the book, there are two areas on which I would now place more emphasis. The first relates to the amounts of information which economic theory requires its actors both to acquire and to process if they are to behave according to its precepts. In strictly limited environments, where the amount of information to be assessed is small, conventional theory can be a reasonable approximation to reality. But this is far from being the case when the economy as a whole is considered.

These informational problems are dealt with at some length in the book. But insufficient attention is given to recent developments in economic theory which attempt to relax the rigid assumptions of orthodoxy and to investigate the implications of more realistic assumptions. Even small deviations from the full panoply of postulates required by conventional theory often lead to outcomes which are quite different from those of the textbooks. It is very encouraging that this work takes place. But many of those carrying it out seem to be unable to shake off completely the deadweight of the past, and still look to the orthodox free market model as the Platonic ideal to which we should aspire. The world itself may have fallen from grace, and have properties far removed from those of conventional economics. Yet orthodox models remain the benchmark against which many of these more realistic models are compared.

The second area of potential revision concerns the process by which the individual actors in economics—whether as individual consumers or workers or as companies- relate to each other. This has occupied much of my time since this book was first published.

In almost all the published work on economic theory, whether within or without the conventional view of the world, the tastes and behavior patterns of individual agents—the phrase used habitually by economists to describe both people and firms—are fixed. An individual is assumed to have certain preferences about, say, the available range of consumer products. He or she is presumed to make a rational choice about which ones to buy, on the basis of the prices of the products and on the amount of his or her income or wealth.

In conventional theory, the behavior of other people alters the behavior of any individual *indirectly*. The choices of others affects the prices of products, and the individual decides what to buy on the basis of these prices. Undoubtedly, this does happen. But it is a very partial and incomplete account of how behavior is influenced. Almost everyone but a saint has other motivations. We observe the things our friends and neighbors buy, and *alter* our own behavior in response. The brand new car in the next door drive leads many to covet one for themselves. In short, their tastes and behavior are not fixed, but are influenced *directly* by the behavior of others.

When the foundations of conventional economics were being built, as long ago as the second half of the nineteenth century, the leading thinkers and those who followed them were perfectly aware of this pervasive fact of life. But the mathematical techniques which would enable them to handle it in theoretical models were simply not available to them at that time. They were therefore obliged to simplify by ignoring the issue. But the founders of economic theory knew all along that their models were based upon assumptions which often ignored important elements of reality. The writings of Alfred Marshall, the great British economist whose work straddled the decades around the turn of the century and who is, on reflection, unjustly neglected in this book, make this absolutely clear.

But this level of awareness has been lost to many current economists. So much of their own intellectual capital and reputation is bound up with orthodox theory that they have forgotten that their work is based on a dramatic simplification of reality. People live in a society, and their actions are constantly influenced by those of others.

The techniques required to deal with this factor have only recently become feasible to implement through the massive development of, and access to, computer power. An awareness of this may have been the source of the alleged remark of the great physicist Max Planck to Keynes in the 1930s. Urged by Keynes to apply his mind to the problems of economics, Planck thought for a moment and said ' No, the math is too hard'. Of course, the level of math used both then and now in conventional economics was trivial to a scientist of Planck's stature and ability.

A world in which individuals react directly to the behavior and actions of others is utterly and completely different from the world of orthodox economic theory. It is also far more realistic. It is this concept which lies behind the book on which I am presently working, and whose elaboration must await publication of that volume.

All this is not to say that conventional economics is completely useless, which some of the more fervent readers of this book appear to believe. Much of the environmental criticism of contemporary economic activity, for example, is given intellectual force by the use of ideas developed in economics. But in many ways, economics at present is like physics before Newton. It is not a completely empty box, and some important insights have been developed. Indeed, a more widespread awareness of these would markedly improve the quality of public discourse on policy. But it is a limited and, ultimately, a flawed account of how the world actually behaves.

An encouraging sign is the rapid fall, on both sides of the Atlantic, in the number of students who want to study economics as it currently exists. Conventional economics is supposed to understand the workings of the free market, and one would imagine that it is the orthodox who would be the first to react to this signal which is being sent by an important segment of their customer base. But this is far from being the case.

Too much of economics has deteriorated into intellectual games subsidized at the expense of the taxpayer. A better understanding of economies and societies will inevitably involve difficult ideas and concepts for, as Max Planck hinted, these human systems are in many ways more complex then the physical universe itself.

The best economists are fully aware of the limitations of their discipline. It is an exciting time, for more and more attention is being paid to developing views outside the mainstream which give a better understanding of the world. Progress is slow, in part because of the difficulty of the task, and in part because of the fierce resistance of the bulk of the economics profession to criticism, whether implicit or explicit, of the ideas which they have all labored so hard to understand.

We live in paradoxical times. At one level, the Western world enjoys material living standards beyond the wildest dreams of those who, for example, lived through the problems of the 1930s. In the Far East, successful economic development is beginning to relieve millions upon millions of people from lives of ceaseless drudgery and poverty. Yet, side by side, the problems of Africa worsen, and in the countries of the West themselves, social divides deepen. Even the lives of many amongst the affluent majority are blighted by new levels of uncertainty.

The ultimate purpose of the discipline of economics, or of political economy as its founding father, Adam Smith, called it, both was and should be severely practical. Smith's own masterpiece, *The Wealth of Nations*, was intended to provide an account of why some nations were wealthy whilst others remained poor. Insights into the success of the former might help the latter escape their poverty. And the study of how economies work remains as important as ever, in order to illuminate both long-standing and new problems which societies face as we move into the next century.

Paul Ormerod
London, June 1997

PART I

THE PRESENT STATE OF ECONOMICS

CHAPTER I

Economics in Crisis

The world economy is in crisis. Unemployment in Western Europe rises towards the 20 million mark. America faces the deep-seated problem of the twin deficits, the federal budget and the balance of trade. Vast tracts of the former Soviet empire are on the brink of economic collapse. Japanese companies, faced by the deepest recession since the war, are on the verge of breaking the long-standing and deep-rooted social convention of lifetime employment.

The orthodoxy of economics, trapped in an idealised, mechanistic view of the world, is powerless to assist.

In Western Europe, the economics profession eulogised the Exchange Rate Mechanism and monetary union, despite frequent bouts of massive currency speculation and the inexorable rise of unemployment throughout Europe during its years of existence. Teams of economists descend on the former Soviet Union, proclaiming not just the virtues but the absolute necessity of moving to a free-market system as rapidly as possible. Such prescriptions involve the establishment of market economies of greater purity than those contemplated by Ronald Reagan and Margaret Thatcher. But despite governments in the former Soviet bloc doing everything they are told, their economic situation worsens.

From the pensioned security of their vast bureaucracies, economists from the International Monetary Fund and the World Bank preach salvation through the market to the Third World. Austerity and discipline are the hallmarks of the favoured policies of the IMF throughout the world, yet its own salary bill has risen by 38 per cent in the last two years, and is budgeted to rise by a further 22 per cent in 1994.

On a more mundane level, economic forecasts are the subject of open derision. Throughout the Western world, their accuracy is appalling. Within the past twelve months alone, as this book is being written, forecasters have failed to predict the Japanese recession, the strength of the American recovery, the depth of the collapse in the German economy, and the turmoil in the European ERM.

Yet to the true believers, within the profession itself, the ability of economics to understand the world has never been greater. Indeed, in terms of influence in the world the standing of the profession appears high. Economics dominates political debate, to the extent that it is scarcely possible to have a serious political career in many Western countries without being able to repeat more or less accurately its current fashionable orthodoxies. Television seeks out the views of economists on Wall Street and in the City of London, anxious that the viewing public should be informed of the impact of the latest monthly statistic on the entire economy over the coming years. The numbers of students seeking to read economics grew dramatically during the 1980s.

Academically, the discipline seems to have developed enormously, particularly over the past decade, the mathematical sophistication especially having increased in terms both of theoretical work and of the approved methodologies of applied economics.

Of course, disputes still exist, such as the well publicised arguments between monetarists and Keynesians as to how the economy as a whole operates. For example, the former argue that increases in government expenditure will ultimately have no impact on the overall level of economic activity and employment. Both sides agree that such increases can have a positive effect on a time horizon of two or three years. Keynesians believe that some of this impact persists. But such tiffs merely conceal the large body of shared belief which characterises present-day economics. The old joke that twelve economists in a room could be guaranteed to hold twelve different opinions, and thirteen if one of them were Keynes, is becoming less and less true. An intellectual orthodoxy has emerged.

Increasingly, the subject is taught not as a way of learning to think about how the world *might* operate, but as a set of discovered truths as to how the world *does* operate. The content of degree courses is becoming increasingly standardised. Substantial and impressive textbooks exist, both in micro- and in macro-economics, consisting in the main of the mathematical technique of differential calculus applied to linear systems.

It cannot be stated too often that very little of the content of such textbooks is known to be true, in the sense that many of the statements in textbooks on, say, engineering, are known to be true: formulae for building bridges exist, and when these formulae are applied in practice, bridges in general remain upright. The same does not apply in economics and yet the confidence of the true believers in economics has grow'd and grow'd like Topsy. As they themselves would doubtless prefer to say, to give the description an authentic mathematical air, it has grown exponentially.

Sociologists and psychologists have documented many case studies

4

concerning the reactions of groups when views which they hold about the world are shown to be false. In such situations, far from recognising the problem, a common reaction of individuals is to intensify the fervour of their belief.

A classic study of this kind, *When Prophecy Fails*, published in 1956, was carried out by American psychologists. It describes the experiences of researchers who joined a group which was making specific predictions of imminent catastrophic floods. When the floods failed to appear, the group, far from disbanding, intensified enormously its efforts to convert others to its beliefs. Another example is provided by James Patrick, a young sociologist who infiltrated a gang of Glasgow youths in the late 1960s.* These gangs, while being almost model citizens by the standards of the American inner city, were notorious for perpetrating acts of violence, mainly on each other but occasionally on the public at large, which were thought extreme in Northern Europe. The gang believed as a point of honour that no member would betray another to the police. Yet, as the author noted:

One prominent member of the gang was arrested and within twenty-four hours all other members had been questioned by the police. The inference was obvious to everyone except the gang. Yet their misplaced belief in gang loyalty was not discarded or even diminished, but became all the more extreme and passionate.

The intensity of faith shown by most professional economists is well illustrated by two passages from *Liar's Poker†* by Michael Lewis, who began his career as a successful trader on world capital markets. His descriptions of how such markets operate are in many ways far removed from the received wisdom of orthodox economics. The first passage deals with the aspect of the growth of economics as a discipline. Writing about the major US universities in the mid-1980s, Lewis states:

[An effect] which struck me as tragic at the time was a strange surge in the study of economics. At Harvard, the enrolment had tripled in ten years. At Princeton, in my senior year, for the first time in the history of the school, economics became the single most popular area of concentration. And the more people studied economics, the more an economics degree became a requirement for a job on Wall Street. There was a good reason for this. Economics satisfied the two most basic needs of investment bankers. First, bankers wanted practical people, willing to

---

*L. Feininger, H. Rieken, S. Schuster, *When Prophecy Fails*, University of Minnesota Press, 1956, and James Patrick, *A Glasgow Gang Observed*, Eyre Methuen, London, 1973.
†Michael Lewis, *Liar's Poker*, Coronet Books, 1990.

subordinate their education to their careers. Economics seemed designed as a sifting device. Economics was practical. It got people jobs. And it did this because it demonstrated that they were among the most fervent believers in the primacy of economic life.

Economics allowed investment bankers directly to compare the academic records of the recruits. The only inexplicable part of the process was that economic theory (which is what, after all, economics students were supposed to know) *served almost no function in an investment bank.*

In other words, at the very centre of world financial markets, where the principles of the free market should be at their clearest, economics as an intellectual discipline served almost no practical function.

The second example from Lewis's book provides even more food for thought, both as an intellectual challenge for economics and as an illustration of how the study of the subject can affect a person's mind. A fundamental belief in economics for many years has been that the price of a commodity – whether it is bananas or people – is determined by the relative levels of demand and supply. The higher the demand relative to supply, the higher the price.

At an early stage in Lewis's career on Wall Street, during his training programme, a group of his colleagues was asked why they were so well paid. 'A person who had just taken an MBA from the University of Chicago explained: "It's supply and demand. My sister teaches kids with learning disabilities, and earns much less than I do. If nobody else wanted to teach, she'd make more money."' In fact, as all the trainees were acutely aware, there had been intense competition to secure places on their programme. Over 6000 people, most of them from economics programmes at the major American universities, had applied for just 127 places on the Salomon Brothers' training programme. Yet as Lewis drily remarks: 'Paycheques at Salomon Brothers spiralled higher in spite of the willingness of others who would do the same job for less.'

In other words, an apparently intelligent graduate from one of the major economics courses in the United States was able to assert, thanks to his understanding of the principles of economics, and in particular the law of supply and demand, that the reason he as an investment banker was paid a salary many times higher than that of his sister who taught children with learning disabilities was that fewer people were available to do his job, relative to demand, than was the case with his sister's. And this was despite overwhelming evidence on a daily basis that the empirical foundation for such an assertion was worthless.

6

Indeed, orthodox economics is quite unable to answer a simple question such as this, other than by resorting to definitions of supply, demand and price which degenerate into tautology. Transparently, many more people relative to the level of demand are willing to supply their labour to the financial markets than are willing to become teachers, yet the price of the former product (the salary) is many times that of the latter. Of course, the interchange of supply and demand can affect prices, but not always to the exclusion of other factors operating on price.

Of course, it may be unfair to castigate economics on the remarks of a single MBA graduate from Chicago. Yet the question he was asked, and answered so well in terms of economic orthodoxy, remains: Why are people operating in, say, financial markets paid far more than, say, schoolteachers or academic economists? There are answers to this question, but none of them involves the 'fundamental' principle of supply and demand.

James Tobin, the American Nobel Prize winner in economics, has questioned very seriously whether it makes sense from the point of view of American society as a whole to divert so much of its young talent from the top universities into financial markets. This debate is not new. John Maynard Keynes considered the same question in the 1930s, and expressed the view that on the whole the rewards of those in the financial sector were justified. Many individuals attracted to these markets, Keynes argued, are of a domineering and even psychopathic nature. If their energies could not find an outlet in money making, they might turn instead to careers involving open and wanton cruelty. Far better to have them absorbed on Wall Street or in the City of London than in organised crime.

Keynes, it should be said, saw the world through the eyes of the gentleman scholar of the pre-war period, through the double negative, the subjunctive, and through irony. But he could when he chose be ruthlessly direct in his criticism. In fact, he likened the financial markets not merely to a casino, but to the childhood games of Snap, Old Maid or Musical Chairs – 'a pastime in which he is victor who says Snap neither too soon nor too late, who passes the Old Maid to his neighbour before the game is over, who secures a chair for himself when the music stops'.

Fervency of belief in the 'theorems' of economics is by no means confined to MBA students. An exchange at a seminar held in March 1993 at the prestigious Ecole des Hautes Etudes Commerciales in France is illuminating. The 500 students were addressed on successive days by distinguished French economists. The proceedings opened with

Maurice Allais, Nobel Prize winner in economics and now in his eighties, presenting what *Le Monde* described as '*le choc Allais*'. It is an article of faith in orthodox economics that free trade between nations is wholly desirable. But to the horror of the audience, Allais attacked the proposition that free trade was in general beneficial. Indeed, he argued that it could be of benefit only in certain very special circumstances. Denouncing the Maastricht Treaty, Allais pronounced that free trade would have favourable effects only when carried out between regions which were at comparable levels of economic development. He condemned roundly 'the free-trade policies of the European Commission'.

Two days later, Jacques Attali took the platform. At the time president of the European Bank for Reconstruction and Development, and the man of whom President Mitterrand of France reportedly said, 'I . . . am a page of history and you are merely a footnote', Attali lost no time in restoring orthodoxy. Quick to point out that Allais had once been his professor, but even quicker to denounce anti-free-trade views as unequivocally '*stupides*', he asserted that 'every obstacle to free trade is a factor which leads to recession'.

It may, of course, be mere coincidence that at a time when barriers to trade within the European Community are lower than ever before – indeed, the much publicised 1992 programme removing many trade restrictions has now come into force – Europe is entering not a boom, but a sharp recession!

To the detached observer, noting the contrast between the actual behaviour of the world and the confidence of orthodox economists to understand it, a number of analogies spring to mind. But the one which is uppermost, and which lingers persistently, is the story of 'The Emperor's New Clothes'. Or, as people during my childhood in the north of England used to say, more bluntly, 'There's none so blind as them as can't see.'

It was not always so. The great classical economists, writing in the late eighteenth and early nineteenth centuries, struggled to understand the dramatic impact on the economy and on society of the Industrial Revolution. But, as we shall see, they did so with an analysis very firmly rooted in reality, addressing questions of great practical import.

In fact, encouraging signs within economics have started to appear again in recent years.

At one level, the tremendous growth in students reading economics which took place during the 1980s seems to have peaked. At Harvard

University, government has recently overtaken economics as the most popular first-degree subject. And, outside academia, membership of America's National Association of Business Economists is falling, although there are still 100,000 people who describe themselves as economists in America. More important, not all economists lack doubts, and an increasing minority are prepared to articulate them, at the risk of incurring professional odium, and to investigate different approaches and different methodologies. The fundamental postulates of the discipline are being called into question as some of the most imaginative economists seek to restore the link with reality which characterised the work of the classical economists.

Some of their most innovative work, often carried out in conjunction with scholars from other disciplines such as the behavioural sciences, artificial intelligence and biology, and using new techniques and new approaches, both exposes the incurable weaknesses of orthodox economics and offers real hope of progress.

We shall see, in the course of this book, how and why economics was hijacked in the nineteenth century by an approach which still today forms the basis of the subject. The new method of analysis was based on a desire to raise the mathematical precision of economics, so that it could enjoy the status and prestige of the physical sciences in the Victorian era. Ironically, as the fervour of belief of conventional economists intensifies, the mechanistic view of the world embraced by economics is seen as less and less relevant by the biologists, chemists and physicists of the 1990s.

The concept that free trade is unequivocally beneficial goes back to the very beginnings of the study of economics as a serious and separate discipline, to the late eighteenth and early nineteenth centuries. During the eighteenth century, a dramatic transformation of the world had begun. Slowly at first, and initially confined to Britain and parts of North-West Europe, the Industrial Revolution launched the world on to a path of sustained growth and economic expansion, with unprecedented levels of trade between nations.

In the late twentieth century we have become accustomed to the process of growth. Annual rates of growth of 2 per cent a year, for example, whether in America or Europe, are regarded as being insufficient to meet the growing demands of society. But for much of human history, a sustained expansion of the economy by 2 per cent required not just a year but decades to achieve.

Historically, although there were long-term fluctuations' in economies, these were for the most part dependent upon shifts in weather patterns which determined the productivity of the harvest. Individual economies could also expand by military conquest and by plunder, which was essentially the basis of the prosperity even of the Roman empire. The conquests of Attila the Hun, who has entered popular mythology as the embodiment of terror and destruction (although Verdi's opera presents a more balanced view of this complex character), are a good example of this form of expansion. Sustained internal economic expansion, however, through the accumulation of capital and through technological progress, was very slow.

One recent study, by Angus Maddison,* estimates that in what are now the Western economies, during the 1000 years between AD500 and 1500, GDP grew on average by only 0.1 per cent a year. Using straightforward compound arithmetic, this growth rate implies that in 1500 the volume of economic activity in the West was between 2.5 and 3 times as great as it had been in 500. To put this in perspective, the Western economies grew as much in percentage terms between 1950 and 1970 as they did between 500 and 1500. And given the much higher base at the start of the 1950s, the absolute increase in the volume of goods and services produced was enormously greater.

Growth began to accelerate around 1500, and between then and 1700 Maddison estimates that total economic output in the West almost doubled. But an even sharper rise in growth then took place, to over 0.5 per cent a year during the eighteenth century. In the more advanced economies, such as Britain, growth was of the order of a full 1 per cent a year.

Such growth was dramatic. It was sufficient to ensure marked changes could be observed during the lifetime of an individual. It was also sufficient to exceed the surge in population which was taking place, and so ensure an expansion of average living standards. The sheer magnitude of the growth was without precedent in human history. It is almost impossible today to capture the wonder and excitement which was felt at the scale of the changes taking place in the economy and in society.

The process of growth fascinated the great early thinkers on economics, such as Adam Smith, Thomas Malthus, David Ricardo and Karl Marx. The central theme of their various works was an attempt to understand and explain both why it was happening and whether and

*Angus Maddison, *Phases of Capitalist Development*, Oxford University Press, 1982.

how it might continue, if indeed it could, for Malthus in particular was pessimistic.

Since it was in Britain that the transformation wrought by the Industrial Revolution was initially the greatest, it was primarily there that the early classical economists analysed the process of economic growth. But as industrialisation spread, so too did the new discipline of economics, and gradually through the nineteenth century citizens of other countries – such as the Austrian Böhm-Bawerk, the Swede Knut Wicksell, Léon Walras in Switzerland and Irving Fisher in America – began to make major contributions to the subject, challenging Britain's pre-eminence in the field.

In fact, the early economists concerned themselves with a wide range of highly practical questions. Moreover, scholars from a range of disciplines felt able to contribute to the discussions within political economy. Jeremy Bentham and the Mills, better known as philosophers and political theorists, and the historian Carlyle, for example, were all involved in these debates. Economics was not seen to be an exclusive preserve of professional economists.

To understand the world better, the early thinkers introduced the important concept of theoretical models, abstract versions of the economy which extracted the essentials of the problem under consideration, but which at the same time, by simplification from reality, made analysis easier. By this method of systematic and logical analysis, great steps forward were made in establishing the basis of modern economics. But despite this theoretical analysis, economics remained firmly based in reality. By no means everything they wrote has stood the test of time. But the overriding concern of these men was to understand the world which they could see about them.

Born in 1766 to wealthy parents, Thomas Robert Malthus was educated at Cambridge where, according to an early editor of his collected works, 'he was generally distinguished for gentlemanlike deportment'. Taking holy orders in the Church of England, this gentleman-scholar corresponded actively with Ricardo and achieved distinction on a European scale, being elected to the French Institute in Paris and the Royal Academy in Berlin before his death at the age of seventy. Writing at the end of the eighteenth century, he observed the explosion in population which was taking place, and drew his own gloomy conclusions.

For Malthus, slow growth in productivity in agriculture meant that any expansion of the population which took place, for whatever reason, was unsustainable. The spectre of death through war and disease permeates his writings, but lurking in reserve, as a final arbiter of growth, is famine.

The Malthusian model has a great deal of validity for much of human history, but as we can now see, with the benefit of hindsight, Malthus did not appreciate the potential for massive technological advance in agriculture, which enables the Western world to be fed with a mere handful of its population engaged in agricultural production. Criticisms can also be made of his empirical data, his main concern being the huge expansion of population in what he regarded as the American colonies, much of which was due in fact to immigration rather than to Malthus's worry about the fecundity of the population. But in an important sense, the fact that we now believe him to have been wrong does not matter. He was trying to understand, by analytical means and using empirical evidence, a phenomenon of great import to society.

Some twenty years before Malthus was writing, a quiet Scottish academic published a book whose profound influence is still with us today. Adam Smith is now seen as the intellectual inspiration of the New Right in Western politics. The drive to privatise nationalised industries and functions carried out by state bureaucracies, and the insistence on the primacy of free-market forces, which has dominated Western politics in the past decade, are carried out with fervent invocations of Smith's name. His major economic work, *The Wealth of Nations* (1776), is indeed intended to demonstrate how the pursuit of enlightened self-interest by individuals and companies can benefit society as a whole. The book is a tremendous analytical achievement, setting up a model of how the economy is thought to operate and develop, and supporting the theory with an enormous sweep of contemporary and world historical evidence.

Smith's work was not a piece of abstract theorising, but was firmly rooted in reality. Indeed, the whole purpose of *The Wealth of Nations* was to understand how economies worked, and why some countries were so much wealthier than others. The full title of the book shows quite clearly Smith's intention. Almost invariably abbreviated now, it was published as *An Inquiry Into the Nature and Causes of the Wealth of Nations*.

In the best scientific tradition, Smith observed the world, and then sought to explain it. Observation came first, theory second.

Contrary to the general perception, *The Wealth of Nations* is by no means a pure eulogy of and apology for free-market forces. Margaret Thatcher famously declared, 'There is no such thing as society.' But such a sentiment would have been completely alien to Adam Smith, who attached great importance to the concept of society. Indeed, before *The Wealth of Nations* appeared, he was already famous for his previous great work, *The Theory of Moral Sentiments*.

A central theme of *Moral Sentiments* was precisely to show how there are propensities in human nature which incline us towards society, such as fellow feeling and the desire both to obtain the approval of others and to be worthy of that approval. For Smith, these sentiments exercised a crucial influence on the self-control and restraint of individuals in their behaviour towards others.

Indeed, he believed that many behavioural problems would be eliminated if only people could see themselves more clearly 'in the light in which others see us'. Importantly, the tendency for individuals to control their behaviour because of the opinions of others was not seen as a utilitarian act, but one which arose quite naturally.

In other words, self-restraint could arise in a system in which people followed purely their own self-interest, simply because of the practical value of such restraint. Life would be intolerable if everyone pursued a career of fraud, pillage and murder. But for Smith, self-control was not dependent upon such self-seeking calculations, but was a natural, integral part of human nature.

The moral climate in which the economy and society function is also an important theme in *The Wealth of Nations*. The enlightened pursuit of self-interest is seen as the driving force of a successful economy, but in the context of a shared view of what constitutes reasonable behaviour. For Smith, an important role of the state was to assume powers which could be used if necessary to support the moral framework. This did not simply extend to the system of justice, or even to legal provisions for the state to deal with monopoly powers. Smith was particularly concerned, for example, with the quality of life of the labouring poor. He defined living standards in terms not only material, but also moral, arguing that the principles of industrial organisation on which material prosperity was based required workers to become increasingly specialised and narrowly focused in their working lives. This process – the principle of the division of labour, in Smith's famous phrase – brought enormous benefits in material terms. But at the same time, it rendered many individuals 'not only incapable of relishing or bearing a part in any rational conversation, but of conceiving any generous, noble or tender sentiment, and consequently of forming any just judgment concerning many even of the ordinary duties of private life. Of the great and extensive interests of his country he is altogether incapable of judging.'

Smith argued that the state had the very important duty to tackle this problem, by providing a level of education sufficient to render every citizen capable of exercising an appropriate level of intellectual and social 'virtue'. The state should even extend its range of activities into the cultural sphere, in order to raise the overall intellectual level of the population, to the benefit of all.

The importance to Smith of the overall set of values in which the economy operates is generally ignored by his followers in the late twentieth century. His economics, based upon individual self-interest, is remembered, but his moral framework is not. Yet societal values are an important theme, and one which will be revisited in the second part of this book, in the context of understanding post-war economic performance. Differences both across countries and within a particular country over time in value systems and the degree of social cohesion are important in understanding, for example, the behaviour of unemployment since the war.

In sharp contrast, modern economics views the economy as something which can be analysed in isolation. There are few greater insults in an orthodox economist's vocabulary than to describe someone as a sociologist. The institutional setting, the historical experience and the overall framework of behaviour are ruthlessly excluded from contemporary economic theory.

In the years following Adam Smith's great book, the pace of economic development quickened even further. In the first two decades of the nineteenth century, the remarkable David Ricardo applied himself to an analysis of contemporary economic questions, of which economic growth remained the most important.

Ironically, it is the shy and retiring academic, Adam Smith, who is today by far the better known of these two outstanding minds. Indeed, it is even possible to obtain a respectable degree in economics with only the haziest notion of Ricardo's existence. Yet to his contemporaries in the emerging world power of Britain, Ricardo was a truly outstanding figure, whose premature death at the age of only fifty-one in 1823 was a major loss to society. He made an enormous amount of money on the Stock Exchange, and even more as a loan contractor during the Napoleonic Wars. He retired from money making in 1815. One outlet for his energies became politics, and in 1819 he entered the House of

Commons, taking advantage of the then prevailing attitude in British politics by purchasing a constituency in Ireland, which he never visited, for the sum of around £1 million at today's prices. Despite this rather unusual, to modern eyes, method of gaining a seat, Ricardo established himself very quickly as an important authority on questions of economics in Parliament.

Like Smith, Ricardo's intellectual interests ranged widely across social and economic problems, or, as he perceived them to be, questions of political economy. These were not to be studied loftily, above the hurly burly of political debate. The whole purpose of the subject was to improve human welfare through a better understanding of how the economy operated. His major work, entitled *Principles of Political Economy and Taxation*, appeared in 1817.

In the early years of the nineteenth century, Britain was engaged in a military struggle with Napoleon, on a scale which is dwarfed only by the global conflicts of our own century. This had a huge impact on British public finances, as military expenditure rose dramatically and the government was obliged to borrow on an unprecedented scale. Ricardo addressed a number of pressing practical issues, such as the stability of the currency at a time when the government was printing money to finance its deficit, and the question as to whether a deficit in the public finances was better dealt with by borrowing or by taxation.

On the question of trade, he extended the analysis made by Adam Smith. Given the great practical importance of this issue in the early nineteenth century, it is worth spending some time on the subject.

One question which intrigued the early, classical economists was why trade between nations should take place at all. This was not merely an abstract area of intellectual speculation. Powerful bodies of opinion believed strongly in the regulation and protection from foreign competition of both industry and agriculture, policies which deterred rather than promoted trade. In thinking and writing about trade, Smith and Ricardo were addressing a contemporary problem of major political and economic importance.

The Corn Laws in Britain were the prime example of such an issue. They gave a high degree of protection to British agriculture, and were an absolutely central political question in the first half of the nineteenth century.

During the Napoleonic Wars, the supply of corn to Britain from the rest of Europe had been cut off and the price of wheat tripled. The poor, whether urban or rural, suffered terribly as a result. But landlords and farmers benefited enormously. With the defeat of Napoleon, imported corn once again became available, and prices fell. The Corn Laws' were hurriedly passed to restrict imports, and to enable prices to stay high. The urban population, of all classes, was violently opposed to the laws, often literally so, and a number of major riots took place. In contrast, landowners both great and small were very strongly in favour. The ultimate abolition of the Laws, a quarter of a century after Ricardo's death, was an issue of such importance that the Conservative Party split on the question, and as a result was out of power for a generation.

In *The Wealth of Nations*, Adam Smith demonstrated that it was in general advantageous for a country to specialise in the production of those products in which it held an absolute advantage over other countries. In other words, its areas of production were those in which it could produce more efficiently than others. If two countries could each produce a different product more efficiently than the other, then it would be to the advantage of both for each to specialise in producing the efficient product, and for trade to take place between them. In general, Smith argued, this would be better for both countries than if each tried to produce both products.

Ricardo went much further. The thirty to forty years between the successive editions of *The Wealth of Nations* and the appearance of *The Principles of Political Economy* had seen a further dramatic acceleration in economic development, particularly in Britain. As industrialisation proceeded, it was entirely possible that for a time Britain held an absolute advantage in the production not just of manufactured goods but also, thanks to mechanisation and technological improvements, in agriculture as well. In other words, Britain could produce a wide range of goods more efficiently than anyone else. Yet trade still took place.

Ricardo explained this by the theory of comparative advantage, which is still the basis of international trade theory in economics today. Imagine that a country, such as Britain in the early nineteenth century, had such a lead in technological development that it could produce any given product more efficiently than any other country.

The theory says that even in these circumstances everyone could benefit from trade. The most efficient country should concentrate its resources on producing those goods where the gap between its efficiency and those of competing nations was the greatest. The less efficient countries should produce those products where the gap was smallest. In this way, more resources could be concentrated on those goods which could be produced the most efficiently of all.

The practical application for Ricardo was clear. Britain could produce both corn and manufactures more efficiently than other countries. But Britain's comparative advantage was much greater in manufactures. In other words, the gap between the efficiency of Britain in producing manufactured goods and that of the rest of the world was greater than the gap between Britain and the rest of the world in the efficiency of their agricultural production. By concentrating on manufactures, Britain could obtain the necessary amount of corn to feed its population from abroad far more cheaply than if it were produced at home. For Ricardo, this constituted a devastating argument against the protectionism of the Corn Laws.

Ricardo was careful to point out that his theory was dependent upon the assumption that funds available to invest in industry ('capital', for short) did not flow freely from one country to another. While capital then moved reasonably easily between regions in any one country, the same did not apply between different countries, even within Western Europe. Ricardo wrote of the 'fancied or real insecurity of capital, together with the natural disinclination which every man has to quit the country of his birth, and intrust himself to a strange government and new laws'. He approved of these restrictions on capital mobility, and stated that he would 'be sorry to see them weakened'.

In contrast, at the end of the twentieth century, capital is for the most part highly mobile. There are still areas where the risk of losing one's investment through expropriation of assets by the state exists. And small and medium-sized companies may well be deterred from investing abroad by local customs. Southern Italy, for example, is not an area to which the foreign entrepreneur is naturally drawn. But for large corporations, to all intents and purposes, capital is mobile throughout the world. Investments can be carried out almost anywhere, and indeed governments vie with each other for the privilege of large companies investing in their country.

Despite the fact that an important assumption behind Ricardo's trade theory, to which he himself drew attention, no longer holds empirically, the orthodoxy of free trade and free markets still prevails in contemporary economics.

The question which undoubtedly most intrigued the great classical economists was that of economic growth. It was this that was making a dramatic difference to both the economy in particular and society in general.

Writing in the early decades of the nineteenth century, Ricardo was by no means certain that growth on the scale he observed could continue. One reason for this was the influence of Malthus on his thoughts about the productivity of agriculture, which led him to suspect that ultimately the growth process might break down through the inability of the economy to support the growth in population.

But Ricardo thought hard about the conditions under which the remarkable transformation in the economy which he observed could continue. An important aspect of this for him was the distribution of national income between profits, wages and rent, or the income from land and property. For Ricardo, the possibility existed that profits would become too low to sustain growth.

Profits were seen as extremely important to economic development by the early economists. Without an adequate level of profit, for example, investment in new machinery and equipment and in new methods of transport such as canals and railways would not be enough to sustain growth. The role of profits in modern economics has faded over time, which is not to say that their true influence in the economy has changed in any way. On the contrary, the neglect of the impact of profits on the behaviour of the economy is a crucial weakness of modern economic analysis, whether Keynesian or monetarist, and it is a theme developed in the second half of this book.

The first economist to appreciate fully the profound qualitative change in the economic system which industrial capitalism brought about was Karl Marx. Marx drew not only on the experience of industrialisation in his native Germany, but also on events in Britain, where he spent the latter part of his life in political exile. The political aura which surrounds his name through its appropriation by the Soviet Communists makes it difficult for many people to approach his writings in the same way as they would those of, say, Adam Smith. But he was writing in the same intellectual, scientific tradition of setting up theoretical models, not in a purely abstract way, but as a means of trying to understand actual economic events.

Marx had the advantage of writing thirty or forty years later than Ricardo. Industrialisation and growth, far from faltering, had progressed by leaps and bounds. What appeared as a new phenomenon to Ricardo, which might at any time disappear, was seen by Marx to have become a permanent feature of society. He concluded that the build up of investment in factories and rapid technological development, the features which distinguished industrial capitalism from all previous societies, would guarantee growth in the long run. And on this point, Marx was right.

Marx did have doubts about the ultimate sustainability of growth. If technical advances and the dissemination of new techniques slowed down, the only way to sustain expansion would be to invest in greater and greater amounts of machinery and buildings, the fixed capital of industry. And eventually, as the size of the stock of this capital grew, the rate of profit available on yet more new investment would inevitably fall. So the two engines of growth, technological advance and the expansion of the stock of fixed capital in machines, vehicles and so forth, would break down.

A vast and esoteric literature has developed over subsequent years on Marx's concept of the falling rate of profit. Whether the rate of profit has fallen or not, technological progress is as rapid as ever, and economic growth continues. Marx himself allowed this as a distinct possibility, and his model of economic growth by no means implied an inevitable break-down of the economic system.

A further important innovation by Marx was to analyse business cycles. We are now familiar with the way in which our economies move through periods of boom, followed by recession, and so on. Much of contemporary macro-economic policy has the intention of modifying and controlling these fluctuations – with, it has to be said, little success. But in the first half of the nineteenth century, such short-term cycles were an entirely new phenomenon. Marx again formulated an analytical model to try to account for them.

In the twentieth century, John Maynard Keynes has been the most important scholar working in the tradition of the classical political economists. This does not mean that he agreed with everything they wrote. But his interest, like theirs, was in the analysis of the great issues of his day, the greatest of which in the inter-war period was not growth but unemployment, a problem so acute at the time that in desperation the Germans turned to Hitler and to fascism. The very future of Western democracies was placed at risk. Keynes was concerned not just to understand unemployment intellectually, but to put forward practical suggestions as to how the problem could be solved. He believed fervently that, for all its faults, Western liberal democracy offered the best hope for the world, and he saw himself working to save it.

Keynes, a Fellow of King's College, Cambridge, had enormous influence with governments around the world on a range of issues from the early 1920s until his death shortly after the Second World War. He fought an unremitting struggle against what he saw as the baleful and malign influences of orthodox economics, which taught that, even with rates of unemployment of more than 20 per cent in both America and Germany, governments should not intervene in the economy, to avoid interfering with the workings of the free-market mechanism.

Keynes, like Adam Smith, believed that market economies could be an enormous force for good in terms of their efficiency and the resulting prosperity which they could bring through economic growth. But he was contemptuous of orthodox economic theory, despite its ostensible concern to analyse the workings of markets, because he regarded such theory as offering a seriously misleading view of how the market economies of the West actually worked.

Like all great thinkers, Keynes's teachings have become distorted by many of his followers, and, as we will see in later chapters, there is an important distinction to be made between his own economics and much of what is now described as Keynesian economics. Indeed, the latter has been safely absorbed by, and neutered within the framework of the orthodox economics of today.

Not everyone can be a Malthus, or a Smith, a Ricardo, a Marx or a Keynes. But economists can aim to emulate the distinguishing feature of their works, namely the attempt to understand the world around them and the great practical questions of the day.

An internal culture has developed within academic economics which positively extols esoteric irrelevance. Despite a new emphasis in some of the very best work now being done, particularly in the United States, on confronting theory with empirical evidence, a relatively low status is given to applied work, involving the empirical testing of theories, in contrast to pure theoretical research.

Of course, this attitude is not unique to economics. Some of the greatest minds of world history have worked on theoretical physics, for example, and theory has a high standing in many disciplines. But in economics, pure theory is held to describe how the world actually operates. There is no perceived need to examine this empirically.

In other disciplines, the need to test theories is strong, and indeed some of the greatest theorists, Archimedes and Isaac Newton, for example, seem to have had a fairly acute sense of empirical observation as well. Of course, it is possible to make advances by pure thought, without reference to observation. But such opportunities are distinguished by their rarity. The truly great thinkers allow mundane events such as lying in a bath or sitting under an apple tree to inform the development of their theories.

Usually, it is only by attempting to describe an observed phenomenon by setting up a theoretical model, and then checking its empirical relevance as thoroughly as possible, that scientific progress can be made. The more situations in which the model can be applied successfully, the greater the confidence in the theory, and the greater the respect in which it is held. Newton's theory of gravity is seen as so outstandingly brilliant precisely because it can explain such an enormously wide range of events.

In contrast, many theoretical economists today bring to mind Shadwell's 1676 Restoration comedy, *The Virtuoso*. The Virtuoso himself, an eminent theorist about almost anything which moves, is, for example, held to be the greatest swimmer in the world. But he never actually swims in water. He simply lies on a table and follows to perfection the movements of a frog which is dangled on a string in front of him. At least the Virtuoso, by observing the frog, has the merit of allowing empirical reality to impinge on him to a modest extent.

Contemporary orthodox economics is isolated. It is isolated from its roots in the late eighteenth and early nineteenth centuries, when economists were by no means afraid to theorise, but did so purely to illustrate and understand the great practical issues of the day. Its method of analysis is isolated from the wider context of society, in which the economy operates, and which Adam Smith believed to be of great importance. And its methodology, despite the pretensions of many of its practitioners, is isolated from that of the physical sciences, to whose status it none the less aspires.

CHAPTER 2

Measuring Prosperity

The study of economics within a social context is of great importance, with the potential to be an enormous force for good. The classical economists of the late eighteenth and early nineteenth centuries sought to understand the world not purely out of intellectual interest, but to address questions of practical significance in the fervent belief that a better understanding of the workings of the economy could improve human welfare.

The major interest which the classical economists shared was the analysis and understanding of economic growth. Even for Adam Smith, writing at the very onset of the Industrial Revolution, the world was being transformed by rates of economic growth which were entirely unprecedented in human history. The importance which the classical economists attached to the phenomenon of growth has been amply justified by subsequent events. Growth has transformed our world completely, and in the late twentieth century we have become accustomed to the idea of rates of growth which alter dramatically the prosperity of a nation during the lifetime of any individual.

And so pervasive has the influence of growth been that in recent decades environmentalists have begun to question whether the costs do not outweigh the benefits.

But it is hard to deny that, for example, the average person in Western Europe or North America is much better off now materially than the average person was in the 1930s. There are periods of recession, when growth from one year to the next is close to zero or even slightly negative, but over the course of a decade all Western economies have shown rates of growth which have been consistently positive for the best part of two centuries, and in the case of the early industrialisers, such as Britain and the Netherlands, three centuries.

Even modest annual rates of growth compound very rapidly. An average growth rate of just 3 per cent a year is sufficient to double the size of the economy in just twenty-four years.* Most developed economies achieved

---

*At first sight, it might seem that the answer should be a little over thirty-three years, for doubling implies an increase of 100 per cent, and 100 divided by three gives the answer

average annual growth rates considerably above 3 per cent during the 1950s and 1960s. Of course, Japan and many countries in Europe were starting from a temporarily low base, with poor living standards as a result of the devastation of the war. But growth rates of 5 per cent a year were not uncommon, and at such a rate the economy doubles in size every fourteen years.

More recently, growth has slowed in all Western economies. During the 1980s, for example, growth in both the United States and in the European Community averaged just over 2 per cent a year, and even in Japan just over 4 per cent, a very marked slow-down compared to the 10 per cent per annum growth registered by that country for much of the 1950s and 1960s. But even at these rates of growth, the size of the economy expands visibly during a relatively short period of time. At 2 per cent growth a year, an economy doubles in size in just thirty-five years.

The benefits of growth are not simply a matter of increased material possessions, nor even of services, such as holidays, consumed. It enables far more leisure time to be taken. Improvements in the efficiency of production mean that more goods and services can be produced with the same amount of labour input. Alternatively, such improvements can be used to produce the same amount of goods with much less labour. In practice, we see a mixture of these two effects. The amount of goods and services produced increases, and the amount of labour input falls.

In many ways, it is this byproduct of growth, increased leisure, which has had the most liberating and enriching impact on the citizens of the West. For the majority of the population, economic growth has brought freedom from the sheer physical drudgery of existence which long hours of work have usually involved.

There are three ways in which this has happened. First, increases in economic efficiency have brought about a shorter working lifetime. Most people are no longer condemned to work until they are physically incapable of so doing. Retirement ages have fallen markedly during the twentieth century.

Admittedly, there is now a debate in the West about reversing the trend to earlier retirement, because of the worries of being able to finance the rising number of elderly people. In many Western countries,

---

thirty-three and a third. But the principle at work is not simple, but compound arithmetic. As the economy gets bigger, each additional percentage point of growth represents a larger and larger increase in the absolute amount of goods and services which are produced.

such as Germany, by the early years of next century over half the population will be aged over fifty.

But at the opposite end of the age scale, children aged five no longer work in factories or are sent up chimneys. They are in education, where they supposedly remain until well into their teens and, in many cases, into their early twenties. And the pressure in all developed countries is to send more and more people into higher education.

On a more mundane but nevertheless important level, economic growth enables both fewer hours per week to be worked, and longer holidays to be taken. The annual hours worked per person have fallen steadily. In the early 1890s, the average annual hours worked in the West came to around 2800. With just one week of holiday at times of religious festivals, this translates to a working week of some fifty-five hours.

By the early 1990s, annual hours had fallen on average to around 1700. The precise figure varies from country to country, and the Japanese in particular notoriously still work well in excess of 2000 hours a year. In America and Britain the figure is about 1600, and in Sweden closer to 1400.

Different countries also have different priorities about the length of annual holidays, but on the European model 1700 hours of work a year means that a total of six weeks holiday can be taken, and on average only thirty-seven hours a week need to be worked. Compared to the position a century ago, this represents a enormous expansion in effective leisure time.

Allowing for the time spent on sleeping and on the essential task of eating, not much more than 100 hours a week are available to the individual. For women workers of the industrial world in the textile mills or munitions factories a century ago, effectively the whole of this time was taken in work and laborious domestic chores. Genuine leisure time was zero. Shorter hours of work, together with labour-saving devices in the home, and even the small changes we have seen in the attitudes of men towards domestic responsibilities, have created the possibility of effective leisure time for working women.

All in all, a person born in the West today can expect to spend, over his or her lifetime, well under half the amount of time in paid employment spent by a person born a century ago. More time will be spent in education, there will be shorter working weeks, longer holidays, and a longer retirement.

This increase in leisure time brings its own problems. Adam Smith's exhortation to the state to equip its citizens with the mental capacities and skills to enjoy culture and understand the issues of government becomes more important than ever before. With the collapse of the Soviet empire, the totalitarian vision of the future portrayed in George Orwell's *Nineteen Eighty-Four* appears to have vanished as a possibility. In many ways, an even greater challenge is to ward off the threat of the world portrayed in Aldous Huxley's *Brave New World*, a prosperous and leisured society which is strictly segmented by intellectual capacity, and in which the bovine majority live the life of well-fed cows.

Different economies have used the proceeds of economic growth in different ways. While the Japanese, as we have seen, continue to work much longer hours than is the norm in the rest of the developed world, elsewhere other priorities exist. In Europe, the proceeds of economic growth have largely gone to those with jobs, whereas in America they have been used to create more jobs. Since 1980, the economies of both the United States and the European Community have grown, coincidentally, by almost exactly the same amount, by just under 30 per cent. In the EC, the numbers in employment have grown by only 5 per cent, but in the United States economic growth has been accompanied by a rise in employment of 18 per cent.

The benefits of growth are plain to see. But in recent decades some people have begun to question the foundations of classical and orthodox economics on the question of growth, asking whether its benefits are being wisely used and distributed and, at a more fundamental level, whether its costs – particularly in environmental terms – do not outweigh the benefits. What may be termed the Green critique of growth is powerful. More precisely, the word 'critique' should appear in the plural, for there is a number of quite different dimensions to it. No single source of intellectual authority exists within the movement, and environmentalism embraces many different strands of opinion. All of them require, in different ways and with different degrees of intensity, alterations in behaviour and in the priorities which as a society we attach to the various outcomes.

To take a simple example, in the United States around $60 billion a year is spent on personal beauty care. In the United Kingdom, over £1 billion is spent on pet food. Yet in both countries the public has been told repeatedly that there is no money available for the provision of better public health care or better public education.

In one sense, this seems to be true. People appear to choose to keep their money and spend it on beauty care or food for cats and dogs, rather than pay higher taxes which might be used to finance better public services. If they had a different set of priorities, as Greens would urge, they would spend their money differently.

In practice the choice is not presented as clearly as this. For example, the electorate might feel, not without a certain justification, that higher taxes might be appropriated by workers in the public sector to increase their wages or the size of their empires, rather than be used to improve services to the public. If a guarantee could be given that tax receipts would not be abused in this way, more people might be willing to pay more taxes and let Fido live on scraps rather than deluxe dog meat. Yet at any point in time, this particular possibility might not exist as a political option. It is either dog meat or taxes.

Orthodox economics, with its reliance on the primacy of the market mechanism, ignores such difficulties. The preferences of consumers are held to be revealed through their choices of goods and services, and the market mechanism ensures that these preferences are met.

A great deal of the Green critique of society consists of a desire that the priorities of consumers and governments should be different. Of course, these might range from a relatively limited wish for more effective control of air and noise pollution, to alterations in relative pay in terms of the contribution of different groups to society, to even more fundamental changes in the operation of society.

To say this is not to minimise in any way the importance of the debate which environmentalists have initiated, or to ignore the powerful vested interests which exist and which profit from the current set of priorities in the West. However, a lengthy discussion of the environmental critiques of Western society is of less concern here than the implications of such approaches to the central theme of this book, the crisis in the discipline of economics.

In fact, while some of the arguments in Green circles pose a fundamental challenge to orthodox economics, others can be accommodated comfortably within the framework of the discipline.

Many readers sympathetic to the environmental approach might feel, in a reversal of Groucho Marx's aphorism, that if this particular club would accept them as members, they must be doing something wrong.

But the implications of such an accommodation of Green ideas for the conduct of economic policy, as opposed to the academic discipline of economics, could be profound.

To illustrate this point, a certain amount of patience and persistence is required, for we must delve into a subject far more tedious than that of economics, namely accountancy. Or, more precisely, the use of accounting principles in economics.

First of all, we need to strike a note of caution. The definition of growth is intended to capture real movements in the amounts of goods and services which are produced, or real movements in material living standards. The total value of production in an economy can change either by the prices of products changing, or by the physical amount of production changing. It is this latter point which is of interest. An economy could grow very quickly in terms of the total value of its output merely by having a rapid rate of inflation, while the actual amount of goods and services produced might not change, or might even fall. In other words, changes in the value of goods and services brought about simply by increases in prices have to be disallowed.

The concept of growth has been mentioned many times, with no precise definition being given. There is a good reason for this. For, unlike many measurements in the physical sciences, there is no unique way of measuring either the size of an economy at a particular point in time, or its growth over time.

Economists often seek to mystify rather than enlighten the public, and nowhere is this accomplished better than with economic data. Certain conventions have been adopted within economics for measuring an economy's size and growth, and they do seem to have a certain degree of validity. The American economy is clearly bigger than that of, say, France or Germany. And anyone visiting Switzerland will receive the impression that the people there are distinctly better off than those in most other countries in Western Europe. The conventions used to measure the size of economies – used to construct their national accounts – reflect these impressions.

But an economy cannot be put in a pair of scales or have a tape measure wound about it to measure its size. The size has to be estimated. And in the process of estimation, decisions have to be taken not only about what evidence to use, but also about what should and should not be included in the definition of size in the first place.

A recent example of such an estimate was the decision of the Italian authorities in the 1980s to make a more realistic assessment in their national accounts of the size of the black economy in Italy. Tax evasion has vied with soccer as the national sport in Italy for many years, and as a result many economic transactions went entirely unrecorded by the government.

At a stroke, the size of the Italian economy, its Gross Domestic Product or GDP, rose by 20 per cent. The Italian press feasted for weeks on *il sorpasso* – the fact that in terms of income per head Italy had now surpassed the United Kingdom – but, of course, reality had not been altered by this change of accounting definition. The Italian economy remained exactly the same the day before the change as it was the day after. The only thing to change was its national accounts, which now gave a more accurate picture of the true prosperity of Italy.

The choice of factors used to define the size of an economy reflects the general preoccupation of economics with monetary transactions, in other words, with things that are bought and sold for money. And the particular factors which are emphasised are those which were thought to be especially important in the economies of the 1930s and 1940s, when the modern conventions of national accounts were first established.

But there is no reason in principle why other factors, such as environmental ones, should not now be thought to be especially important and hence included in the national accounts, despite the fact that many of them, such as pollution, exist but are not bought and sold. Similarly, work done within the household is not given any value in the current conventions used to construct national accounts. So the various daily tasks of cooking, cleaning, washing, ironing and child care are assumed to add no value to the economy.

At one level, this is patently absurd. In a purely utilitarian sense, clothes which are not washed, for example, will wear out and lose their value more quickly. The act of washing, by preventing value being lost, adds to the overall size of the economy. This is to say nothing of the value to be attached to personal hygiene. In Jerome K. Jerome's *Three Men in a Boat*, three young men decide to have a rowing holiday on the River Thames. A long discussion about the desirability of washing clothes, with all its effort and inconvenience, takes place. The decisive factor is the general wish to have the author's friend, Harris, clean and fresh around the boat. Unfortunately, this elusive but undoubtedly tangible benefit would not be measured in the national accounts.

The reason why household chores are excluded from the concept of value as defined in the national accounts is that economics, from whatever perspective, is essentially about the workings of economies, of whatever kind, in which monetary transactions take place – in other words, in which people buy and sell goods and services for money. Hiring a servant to do the cooking is a money transaction – the cook is paid – and so is taking shirts to the laundry. But cooking for the family, or washing and ironing one's own shirts is not paid.

In developed economies it would be easy enough to make a rough estimate of the value of these chores, and add the figures to the size of each economy. The result would be to give a more accurate picture of the value produced within each economy.

But nothing would have changed in reality. The new accounting conventions would not create extra resources in the economy, to be used to generate jobs or pay for public services or whatever. The change would be purely definitional with no practical consequences, just like the Italian reassessment of economic prosperity.

In developing economies, a far higher proportion of total transactions takes place within the household compared to those in the money economy. In a subsistence economy, a great deal of food production, for example, will never be bought and sold in the market, but is consumed by the community in which it is produced. Its value is therefore not reflected in the national accounts of these economies. Thus – while not in any way seeking to deny the existence of serious poverty and hardship in many developing economies – present accounting conventions underestimate their per capita incomes precisely because they do not take account of economic activity which takes place outside the market.

The particular focus of the national accounts is on measuring the amount of spending on goods and services carried out by the various sectors of the economy: by consumers, by companies, and by the public sector.

The reason for this emphasis is historic. The first serious efforts to construct national accounts took place in the 1930s and 1940s, when the ideas of Keynes were fashionable in economics. These ideas and their relevance to current circumstances will be discussed later in the book. The point to be made here is that, in essence, Keynes believed that the high unemployment in the West in the 1930s was due to a lack of demand in the economy. His reasoning was rather more subtle than is conveyed by this simple statement, but the amount of spending in the economy – the demand for goods and services – was thought to be the key driving force. It was therefore natural that the early national accounts should focus exactly on the level of spending, on the level of demand in the economy, and be organised around this concept, which has remained the focus of the accounts ever since.

But there is nothing immutable about the construction of the national accounts, about what does and what does not constitute economic activity.

Areas such as defence and the operations of the taxation authorities are undoubtedly part of the economy. People are employed in them, and these sectors buy resources from other sectors of the economy. But the outputs of these sectors are not traded. They are paid for by the taxpayer, but no taxpayer, either as an individual or as part of a group, buys them in the market place. The armed forces, for example, are provided collectively to the nation. There is a cost to this provision, financed through taxation, but there is not a price. In other words, one cannot go to the local supermarket and choose to buy, say, a share in a nuclear bomb for so many dollars, while at the same time deciding not to buy the marines. There is no option but to pay one's tax and 'buy' the whole package – although even this appeared threatened at the height of the consumer boom of the mid- to late 1980s, when a leading British computer retailer, Alan Sugar, declared that he would sell not just personal computers but personal nuclear weapons if they were available.

To overcome this problem, of assigning value to activities which are not traded in the market, a variety of assumptions is made. Since the value of the output of these sectors cannot be measured, for it is not bought and sold in the market and no price is put on it, the usual approach is to link it by some simple formula to the value of the inputs into the relevant sector. And the inputs can be measured. For example, the number of people employed in the armed forces is known, as is the cost of employing them. This information is then used to estimate the value of the output of the defence sector.

The assumptions used to make these estimates are now largely a matter of convention. Care and thought have gone into them, but there is no single right way to go about dealing with this problem. In a sense, as long as a reasonable solution is adopted, it does not really matter.

All this is very relevant to the Green argument. For there is no intellectual reason why the national accounts as currently constructed could not be amended to incorporate environmental costs and benefits. As with the armed forces, there is no unique way of doing this, but a set of conventions could readily be assembled so that the task could be done.

Indeed, particularly within the United States, such work has to a substantial extent already been done by imaginative economists. As far back as 1971, an important conference was held, entitled, in the literal way of economists and accountants, the Conference on Income and Wealth. Even then, many of those who attended felt that the emphasis in the national accounts on market transactions was too narrow, and that, among other things, environmental costs and benefits should be considered.

The following year, James Tobin and his American colleague Bill Nordhaus constructed a Measure of Economic Welfare (MEW) for the American economy, which they contrasted with the conventional measure of economic activity, Gross National Product (GNP).*

Although not directly concerned with environmental issues, MEW made a number of important adjustments to GNP. For example, value was ascribed to leisure and to household work. And costs were attributed to some aspects of urbanisation, such as commuting to work, which appears as a positive addition to GNP. Almost all commuting is by car or by public transport, and the services provided by the use of cars, buses or trains are valued and added to the measure of GNP. Tobin and Nordhaus argued that if more people spent longer travelling to and from work, this would not satisfy more human wants. Commuting is a regrettable necessity, rather than a contribution to human welfare. Accordingly, they subtracted the costs of commuting from GNP. Even so, over the long period examined in their paper, from 1929 to 1965, Tobin and Nordhaus found a strong correlation between their measure of MEW and the conventional measure of GNP. Both had grown substantially.

This is not surprising. Leaving aside statistics, the testimony of those who grew up in the 1930s, particularly in the depressed regions of Europe and America, is sufficient to show that human welfare in the developed world has improved dramatically. Conventional GNP, for all its imperfections, has some value as a measure of welfare.

But although MEW, like GNP, did grow over the period in question, it did so more slowly than GNP. In per capita terms, its annual growth was only 1.1 per cent over the 1929–65 period, compared to the 1.7 per

---

*European readers in particular will see the symbols GDP (Gross Domestic Product) used more frequently in media discussions of economics than GNP. There is a small difference between the two concepts, which even in a discussion on economic accounting principles is too mind-numbingly boring to bear repetition. But for all practical purposes, in most economies, they are the same, particularly when comparing not just the size of the economies but their growth rates over time.

cent of GNP. And most subsequent attempts to incorporate non-marketed factors in the definition of the national accounts give growth rates which are less than those obtained by the conventional measure.

For example, a recent series of adjustments to GNP was made by Herman Daly and Richard Cobb in their book *For the Common Good* (1989). Daly and Cobb examined the American economy from 1950 to 1986, and constructed an Index of Sustainable Economic Welfare (ISEW). The emphasis in their work is very much on the concept of sustainability, and environmental factors play an important role in their calculations. Deductions from the value of economic activity in any given year are made to take account of the costs of depletion of non-renewable resources and of long-term environmental damage.

On a per capita basis, the ISEW rose by only 0.9 per cent a year, compared to the 2 per cent of the conventional GNP figure. This was a larger gap than that between the Tobin–Nordhaus MEW and GNP, but the two are not dissimilar. Broader definitions of welfare therefore seem to imply that between 0.5 per cent and a full 1 per cent should be deducted from conventional GNP growth rates to get a realistic picture of what is happening to the overall welfare of society. Over a long period of time, we are getting better off, but not quite as quickly as the usual measure suggests.

This point is supported by cross-country comparisons of income per head in any given year. For example, UNICEF, the United Nations agency for children, measures the relative wealth or poverty of nations using quality of life indicators for children, such as under-five mortality and the proportion of children receiving at least four years of primary schooling. In general, the ranking of a country by per capita GNP is a good indicator of its ranking by quality of life. The broad ranking of countries is left unchanged by these adjustments. Money still counts. Europe and America are still very high in the rankings. But in comparison with the quality of life which would be expected given their GDP levels, countries as diverse as Sri Lanka, China and Kenya score highly.

The importance of adopting amendments to the national accounts along the lines of any of the studies discussed above would not really lie in the precise figures which emerged. Rather, an important stimulus would be given to alter the emphasis of government policies.

Governments like to see strong growth. One purely venal reason for this is that, around the world, whenever it happens, governments love to take the credit. Curiously, in recessions, when growth falters, it appears to be due to world events, which the government is naturally powerless to influence. Indeed, so prevalent is this phenomemon that a new law of economic growth in Western democracies could almost be formulated: when growth is strong, the policies of the domestic government are seen to be working; when growth is weak, the policies of the domestic government are still working, but are being overshadowed by world events.

On a less cynical note, the inclusion of more non-marketed factors in the national accounts, such as the cost of pollution or the cost of traffic congestion, would encourage governments to take these problems more seriously and try to do something about them. There is no guarantee that they would succeed, and they may quite readily make matters worse. But attention would be paid to problems over which there is increasing concern, particularly in urban areas.

A redefinition of the national accounts would result in a switch of emphasis in government policies. The whole paraphernalia of interest rates, government deficits, the money supply and exchange rates, factors which feature large in the financial media but which in this book are still hovering in the wings like Rosencrantz and Guildenstern, would still be used. But they would be joined by a series of taxes and subsidies, each designed to enhance the value of the new components in the national accounts.

Far from being a challenge to conventional economics, expanding the basis of the national accounts might even enhance the importance of the subject in official circles.

The ability of orthodox economics to understand the workings of the economy at the overall level – the macro-level in the technical phrase – is manifestly weak (some would say it was entirely non-existent). This is not to say that the subject is a completely empty box. At the detailed level – the micro-level – economics might be able to offer certain insights. In terms of understanding the impact of various taxes and subsidies, designed to deter or encourage the consumption of particular goods or services, a combination of theory and applied work can sometimes be useful. It is when economics strays from the particular into the general that its weaknesses are exposed more ruthlessly.

But the real challenge which environmental thinking poses to economics is entirely different.

The fundamental building block of economics is Rational Economic Man. It should be said that even economists are not completely immune to social trends, and in recent years women too have been given the doubtful privilege of being embraced in the definitions of how a rational economic person ought to behave.

The view that society is made up of individuals acting on the rational calculation of their own self-interest pervades modern economics. Indeed, to an economist, just as to Mrs Thatcher, there is no such thing as society, only the individuals who constitute it.

As we saw in the previous chapter, this notion was quite alien to the philosophy of Adam Smith, now eulogised as the intellectual discoverer of the powers of the free market. For Smith, the restraint of public morality on individual behaviour was innate. When events such as industrialisation conspired to erode this framework, the state had a very clear duty to try to rebuild and strengthen it.

An insight into the economist's view of the world is given in a 1993 paper by Frank, Gilovich and Regan of Cornell University. The authors, one an economist and the other two psychologists, used the methodology of behavioural studies in experiments with first-year graduate students.

In one particular game, the students were divided into pairs. One was an allocator, the other a receiver. The allocator was given $10 and told to divide the money between the two. The receiver could either accept this division, or reject it. If rejected, neither player received anything.

In fairness, the money will be divided equally. In pure self-interest, the allocator will propose a division heavily weighted in his or her own favour. The receiver then has a choice whether to accept a small sum, or nothing at all by rejecting the deal.

The research found, in a dry but cutting phrase, that the economics students 'performed significantly more in accord with the self-interest model' than did the non-economists.

Even more telling was a different experiment. In this, the students were each given some money and asked to divide it into two accounts. One of these was a private account, to be kept by the individual. The other was a public account. Once all the decisions had been made, the students were told that the money put in the public account would be increased by an injection of more cash from the organisers and would then be divided equally among all the students.

For the group of students as a whole, the best solution is a fully co-operative one. Everyone puts his or her entire amount into the public account, and then receives an increased amount thanks to the generosity of the organisers in donating to the public account. But for a self-interested individual, the best procedure is to put all his or her money into the private account. In this way, the individual keeps all the money, and gets a full share of the public account money to which everyone else has hopefully contributed.

The students studying economics contributed on average 20 per cent of their initial money to the public account. The non-economists contributed no less than 50 per cent.

The most interesting aspect of the study for many readers might well be the way in which it reveals economists as anti-social reincarnations of Ebenezer Scrooge. But more important is the strong evidence it provides against the core model of behaviour in economics. People appear to co-operate far more frequently than the postulates of self-interested rational calculation allow.*

This is the real challenge which environmental thinking poses to the economic orthodoxy. The benefits of co-operative behavour are a key proposition of environmentalists, who, in sharp contrast to the individualistic behavioural model of orthodox economics, have stressed from the outset the fundamental interdependence and interconnectedness of human actions. Any action taken by an individual today can have consequences for other individuals either today, tomorrow, the day after tomorrow, or even into the remote future.

The concept of understanding human society as a system containing extensive feedback was introduced into the environmental debate by the Limits to Growth studies in the early 1970s. Decisions taken at any time on any point of the planet could in principle have profound consequences as the complicated series of interconnections worked their way through the system.

The initial technical work was carried out by Jay Forrester at the Massachusetts Institute of Technology in 1970, and the results were published by Donella and Dennis Meadows, Jørgen Randers and William Behrens in 1972. The aim of the project was to analyse 'the complex of problems troubling all nations: poverty in the midst of plenty, degradation of the environment, insecurity of employment, economic disruption' and so on. The research team made it clear from the outset

---

*Robert Axelrod's fascinating book, *The Evolution of Co-operation* (1984), provides strong evidence that co-operative behaviour is far more beneficial than the narrow-minded 'rationality' of economics. Axelrod describes the results of many tournaments held between computer programs playing the game of iterated Prisoner's Dilemma. Simple, co-operative programs dominate.

that all such problems interacted with one another.

The Limits to Growth team argued that five basic factors determined the ultimate limits to growth: population, agricultural and industrial production, natural resources and pollution. A change in any one of these factors had, through complex connections in the system, implications for all the others. The conclusions were that, on then existing trends, the most likely scenario for the planet involved the limits to growth being reached during the next century, which would be followed by a sudden decline in population and production. It was possible to avoid this outcome and to bring stability, but only by people and governments acting co-operatively to generate beneficial rather than harmful feedbacks in the system.

Many criticisms can be – and indeed have been – made of the initial Limits to Growth exercises. Indeed, all of them, fair and unfair, weak and strong, have been made.

One way in particular in which the studies were open to criticism from economists was their neglect of the role of prices. If a resource became in short supply relative to the demand for it, the price would rise. This in turn would stimulate searches to discover more of the resource, often in places which at the previous low price had been unprofitable to investigate. Further, the higher price of the resource would encourage people to use, or even to develop, substitutes for it.

As we shall see, there are many criticisms which can equally be made of the workings of the price mechanism as seen by economic theorists. For example, there is no guarantee that the price mechanism can send the correct signals to people today when complex questions such as the availability of resources in the uncertain future are concerned.

But whatever the particular criticisms, the true and lasting significance of the Limits to Growth work was the development of a fundamentally different approach to understanding the workings of the economy to that of orthodox economics.

Economists see the world as a machine. A very complicated one perhaps, but nevertheless a machine, whose workings can be understood by putting together carefully and meticulously its component parts. The behaviour of the system as a whole can be deduced from a simple aggregation of these components. A lever pulled in a certain part of the machine with a certain strength will have regular and predictable outcomes elsewhere in the machine.

In the basement of the London School of Economics lives a wondrous object. In the 1950s, Bill Phillips, an engineer turned economist, built a machine to teach his students the workings of the economy. Levers are pulled, buttons pressed. Sluice gates open, and liquids of different colours rush round the tubes of the system in a controlled way. This marvellous machine still survives, the very embodiment of the economist's view of the world.

Environmentalists, by contrast, see the world as a living organism. Prodding the system in a certain way in a certain place may sometimes cause the beast to hop in one direction, sometimes in another, and sometimes it will not move at all. The behaviour of the system may well be quite different from what might be anticipated from extrapolation of the model of the behaviour of individuals. Individual behaviour does not take place in isolation. On the contrary, there are impacts on the behaviour of other individuals, which in turn cause feedback elsewhere in the system, and so on and so forth. Behaviour is altogether too complex to be captured by a mechanistic approach.

But it is not just environmentalists who have adopted this complex model as a practical method of analysis. Increasingly, hard-headed mathematicians working in biology, climatology, chemistry and even physics are coming to see it as a more powerful way of understanding the world.

CHAPTER 3

The Roots of Economic Orthodoxy

The opening lines of Dante's *Inferno* capture to perfection the problems encountered by economics from the second half of the nineteenth century onwards: 'In the middle of the journey of our life, I found myself within a dark wood, in which the straight path was lost.'

Economics started with great promise. The classical economists were not afraid to use theory as a method of analysis, but their work was clearly oriented towards practical problems. And economics did not simply deal with economic questions, but with the wider issues of political economy. In other words, the issues addressed by the discipline were chosen precisely because of their political importance and relevance.

During the late nineteenth century, economics began to lose its way, and entered its dark wood, from which it has not yet emerged. Virgil, Dante's companion on his tour of Hell, makes it clear that there is only one way he can escape: '"Thou must take another road," he replied when he saw me weeping, "if thou wouldst escape from this savage place."'

Towards the end of the previous chapter, there was a brief discussion of the 'other road', of an alternative approach to the orthodox view that the behaviour of the economic system as a whole can be deduced by simply adding together the individual parts and that there is therefore no such thing as society.

Almost from the outset of the development of the current economic orthodoxy over a hundred years ago, it should be said, a minority of economists has dissented from the standard view, the most serious intellectual challenge being made by Keynes in the 1930s. Keynes argued forcefully that the characteristics of the world assumed by orthodox theory 'happen not to be those of the economic society in which we actually live, with the result that its teaching is misleading and disastrous if we attempt to apply it to the facts of experience'. But, as we will see in Chapter 7, following his death in 1946 a bastardised version of his own theory was constructed, safely neutered, within the framework of orthodox economics.

But before we look at these arguments, we need to understand how economics came to be in its present position, and to appreciate more fully the severe limitations of the current way in which orthodox economists look at the world.

During the second half of the nineteenth century economics was greatly influenced by the achievements of the physical sciences. Envious of their success and prestige, and aware of the power of mathematics and its influence on their progress, economists turned their analysis in this direction.

The intellectual self-confidence of scientists in the Victorian era stemmed from a mechanistic view of the world. Essentially, they saw the physical world as a machine: a very complicated one, but a machine none the less, whose principles of working could be understood in the same way as the workings of the steam engine were.

Scientists had good reason to hold this view. Their understanding of physical laws, and their harnessing and application through inventions and technological progress, were transforming the world. A powerful example of this was the railway. Using the mechanical principles of the steam engine and of locomotion, scientists in the early decades of the century had made it possible for the first time for humans to travel faster than the speed of a horse. Less than fifty years later, an enormous network of railways spanned the globe.

It can be hard for readers at the end of the twentieth century to grasp the optimism with which these achievements were viewed. Ultimately, our society still rests on scientific advance, but science today is regarded with elements of doubt and fear which would have amazed our Victorian ancestors. Nuclear power eliminates the environmental pollution of fossil fuels and offers a potentially unlimited supply of energy, yet people mistrust the safety of the industry and worry about the long-term consequences of nuclear waste disposal. New drugs offer hope to the sick, yet occasionally we see the horrendous consequences which result from unforeseen side-effects.

Even then, however, at the very forefront of science itself, doubts did begin to emerge as to whether the world was ultimately explicable as a vast but complex machine.

For example, the brilliant Frenchman Henri Poincaré, perhaps the world's leading mathematician in the closing decades of the last century, whose immensely popular books on mathematics were translated into six other languages, discovered the existence of what would now be termed chaotic behaviour. What is more, he found it in physical systems of apparently great simplicity. The distinguishing feature of chaotic systems is that their behaviour is impossible to predict in the long run, a property which cannot be encompassed by a view of the world which regards it as an enormous machine. According to that view, a lever pulled here today will have consequences in different parts of the system over time which, given a sufficient understanding of the workings of a machine, can be understood completely and predicted accurately. In chaotic systems, this is simply not true.

Further uncertainty in the physical sciences was introduced by the remarkable concepts of quantum physics, which even today appear bizarre to the Western mind. Towards the end of the nineteenth century, experiments of increasing sophistication began to raise very serious problems for classical physics in explanations of the world made at the level of the atom and its component parts. In 1900, the outstanding German physicist Max Planck had an insight which laid the foundations for the revolutionary concepts of quantum physics. This theoretical development was not conceived in isolation, but was firmly based on empirical observations, on the need to explain reality.

But these were developments very much at the frontiers of human knowledge. To the practical Victorian engineer or chemist, scientific principles based on the assumption that the world was a well-oiled machine appeared to work. Bridges stayed up. Railway engines moved. The electronic telegraph, an invention in many ways even more important than railways in terms of the speed with which humans could communicate around the world, enabled messages to be sent and received almost instantaneously from Europe to America. And automatic weapons, which gave such enormous military supremacy to the Europeans who invaded Africa, Asia and the Americas, all too clearly worked.

In the past twenty years or so of our own century, the ideas of uncertainty and the inherent difficulty of prediction, and the concepts of sudden change and discrete jumps in patterns of behaviour, even in apparently smoothly running systems, have become far more pervasive in scientific analysis, through the tremendous growth of interest in chaotic and non-linear systems. These latter are important concepts which form a key theme of the discussion in the second half of this book.

Analytically, the scientist of the 1990s would feel very much at home in the world of the classical economists, with its emphasis on dynamic change and marked and irregular fluctuations. As we have seen, even for Adam Smith, analysis of the economy was by no means confined to a world of harmony, brought about by each individual economic agent following his or her self-interest. For Malthus, the economy was very far removed from harmony. Catastrophic and unpredictable impacts such as war and plague were a central feature of human society. From time to time, an economy might escape them for a prolonged period and enter a phase of rapid population growth, only to be laid waste by famine. For Ricardo and Marx the main interest was in the process of growth and change. Neither of them believed that there was any natural harmony in the workings of the economy that would guarantee a smooth process of transition.

It was this view of the world which was lost in the economics that took shape in the final decades of the nineteenth century, and that has since come to dominate the profession.

The analogy of the world as a smoothly running machine has an important implication, in addition to the one regarding its ability to be explained. It refers to a world that is in harmony and in equilibrium. Once started, the machine glides along, each component part contributing to its serene progress. There is no place in this kind of universe for shocks and catastrophes, or even, at a less dramatic level, for any tendency of the machine to break down.

Against this background of the great achievements of physical scientists, economists sought to emulate their work. Around 1870, quite independently, William Stanley Jevons at Manchester University and Léon Walras in Lausanne, both of whom were trained initially as physicists, introduced mathematical systems of analysis, founded on principles used successfully in subjects such as engineering, which remain the basis of much of the economics of today.

Indeed, a great deal of modern economics is the result of applying more sophisticated mathematics to the methodological framework they set up.

Walras's system was probably the more complete of the two, and it is certainly his name which is best remembered in the literature of economics. Even today, the phrase 'Walrasian General Equilibrium' is applied to the core model of economic theory taught to students around the world.

The description and criticism of this model occupy much of this and the subsequent chapter. But, in summary, Walras's approach broke decisively in many ways with the work of classical economists such as Smith and Ricardo.

From an economics that took into account specific institutional, social, political and historical factors, which for scholars such as Smith played such an important role in determining the development of any particular economy, a theory was articulated which was believed to hold in all economies at all times. Growth was simply taken for granted, and the problems of economic fluctuations and unemployment, which featured strongly in the classical writings, simply disappeared. The key issue in Walras's theoretical model was how a given quantity of resources could be allocated most efficiently among individual consumers and individual companies. This had been a subject of interest to the classical economists, too, but it now came to occupy centre-stage, displacing the previous emphasis on the causes and consequences of growth and change.

Despite the highly abstract nature of his theoretical writings, Walras shared one key element of the perspective of the classical economists, for he believed that the ultimate justification for economic theory was its potential to improve human welfare. Indeed, he took an active interest in both applied economics and the question of social reform. A successor to his chair in economics at Lausanne in the mid-twentieth century argued that Walras was diverted from these issues by the mathematics which he used in his theories.

Many people do feel instinctively uncomfortable when mathematics is applied to the analysis of human activities. The description of behaviour in symbols and equations seems in some rather disagreeable way to undermine the concept of free will, which remains deeply rooted in the Western mind.

Certainly the use of mathematics purely for its own sake is something resolutely to be avoided. As Sherlock Holmes himself reminded us: his arch-enemy, Moriarty, was 'a professor of mathematics at a provincial university'. The fictional nature of both these characters does not detract in any way from the strength of the warning.

The great classical economists used no mathematics apart from simple arithmetic. Keynes was probably the most influential economist in the world over the period from around 1930 to 1970, and even today still commands many followers. Yet despite his own extensive training in mathematics he permitted himself the use of no more than a few lines of elementary algebra. One of his leading Cambridge disciples, Joan Robinson, writing in the 1950s, complained subsequently of economists hiding behind 'thickets of algebra'. She would have sympathised with a resolution passed almost a hundred years previously by the Danish economic association, which august body in 1874 declared mathematical economics to be 'officially invalid'.

A casual glance at academic economic journals seems to confirm Robinson's suspicions. Indeed, if anything, they show the situation to have worsened markedly. Whole pages consist almost entirely of mathematical symbols. In some of the journals which are most highly regarded by orthodox economists, such as the British-based *Review of Economic Studies* or the American *Econometrica*, the comment could apply not just to individual pages but to whole articles. Taking the July 1993 issues of these journals at random, we can find an article on 'Implementation in Economies with a Continuum of Agents', containing sub-headings such as 'upper hemicontinuity at the continuum limit', and another entitled 'Existence and Uniqueness of Equilibria when Preferences are Additively Separable', one of whose few concessions to the English language is its opening two sentences:

While the infinite dimension equilibrium existence theory is now well understood, there are few results on the problem of uniqueness. The purpose of this note is to study the particular case of a pure exchange economy where agents' consumption space is $L_+^p(\mu)$ and agents have additively separable utilities which fulfil the hypothesis that agents' relative risk aversion coefficients are smaller than one.

There is a story, perhaps apocryphal, current on Wall Street about a Romanian theoretical physicist now employed as an economist at a leading firm of brokers. On being asked at interview how he had come to be interested in economics, he replied that he had been able to study it only with great difficulty. The communist regime under Ceauşescu had imposed an ideological ban on imported economic journals from the West. But one journal, *Econometrica*, had escaped the censor, on the grounds that its contents could be of no conceivable relevance to anything.

The temptation to use mathemetics is irresistible for economists. It appears to convey the appropriate air of scientific authority and precision to economists' musings. More subtly, its use hides the implications of many of the assumptions which are made routinely in professional work.

To take just one example, the phrase 'assume a continuum of traders' will be encountered in many theoretical papers on the idealised market economy. Not only is the phrase used widely, but it is important in the theoretical models which represent the modern development of the approach first put forward by Walras and Jevons. The precise reasons for this need not concern us just yet, except to say that it is a convenient mathematical assumption to make in many of the models which theoretical economists built, enabling them to develop results by using certain powerful mathematical theorems which would otherwise not be valid. Once this assumption is made, further assumptions are then spelt out in more detail, and, several pages of mathematics later, the conclusion is proved.

But what does this phrase 'continuum' actually mean? It sounds quite innocuous, yet spelt out in words it might lead people to query the realism of any academic paper based upon this assumption, or even to begin to doubt whether the article was worth writing in the first place. For the phrase means that the number of people, whether as individuals or as firms, carrying out trade in this theoretical economy is not just large, but is quite literally infinite. In fact, to be strictly accurate, it even means rather more than this. If one were to start to count the whole numbers – one, two, three and so on – one could go on for ever. There is an infinite number of them. No matter how big the number, there is always one bigger. But mathematicians have the apparently bizarre but nevertheless logical concept of infinities which are even bigger than this infinity! A continuum is exactly one of these. In other words, it is assumed that there is not just an infinite number of traders, in the sense that the set of whole numbers is infinite, but that there is an even bigger number of them than this.

Economists who write such papers are perfectly competent mathematicians. They know precisely what the assumption means mathematically. But its full implication has been obscured by repeated use. Without being able to make this assumption, many elegant papers would simply never see the light of day. It is essential to the solutions of the systems of equations set up in the theoretical economic model.

Despite these important qualifications and reservations, mathematics – if properly used – can be of great value in political economy. Like language, it is simply a tool to assist the process of thought.

Seen in its proper role, as servant, not as master, maths is an invention which can increase enormously the productivity of thinking. In our everyday lives we are familiar with the myriad inventions which enhance productivity, whether at home or at work. The washing machine enables more washing to be done more efficiently in much less time than if it were done by hand. The word processor allows more documents to be produced more quickly than if they were written out by hand.

Similarly, maths can vastly increase the power and effectiveness of thought. Complex problems, which would take many pages of words to describe, can be stated more succinctly, and their implications analysed more clearly, by the use of mathematics than by the use of words. And there are many problems which are quite beyond the power of words to analyse. In the same way that one would use words and not maths to write poetry, maths and not words is helpful in deciding how to send a rocket to the moon.

The method of analysis developed by Walras and Jevons introduced the systematic use of mathematics into economics. But it was not the use of maths by itself which led economics to its present erroneous path; rather, it was as a result of seeking to raise economics to the status of the physical sciences that the pioneers of the new economics in the late nineteenth century adopted the then dominant view of the harder sciences, which saw the world as a smoothly functioning machine. As it happens, this particular picture of the world led to the use of certain kinds of mathematical tools and approaches rather than of others. But at least initially the economics drove the maths, rather than the other way round.

The 'marginal revolution', as it has come to be known within economics, of Jevons and Walras and their successors formalised a part of Adam Smith's work, and demonstrated more rigorously that under certain assumptions the free-market system would lead to an allocation of a given set of resources which was in a very particular and restricted sense optimal from the point of view of every individual and company in the economy.

Smith argued that free markets, in which everyone, whether a buyer or seller, of labour or of produce, followed his or her own self-interest, would lead to outcomes which were to the benefit of all. It was this part of his contribution to economics that was translated into mathematics in the 'marginal revolution'. The mathematics refined and sharpened the assumptions which were required for this result to hold, and, given these assumptions, appeared to prove Smith's conclusion in a more rigorous way than was possible with purely verbal argument.

But in so doing, much of the richness and complexity of the original analysis was lost. Smith's insistence on the importance of the institutional framework and the overall set of moral values in which free markets operate was neglected, for such concepts do not convert readily into the language of mathematics. Neither was his deep interest in the process of economic growth and the processes by which some nations become rich while others remain poor addressed by the new system of economic analysis. The problem of growth was assumed to be solved, and a new central question for economics was therefore assumed: how to allocate the resources generated by growth in the most efficient way.

The use of the word 'marginal' in the description of the new theory does not mean that in some way it is now at the margin of, or in some way irrelevant to, modern economics. As we shall see, the word describes the key feature of the behaviour of people and companies in the approach. Over the years, in fact, the system of thought which it embodies has come to be known as the model of competitive general equilibrium – or Walrasian general equilibrium – but it is still based very clearly on the principles of marginal analysis.

The initial success and attraction of marginal economics were essentially due to three factors.

First, by appearing to demonstrate the superiority of the pure, free-market economy, it served valuable ideological functions. For example, the less interference there was from government in the running of the economy and of society, the closer the real economy would be to the theoretical free-market ideal, and so, it was argued, the more efficient it would be. Business should therefore be free to operate with an absolute minimum of regulation. Further, the less the government did, the smaller the size of the state machine required to carry out its duties, and so the less the amount of money required from taxation to finance its operation. Marginal economics appeared to 'prove' that business should be left as much as possible to its own devices, without help or hindrance from the state, and that the level of taxation should be as close to zero as possible, sentiments which exactly suited the Victorian philosophy of self-help and self-reliance.

The second reason was, as we have seen, that the concepts of harmony and equilibrium on which marginal economics is based were very much in keeping with the scientific spirit of the times.

The third reason for the success of marginal economics was that it represented a formidable intellectual achievement. As an example of abstract human thought, even at this distance in time, it is truly impressive. It appeared, by its use of mathematics and remorseless logic, to be rescuing economics from what was seen as the often complicated and occasionally contradictory verbiage of the classical economists.

The theoretical constructs introduced to economics over a century ago continue to pervade discussions of policy. They provide both a strong bias towards and an apparently strong rationale for policies which move towards the creation of a free, competitive market. For example, the political and social agendas of Ronald Reagan and Margaret Thatcher were powerfully motivated by the logic of free-market economics. Or, to be more precise, free-market economics was used to underpin the ideological preconceptions of these politicians. The deregulation of financial markets in the 1980s in the Anglo-Saxon economies; the deregulation of and increased flexibility in labour markets, a topic which is presently the subject of a fierce debate among the political classes of Europe; the privatisation of state-owned industries; reductions in welfare programmes – all these themes flow from the logic of the theory of competitive equilibrium.

As we noted in the first few pages of this book, disagreements among economists attract considerable publicity. But almost all such disputes concern the behaviour of the economy at the aggregate, macro-level, rather than at the micro-level of individual behaviour. It is the micro-level which is described by the equilibrium model of marginal economics, and which is fundamental to the world view of orthodox economists, regardless of any differences which they might have about how macro-economic policy should be conducted.

By far the most publicised argument in macro-economics is that between Keynesian and monetarist economists, which has persisted ever since the appearance of Keynes's major work, *The General Theory of Employment, Interest and Money* (1936). Keynesians are rather more inclined to believe in market failure than monetarists, and so not only attach more importance to the role of government in trying to regulate fluctuations in the economy through changes in public expenditure and taxation, but believe that even after a period of years such changes can have an effect on economic activity and employment.

The experience of the 1930s, against which Keynes wrote, did raise serious doubts about the continued existence of market economies in the West, particularly in Europe. An unemployment rate in America of more than 20 per cent led to the New Deal, but in Germany such a rate led to Hitler and fascism, and to a deep sympathy among many Western Europeans for the Soviet system. Communist parties came close to power in free elections in both France and Italy.

Such unemployment rates also raised doubts about the validity of free-market economics as a description of reality. Theoretically, under certain assumptions, free markets had apparently been shown to be efficient in allocating all available resources. But in practice, in the market for labour in particular, gross inefficiency prevailed. The number of those seeking work outnumbered by many millions the number of jobs which were available. Supply was much greater than demand.

Despite these difficulties, raised by the actual experience of Western economies, the theory of competitive equilibrium continued to retain its grip on the subject of economics.

The most powerful reason for the continuing appeal of the theory is that, despite their problems, Western market economies are clearly the most successful form of economic organisation yet invented. There is increasing power in the environmental critique of economic development but, as we saw in Chapter 2, mixed economies have delivered enormous benefits to their citizens over the past two centuries.

The model of competitive general equilibrium is regarded as a theoretical, idealised form of the workings of such economies. It is this link, made between the transparent success of Western economies and the theoretical economic model, which sustains the intellectual dominance of the model.

It cannot be emphasised too strongly that, in practice, the competitive model is far removed from being a reasonable representation of Western economies in practice. By definition, any model necessarily abstracts from and simplifies reality. But the model of competitive equilibrium is a travesty of reality. The world does not consist, for example, of an enormous number of small firms, none of which has any degree of control over the market in which it is operating. Small firms may be fashionable at present, but it is the large multi-national companies such as Ford, BP and Sony which dominate the world economy. It is entirely illegitimate to make the link between the model and the observed success of the Western market economies.

The theory introduced by the marginal revolution was based upon a series of postulates about human behaviour and the workings of the economy. It was very much an experiment in pure thought, with little empirical rationalisation of the assumptions. Designed as a logical description of how rational individuals and companies ought to behave, the emphasis lies equally on the words 'rational' and 'individual'. The individual is considered to be the key building block of the system, the behaviour of the economy as a whole being simply the summation of the behaviour of its component parts.

This attitude was articulated with unusual clarity by Ronald Reagan when he was governor of California. In the context of an environmental debate about redwood trees, he made the famous remark: 'When you've seen one redwood, you've seen 'em all.' The idea that there might be quite different qualities in a collection of redwoods which could not be captured by looking at a single specimen was dismissed out of hand.

The key concept for the individual introduced by marginal economics was that of marginal utility. People were held to consume goods and services because of the 'utility' which they derived from them. This theory did not spring fully fledged from the works of Jevons and Walras, but was developed gradually during the final decades of the nineteenth century, with refinements being added in our own century. The most important figure associated with the development of this theory was undoubtedly Alfred Marshall, who occupied a chair at Cambridge University for many years and whose *Principles of Economics* represented for a long time the most comprehensive articulation of marginal economics. But many distinguished economists made important contributions, such as the American Irving Fisher, over several decades, beginning with his 1892 doctoral dissertation on *Mathematical Investigations in the Theory of Value and Prices*.

In the theory, it is not assumed that everyone need derive the same amount of utility from any particular set of goods and services which might be consumed. Indeed, everyone could have quite different preferences. But it was thought to be self-evident that the more of any product which an individual consumed, the less would be the additional amount of utility derived from the consumption of yet more of the same.

One child on a birthday outing might like McDonald's hamburgers, for example, yet be quite satisfied after just one, switching his or her attention to the consumption of several ice-creams. But another child may particularly relish hamburgers, eating three or four of them, and perhaps forgoing ice-cream altogether. The tastes of the two children differ. But whether the preference is for ice-cream or for hamburgers, it seems sensible to think that it is the consumption of the first item of food to be offered that gives the most pleasure. The second is enjoyed, as is the third, or even conceivably the fourth, but the additional enjoyment obtained from each one is that little bit less than from the previous one.

49

In the technical phrase used to describe this assumption, consumption is subject to diminishing marginal returns. The consumption of yet more of a product will never reduce the total amount of utility derived from its consumption, but the extra satisfaction – utility in the technical phrase – derived from each additional amount will diminish as the absolute amount consumed rises.

It was assumed in the development of marginal economics as a theory that every individual would carry out rational calculations and consume an amount of any particular product such that the utility derived from the consumption of the final unit of it – the marginal unit – was equal to the cost of obtaining that unit. At first sight, this does seem to be a plausible description of attitudes towards consumption. The purchase of a first car by a household increases its mobility enormously and is a source of great pleasure, while to have a second, additional, car is often little more than an added convenience. The household does gain extra benefits, but the additional benefits are not as great as those obtained when moving from a situation of having no car at all to having just one.

But, logical and rational as the assumption of diminishing returns may seem, an extension of the example of car ownership illustrates that consumption may not always be governed by this principle. The purchase of a third car, for example, would be unlikely to increase the mobility of most families by very much. Its value would seem to be purely as a source of convenience whenever, say, the teenage son or daughter required a car. But, for some three-car households at least, this is hardly the motivation for the purchase of the third car. More satisfaction might be derived from the acquisition of the third car even than from the first, and certainly from the second, for it is a way of demonstrating to friends and neighbours the unquestionable wealth of the family.

With the example of the Yuppies in Britain and America and Les Golden Boys in France fresh in our memories from the 1980s, the idea of conspicuous consumption as a means of displaying wealth and power should be quite familiar. For some people, at least, consumption is often subject not to diminishing but to increasing returns to scale. The more one has, the more one wants, and the greater the satisfaction obtained from getting it.

Such an observation is not new. The concept of conspicuous consumption was introduced at the turn of the century by the American Thorsten Veblen, in his book *The Theory of the Leisure Class*. Marginal economics did not lack critics, even at the outset, and Veblen was one of the most prominent. His 1904 book, *The Theory of Business Enterprise*, extended his challenge from the theory of consumer behaviour to the theory of how companies operated.

No less a scholar than J. K. Galbraith, recently asked by the *Times Higher Education Supplement* to name the book which had had the most influence on his way of thinking, cited Veblen's *Theory of the Leisure Class*, but Veblen's work has been brushed to one side by the mainstream of the economics profession. Adam Smith emphasised the importance both of the price mechanism and free markets, and of the social and institutional frameworks in which they operated. Analysis and description were inextricably linked. In essence, the economists of the marginal revolution emphasised the former part of Smith's work and made it more rigorous, while those such as Veblen stressed the importance of the latter part, of institutions and of social and cultural values. But the remorseless, mathematical logic of the marginal school carried the greater appeal to the economics profession.

For individuals, consumption was held to be subject to diminishing marginal returns. For companies, it was assumed that production was carried out with diminishing marginal returns to scale.

The process of production and the state of technology was assumed to be as follows. A certain quantity of any given product could be produced with a certain combination of inputs – factors of production – such as labour, capital and land. The use of a greater amount of these factors of production, either alone or in combination, would increase the total which could be produced. But it was assumed to be logical that the additional amount which could be produced for any given increase in the inputs would diminish as the scale of production increased. Firms would produce an amount such that the marginal revenue obtained – the revenue from the sale of a unit of output – would equal the marginal cost of its production.

The existence of diminishing returns to scale of production in this model would tend by itself to limit the size of individual firms, or at least limit the size of any particular process of production. If, as the scale of operations expanded, less and less could be produced by the use of extra inputs, there would be little incentive to create large factories.

Suppose, for example – although it is a big supposition to make – that the techniques of mass production of cars had never been invented. Henry Ford never existed. Instead of the enormous factories, the world-wide distribution and marketing networks which characterise the car industry in reality, a quite different structure would be seen. The production of cars would resemble the production of fine claret in the vineyards near Bordeaux. There would be a large number of producers, each assembling carefully crafted products, each subtly different from those of its neighbours. But the market for any single product would be very small, and the size of firms severely limited by the available technology.

But the theory of marginal economics went even further than this in its assumption of a world of many small firms. In the real world, for example in the production of claret, each producer, or vineyard, has its own unique set of qualities which differentiates it from the rest. Even though the company is small, limited by the technology of production, it can nevertheless exercise some degree of control over its limited market by appealing to its own unique qualities. Brand loyalty can be built up, and the price of the product increased by exploiting that loyalty, as any lover of claret will testify.

In the theory of marginal economics, by contrast, it was assumed that all the small firms in any given market produced identical products, with no single firm being of a size to influence the price of the product being sold. In other words, as if all the vineyards and all the claret produced in France were exactly the same.

The world of marginal economics was and is a world of many small firms. As we saw earlier in this chapter, the more sophisticated mathematics applied nowadays to the competitive equilibrium model often makes the assumption of a 'continuum' of firms. In other words, of an infinite number of companies!

When first developed, the theory of both individual and company behaviour employed the mathematical technique of the differential calculus – high-school algebra – invented some two hundred years previously and widely used in the harder sciences. In fact, it is through this technique that the theory is still taught to most students up to first degree level throughout the world.

The application of differential calculus to the axioms of behaviour discussed above produced what was regarded at the time as an outstanding analytical advance. Adam Smith's notion of the Invisible Hand, of the power of competitive market forces in co-ordinating the myriad individual economic decisions into an efficiently functioning system, appeared to be proved mathematically.

Ironically, at precisely the time when the theories of marginality and diminishing marginal returns were capturing the academic discipline of economics, the United States was moving towards world economic dominance by exploiting the unprecedented and massive *increasing* returns to scale of production and distribution which its rapidly expanding economy permitted. In other words, by taking advantage of the benefits of being big.

A large number of the companies which were to become household names in the United States in the twentieth century grew enormously and established their market strengths in the final decades of the nineteenth century. Quaker Oats, Campbell Soup, Heinz, Procter and Gamble, Schlitz and Anheuser Brewing, Eastman Kodak, American Telephone and Telegraph, Singer, Westinghouse, Union Carbide – all these are examples of companies which took advantage of increasing returns in production and distribution at that time to establish themselves on a national, and in some cases international, scale.

In 1870, the population of America was 39 million, not much more than that of Britain at 31 million. American income per head of the population was around 80 per cent of the British level, which was then the highest in the world. The combination of a higher population and a lower income per head meant that the size of the American domestic market was virtually identical to that of the British.

By the onset of the First World War, this had changed dramatically. America had overtaken Britain as the leading economy in terms of income per head. From being 20 per cent below the British figure in 1870, America was by then 20 per cent above. And while the population of Britain had grown by only 14 million over this period, in America the growth was 58 million. Indeed, the growth in the American population was of itself much bigger than the total size of Britain's population.

From a position of equality in 1870, by 1913 the American domestic market was over two and a half times that of its main European rival, Britain.

Such a market was of a size entirely without precedent in world history. It offered tremendous opportunities for the exploitation of increasing returns to scale. Companies found, contrary to the precepts of marginal economics, of which they were blissfully ignorant, that the bigger the scale of operations, the more could be produced, and the more profit could be made from the additional marginal unit of production.

Advances in technology made these leaps in economic progress possible, which in turn provided the finances not just for further investment in plant and machinery but for yet more research and development. These positive feedbacks placed the Western economies, and particularly that of America, on a virtuous circle of growth.

Two factors of great importance were, first, the massive expansion of the railway system, not just in America but also in Europe, which meant that enormous volumes of goods could be moved at unprecedented speed, and, second, the invention and installation of the telegraph, the impact of which has perhaps not been dwarfed even by the revolution in electronic communications through which we are living today. With communication possible virtually instantaneously between distant places, commands could be given, orders for purchases placed, and so on, in a way which until then had been quite impossible.

Similar developments took place in Europe, but it was in America in the last quarter of the nineteenth century and the early years of the twentieth that the most dramatic advances occurred.

In part, the shape and size of American industry which emerged from this period, and which created the conditions necessary for world economic dominance, were due to historical accident – or, rather, to a particular piece of legislation, the Sherman Antitrust Act, which, if we had the facility to replay history many times in a laboratory experiment, would not be seen as at all inevitable, but which had the most profound consequences.

The dynamic combination which the new size of markets permitted, of technological innovation, investment, and exploitation of increasing returns to scale, meant that there was downward pressure on the prices of manufactured goods. Modern examples of this process are video recorders and personal computers, the latest models of which not only offer better quality than their counterparts of ten years ago, but are available at much lower prices. Technological advances permit improvements in quality, and the creation of mass markets enables the cost of production of these products to fall dramatically, as manufacturers are able to take advantage of increasing returns in the processes of production, sourcing, distribution and marketing.

In both Europe and America, in the 1870s and 1880s, there was consistent downward pressure from these 'supply-side' factors on the prices of manufactured goods. On both continents, manufacturers responded by forming trade associations across a wide range of industries. Far from being sources of charitable benevolence, the purpose of such associations was to allow companies to control and organise markets so that prices could be maintained and profits increased.

It was in response to this that, in 1890, the United States Congress passed the Sherman Antitrust Act, which declared such associations and combinations of firms to be illegal. This form of legislation was unique to America, with no counterparts emerging in Europe for many decades.

The response from industry was to formalise such associations through mergers and acquisitions. In other words, instead of working with a large number of other small and medium-size companies to try to control the market by the informal agreements of a trade association, certain companies achieved their aim by the direct process of taking over potential rivals.

The merger and acquisition movement around the turn of the century was on a tremendous scale, and laid the foundation for America's economic dominance. Companies of enormous size were created, which gave even more opportunity for effective management to realise gains from increasing returns to scale.

Of course, American law continued to be firmly against market power exercised through contractual co-operation between companies, but the very scale of the companies created in the years preceding the First World War gave them the ability to achieve market power and control through size and efficiency.

This competitive advantage, once created, proved to be enduring. The longevity of consumer brands, for example, has proved remarkable. Of the top twenty brands in America in 1925, almost seventy years later no fewer than eighteen of them are still the best-selling products in their categories. This does not mean that new, powerful brands have not emerged; they have, but they have been in such markets as training shoes, which were either small or non-existent in the early years of this century.

In many sectors, firms which were the biggest or next biggest in their industry at the end of the First World War have remained so, although subsequent waves of mergers and acquisitions have meant that the survival rates of dominant individual companies is not quite as striking as it is for the individual consumer brands.

Ironically, it was against this background that the grip of marginal economics, an imaginary world of many small firms constrained in size by the technology of production and unable to influence price or shape the market in any way, was consolidated in the economics profession.

Almost from its inception, the theoretical postulates of marginal economics concerning the nature of companies have been a travesty of reality.

Companies operate in a dynamic, uncertain environment. They seek to influence demand by complex marketing strategies, from advertising to pricing policies. They try to gain advantage over their competitors by research into new products and new techniques. They innovate across the whole production process, from the philosophy and structure of management to the physical organisation of the workplace. They make mistakes, but it is only by constant questioning of existing practices and by constant change that they succeed.

The benefits of success are substantial. In many areas of activity, companies experience increasing returns to scale, not the diminishing marginal returns of economic theory. An advantage over competitors, once gained, can be further exploited and enhanced. To him that hath, more shall be given.

In the Gulf War of 1991, it really did not matter how many tanks or how many aircraft were available to Iraq. The technological superiority of the Allies was such that the Iraqi armed forces could be destroyed almost at will.

Economic competition between companies, particularly large ones, bears a strong resemblance to this military world. Competitive advantage is not something which falls from the skies like manna from Heaven. It has to be created and earned, but once earned it can be used to ensure a position of enduring dominance. However, according to orthodox economic theory, this should not happen, since if any single firm were able to gain an advantage at any point in time, competitive forces would rapidly ensure that this state of affairs would be purely temporary.

In a world of diminishing returns, there are strong restrictions on the ability to reinforce competitive advantage, whether through the techniques and organisation of production, the purchase of supplies, or through the structure of distribution and the process of marketing. After a certain point, the cost of making each additional unit of production rises. By definition, discounts are not available for bulk purchase of supplies. Efficient national and international channels of both distribution and marketing are assumed not to exist.

Economists tend to see the entry of firms into markets as something which takes place easily, and any 'supernormal' profit streams which come into existence are eroded by such entry and the resulting competition which it creates.

It may be said in passing that, in the market for strategic advice, the revealed preference of companies is to use management consultants and business-school academics rather than economic theorists. The former group tend to have few, if any, theoretical preconceptions, and draw instead on a wide range of practical experience.

To the economist, this poses problems. Firms by definition are rational, yet they choose to pay large sums of money to people who purport to believe – indeed, many of them truly believe – that their advice can confer distinct and lasting competitive advantages on the beneficiaries. Further, economic theorists are presumed to be rational economic people themselves. Their typical remuneration is small compared to that of business consultants, who proffer what the economist sees as virtually worthless advice. Yet, quite contrary to the doctrines of their discipline, we see very few theorists trying to enter this market to bid away competitively the fees of consultants by conveying the truth. And we see even fewer who succeed.

By far the most complete and detailed empirical account of the development of companies on a global scale has been produced by a non-economist, Alfred Chandler of the Harvard Business School, who over a lifetime of investigation has documented the transformation of capitalism brought about by the growth of giant industrial companies. His magnum opus, *Scale and Scope of Industrial Capitalism* (1990), examines the histories of the 200 largest manufacturing companies in the three leading industrial nations, America, Britain and Germany, over a century, beginning in the 1870s. A wide variety of detailed source material is used, from company histories and published company reports to investment directories and archival records.

Chandler's work is a detailed account of how firms were able to take advantage of the supply-side opportunities created towards the end of the nineteenth century, and of how, once acquired, the advantage was consolidated in subsequent years and through subsequent periods of rapid innovation. He shows that, far from being passive recipients of the technological environment and the markets in which they operated, successful firms implemented strategies which actively shaped the markets and their structure. For example, before the First World War, firms in the United States which made soap and household detergents relied on selling to wholesalers, who in turn supplied the retailers. In 1919,

Procter and Gamble realised that by supplying directly to the retailer they could exercise much greater control over the steadiness of production in their own factories. Consumer demand for the products was steady, but orders from individual wholesalers could fluctuate widely, requiring periods of overtime in the factories followed by periodic lay-offs. A large investment in sales staff, warehousing and the accounts department was necessary. But the move was very successful, and other companies in the market quickly followed suit, effectively eliminating the middleman wholesalers.

In the car industry, by 1921, Ford and General Motors had already established themselves as the leading companies, not just in America but worldwide. Each invested heavily, both in the techniques of mass production and in distribution and marketing networks. Assembly plants were built across America, in order to reduce the transport costs involved in getting the product to market. In the inter-war years, both expanded rapidly abroad on the same principles, with the difference that GM acquired foreign companies while Ford tended to build its own factories abroad. These years in particular were not without problems for car companies, but at the onset of the Great Depression in 1929 these two were producing well over half the cars in the world.

In electrical machinery, the German companies of Siemens and AEG, along with General Electric and Westinghouse in America, exercised world domination of this important industry for many decades. Even by the turn of the century, the two German companies were operating on a global scale. Extensive sales forces were built up, which not only sold but also provided the production, design and research divisions with information about the needs of their customers. This information was used directly in research and development of new products. Siemens and AEG diversified rapidly and on a large scale into related product lines such as equipment for telephones and for the manufacture of chemicals. In addition, they each either set up or acquired financial institutions for the specific purpose of providing funds to their customers to enable them to buy their products.

Chandler shows that in general a three-pronged strategy was necessary for success. First, there needed to be investment in production facilities large enough to take advantage of economies of scale and scope. Technical innovation itself was not the same thing at all. Then, as now, technical knowledge was widely available. It was the translation of technical knowledge into the productive process by means of investment in new plant and machinery which was the key. Second was investment in product-specific marketing, distribution and purchasing networks. Third was the recruiting and organisation of managers capable of operating the firm efficiently.

Chandler emphasises that it was the combination of these three activities that was necessary for success. British companies, for example, tended to be handicapped by the persistence of family control and management of the company, which failed to ensure that the enormous potential for economies of scale and scope *within* it was realised to the extent it was in America and Germany. The co-ordination and control of complex processes, both in production and in distribution, by a suitable management structure was very important.

Albright & Wilson, which by the end of the nineteenth century had become a large and successful chemical company, mainly making phosphorus for matches, provides one illustration of the problems which family management brought in Britain. Twenty years after American chemical companies had specialised the task of cost-accounting, it was still being carried out in longhand at Albright & Wilson, by the board of the company themselves, taking up days and days of their time. Even the proposed use of a slide-rule at these meetings was frowned upon by the senior member of the family who was present.

Turning orthodox economics even further on its head, Chandler argues that the massive merger movement at the turn of the century was positively beneficial to the American economy, permitting a rationalisation of industry and implementation of the three-pronged strategy, which did not begin in Europe until twenty or thirty years later.

We have seen that successful companies, once established, have proved very hard to dislodge. In orthodox economics, any economies of scale and scope which exist are both immediately available to and immediately attainable by all companies. In reality, it is companies which possess the organisational and financial capacity to exploit these economies which succeed.

An important implication of Chandler's study of several hundred of the world's largest manufacturing companies is that the path which a firm follows over time – or even, given the size of some of these companies, the path which the whole economy follows – is very sensitive to particular decisions made at critical points of time.

Both good and bad decisions can have consequences which persist for decades, as competitive advantage, once gained, is reinforced and magnified. This property of the sensitivity of performance to particular sets of conditions is one which we shall formalise when we consider the behaviour of national economies in the second part of the book; it is especially important in formulating a realistic analysis of such behaviour.

The above point may sound obvious, but until very recently it was almost entirely absent from orthodox economics. The persistence of high levels of unemployment in particular has obliged economists to consider reasons why this should be the case, because according to the model of competitive equilibrium economies should tend towards situations in which demand equals supply, and large imbalances should not persist. Not surprisingly – and this is another point to which we return later in the book – many economists believe that the problem is due to practical restrictions on the operation of the free market, and so the solution to unemployment is to deregulate.

Yet the importance of specific events, of specific institutions, and of the ability of decisions to have consequences which persist for long periods was recognised by Adam Smith over 200 years ago. This is yet another illustration of the tendency among economists to focus purely on the analytical aspects of Smith's work regarding the operation of the price mechanism, and to ignore his wider arguments.

Chandler's book does not deal with the development of industrial capitalism in Japan, which took place later than it did in Europe, although the initial model used in Japan had much in common with the successful model of development used in Germany. In brief, German companies drew on many of the same principles which were used in the United States. The major difference between the countries was in the attitude of the respective governments to industrial collusion. Although American law in general supported any competitive advantage which might be gained by following a successful business strategy, even if this gave a company domination over an industry, co-operation and collusion between companies to achieve the same ends in partnership with each other were outlawed. In Germany, by contrast, the law gave active support to the establishment of industrial cartels.

But perhaps the Chandler view of the world is most relevant to Japanese success when looking at the most recent two or three decades. An absolute prerequisite of industrial success in the first century of managerial capitalism has been the task of company management to define a suitable set of goals for the organisation.

In America, during the long period covered by Chandler's study, the basic goals of managerial firms were long-term profit and growth of the company.

In contrast, in family-owned, personally-managed British companies, the goal was to supply a steady flow of cash to the owners to sustain their expensive lifestyles. Growth itself was not a primary objective, and there was a tendency to consume rather than invest profits. The story remains much the same in Britain of the 1990s. The substitution over the years of pension funds for individual ownership has not altered the bias in favour of short-term income flows at the expense of longer-term investment and growth.

Recent decades have seen the classic goals of companies in America placed under threat. The greatly expanded roles of financial institutions, particularly during the 1980s, led to a new emphasis on short-term performance and financial engineering, which is seen increasingly as having damaged the long-term capability of the American economy. But it seems likely that this will prove a purely temporary phase. Financial institutions are now such important holders of the debt and equity of American industrial companies that their interests now coincide increasingly. It is only by the long-term success of the latter that the former, too, will prosper. Indeed, at the time of writing financial companies in the United States have begun to take an active role in the removal of top executives whose performance they judge to be inadequate (IBM is probably the best-known example).

Even so, the short-term financial wizardry of the 1980s has undoubtedly weakened American industry. By contrast, both German and Japanese companies have retained their emphasis on the classical American goals of long-term growth and long-term profit.

A new general dimension of industrial capitalism has emerged during the past decade, based on micro-electronics and information technology. There is a switch of emphasis away from economies of scale in a range of productive processes, and towards flexibility of production. Flexible production permits economies of scope and product variety at much lower volumes of production than is possible under systems of mass production. The flexible use of fixed capital equipment both makes diversification easier, and shortens the product life-cycle.

It is in the practice of flexible production that Japan excels. Cars can be custom-built, virtually to the individual specification of the buyer. Just-in-time systems of delivery, which have become possible through sophisticated information technology, cut down drastically the level of stocks which need to be held, and enhance the degree of control over the flow of production in the factory.

But the basic principles of corporate success remain unchanged from those identified by Chandler. A strong and reliable stream of cash needs to be available for investment, obtained either from a good flow of internally generated profits, or from a long-term relationship with the financial sector. And high levels of investment are needed to ensure that companies stay at the frontiers of technology in their industries.

Increasingly, of course, the concept of investment has widened to embrace investment in the skills and abilities of the workforce, investment in human capital as well as in the traditional physical capital of machines and buildings. In the pre-Second World War period, successful Chandlerian companies did invest extensively in management. In the 1990s, investment in people is needed at all levels of the company.

Flexible production demands a close relationship with efficient suppliers and efficient distributors. Nissan can now deliver a vehicle chosen from an option range by the individual consumer within ten days. And appropriate management structures need to be in place to manage companies which have become increasingly global in their operations. In the past decade alone, for example, the Japanese have built a successful automobile industry within the United States which is bigger than that of Britain or Italy.

Despite the weight of evidence against the validity of the model of competitive general equilibrium as a plausible representation of reality, its tenets continue to permeate both theoretical economics and economic policy.

Academic and consultant economists from the West – of which Jeffery Sachs of Harvard, who acts as an adviser to the Russian government, is perhaps the most prominent example – descend on Eastern Europe, proclaiming the urgent need to move to free-market economies as soon as possible. Yet tremendous economic dislocation has taken place in many countries where this advice has been followed. In the autumn of 1993, much is being made of the fact that the Polish economy, an early subject of these experiments, is set to grow by some 4 per cent during the course of the year. But the Polish people in the general election have at the same time given their verdict on the collapse of their economy in the immediately preceding years, by restoring many former communists to power.

In an article in the British newspaper the *Independent* in October 1993, Sachs argued that the failure of 'shock therapy' – his phrase – in countries such as Russia and the Ukraine was not due to the idea itself being wrong, but to the fact that it had not been implemented with sufficient rigour. In the Czech Republic, where the advice had been followed more closely, the economy was starting to recover. But this ignores the crucial influence, which Adam Smith emphasised, of the cultural and social framework in which markets operate. Before the war, the old Czechoslovakia had living standards equal to those of the West, and even a brief visit to the country confirms how deeply Western are its roots, located in centuries of the Austro-Hungarian empire. A society like this can be moved more quickly towards a market economy than countries further to the East, in large areas of which, even before the Soviets seized power, markets had never evolved beyond those of rudimentary village agriculture, which have characterised peasant economies for thousands of years.

The advice to follow pure free-market policies seems in any event to be contrary to the lessons of virtually the whole of economic history since the Industrial Revolution. With the possible exception of the first wave of industrialisation in Britain, every country which has moved into the strong sustained growth which distinguishes industrial, or post-industrial, societies from every other society in human history, has done so in outright violation of pure, free-market principles.

Markets, competition and entrepreneurship are all very important, but by themselves they are not enough. Infant industries – even when they have become industrial giants – have sheltered behind tariff barriers; government subsidies have been widespread; there has been active state intervention in the economy; and, perhaps most important of all, successful companies have exercised power and control over their markets.

Even Far Eastern economies such as South Korea and Singapore, which are held up as models of free-market principles, do not in practice conform to the ideal. The governments of these countries possess a degree of internal power which is far greater than is the norm in Western societies, and they are not afraid to use it.

The model of entrepreneurial activity in the product markets, with judicious state support plus repression in the labour market, seems to be a good model of economic development. The People's Republic of China and the Mafia are perhaps the latest examples of this kind. But it is not necessarily a policy menu which would suit everyone, and it cannot be said to be an example of the free, competitive market.

Leaving aside the question of the degree of internal democracy, countries such as Singapore demonstrate the enormous progress which can be achieved with a combination of a visionary government and an entrepreneurial society. In fact, Singapore is a classic example of how competitive advantage can be earned and created. An illuminating article in the *Harvard Business Review* by Rajendra Sisodia in 1992 describes in detail how the economy of the country had been transformed. Its only natural assets are its strategic location and its deep-water harbour. All its energy, and even its water, has to be imported.

Yet in terms of GDP per head, Singapore has risen rapidly to a level higher than that of most of Southern Europe, and higher even than certain regions in prosperous Northern Europe.

Sisodia notes a number of important features of Singapore's economic development. The government has played a key role in several ways. Although the proportion of the workforce directly engaged in the public sector is very small, at only 6 per cent, the influence of government is pervasive.

It was the government, not the free market, which decided that the management and use of information technology was the most critical of all contemporary managerial concerns. Massive investments have been made both in public infrastructure and through the state-owned tele-communications company to ensure that Singapore quite literally leads the world in its use of information technology.

It was the government, not the free market, which decided in the context of its economic plan that the skills of its workforce needed constantly to be upgraded. And it was the government which solved one of the classic problems associated with rapid economic development, namely acute urban traffic congestion, by interfering ruthlessly with the free market in transport in order to ensure the flow of traffic and a relatively unpolluted environment. A quota system for the purchase of new cars was introduced, for which people bid each month in order to be eligible to buy one. A lower priced permit allows cars to be driven only at weekends and at night, with the penalties for breaking the regulations running into thousands of dollars.

The public sector in Singapore has behaved in many ways like an exemplary Chandlerian company. It has had clear goals with which to judge its progress and achievements, and it has invested heavily in a number of dimensions in order to achieve these goals. It has shaped its own markets and has created its own competitive advantage.

Too often in the West, the public sector operates in a bureaucratic way, stifling initiatives, with the workforce itself having the primary interest of preserving the cartel structure which protects its jobs, rather than in serving the public. In Singapore, salary increases of public-sector workers are linked to the overall performance of the economy, an important symbol of the role which the public sector is expected to play, namely through its own efficiency and vision to enhance the effectiveness of the private sector.

The World Bank brought out a report in the autumn of 1993[*] which attempted to challenge the idea that the success of the Far Eastern economies in general was due to extensive co-operation between the public and private sectors, and in particular the idea that government intervention in the economy had been successful. But even this report, which met a barrage of criticism from Far Eastern experts, was obliged to recognise that a key reason for the economic success of the countries was a high level of investment in education by the state, that policies to promote exports, which often involved protection of the domestic market, had worked, and that government intervention in financial markets to support industry had usually been successful.

The New Right in the West have had so many easy targets in the public sector that their eulogy of the free market has attracted widespread political support. But their policy package contains two quite distinct offers. First, the need to eliminate waste and inefficiency in the public sector. Examples of this are both widespread and transparent. But, particularly following the election of Bill Clinton, this can no longer be claimed as exclusive territory by the Right. The title of the influential book by David Osborne and Ted Gaebler, *Reinventing Government*, has been taken up by the administration in the United States as a symbol of their commitment to reduce red tape and improve the efficiency of public services.

The second part of the New Right's policy package has been the belief that free-market solutions are always best. It is this latter view which is profoundly mistaken. Markets and profits are crucial, but the *pure* free-market model itself is deeply flawed.

Of course, markets and incentives do have a very important role to play in increasing economic welfare. A key theme of the second part of this book argues exactly on these lines. The impact of profits in determining the course of the economy as a whole was of the greatest importance to

The East Asia Miracle, World Bank, 1993.

the early classical economists. It is very much neglected by contemporary economic analysis and needs to be restored to its primacy. But to say this is not to recognise in any way the validity of marginal economics.

Criticisms of the relevance of the marginal model to the economies of the West have been made for many years. Indeed, there appear to be so many violations of the conditions under which competitive equilibrium exists that it is hard to see why the concept survives, except for the vested interest of the economics profession and the link between prevailing political ideology and the conclusions which the theory of general equilibrium provides.

The traditional defence against such observations is that, despite the enormous size of many companies, markets operate as if there were many firms, and as if the conditions of competitiveness existed. If a large company is making excessive profits in a particular market, for example, other large companies from outside the market have the financial power and resources to enter the market and thereby ensure that competition prevails.

From time to time, there are examples of such a phenomenon actually occurring. Indeed, in the computer industry the successful challenge to the dominance of IBM has come not from another industrial giant, but from Microsoft, a company which barely existed a decade or so ago. Defenders of the faith are accordingly able to dismiss to their own satisfaction criticisms of the theory which are based upon the apparently glaring contrast between the size and power of companies required by the theory, and the size and power of successful companies in practice.

The theoretical model of competitive equilibrium is a formidable intellectual construct. A similar situation arose, for example, in the Middle Ages, when the belief that the sun revolved around the Earth led to astronomical models of great complexity as scholars struggled to account for ever more discrepancies between the observed paths of the heavenly bodies and those required by the theory.

Eventually, the entire model was laid to rest.

CHAPTER 4

Professional Reservations

The distinguished physicist Erwin Schrödinger, reflecting on the nature of his discipline, once wrote that:

A theoretical science unaware that those of its constructs considered relevant and momentous are destined eventually to be framed in concepts and words that have a grip on the educated community and become part and parcel of the general world picture ... in the long run is bound to atrophy and ossify, however virulently esoteric chat may continue within its joyfully isolated groups of experts.

At one level, this is a charge which seems more relevant to literary theorists than to economists. Over the years, many leading economists have, after all, entered actively into public policy debate, articulating their view of the world and setting out clear policy prescriptions. Keynes in the inter-war years and Milton Friedman in the 1970s and early 1980s have been perhaps the two most prominent examples.

This phenomenon should not be confused with the bombardment in recent years of television, radio and the press by economists employed by financial institutions. With very few exceptions, these outpourings are essentially part of the public-relations and advertising activities of the companies concerned. Indeed, on Wall Street a stipulation in the contracts of a number of economists is that they should secure a certain minimum amount of media coverage for their company. Despite the high salaries involved, employing economists is a cost-effective way for banks and stockbrokers to secure exposure in the media.

But the bulk of economics as a discipline is carried out within universities around the world, with, to paraphrase Schrödinger, small groups of the initiated musing to each other. This lurking mass, despite overwhelming empirical evidence against the validity of its theories, dominates the subject, and even surfaces occasionally to see the light of day. It is this mass which forms the subject matter of the present chapter. Of necessity, we will at times need to use the 'virulently esoteric chat' which surrounds the core model of economics, but this should not detract from our intention, which is not merely to provide an exercise in ivory-tower criticism. Indeed, as we have seen, the model of competitive equilibrium, built on the premise of Rational Economic Man, currently exercises a great deal of influence on the conduct of practical economic policy in the real world.

The whole emphasis of economic policy in the West in the past ten to fifteen years has been to implement free-market 'solutions' to problems. Labour markets must be made 'flexible'. Industries in the public sector should be privatised. Financial markets should be freed of tiresome restrictions and deregulated, both within the domestic economy and in terms of relations with the rest of the world, so that, for example, controls on the movement of capital should be abolished.

The prime movers in the recent fashion for free markets were the right-wing administrations in Britain and America at the start of the 1980s. But many nominally centre–left governments have been unable to resist the pressures. France under Mitterrand, Spain under González, Australia under Hawke and Keating and New Zealand under Lange are all examples of countries in which notionally social-democratic governments adopted most of the policy agenda of Margaret Thatcher and Ronald Reagan.

Following the election of Bill Clinton in the United States, there are signs that the previously irresistible drive towards free-market solutions is being checked, but as the twentieth century draws to a close the dominant tendency in economic policy is still governed by a system of analysis inspired by the engineers and scientists of the Victorian era.

The practical influence of the theoretical model of competitive equilibrium during the past decade or so has been enormous. Certainly, it has been far greater than it was for many years after the Second World War. The phrase 'rolling back the frontiers of the state', coined in the late 1970s in the early days of Mrs Thatcher's leadership of the British Conservative Party, inspired governments around the world during the 1980s, regardless of their political background. The Labour Party in New Zealand, for example, had a tradition of economic regulation and intervention which was almost unparalleled outside the Soviet bloc. Yet in government in the 1980s the party introduced a free-market reform programme that drew the admiration of a former adviser to Margaret Thatcher, who said it had moved more quickly and more brutally to liberalise the economy than she would have ever dared.

In the past decade or so, free-market policies have led to a number of conspicuous failures. Britain, for example, has been at the forefront in

Europe of policies designed to deregulate labour markets, to make them correspond more closely to the flexible free-market ideal. A series of laws has been passed on trade union activity, for example, each one restricting more and more the ability of trade unions to function. But British unemployment remains very high, at over 10 per cent of the labour force, or just under 3 million people. This compares to an average of under 0.5 million in the more regulated, corporatist policy regime of the 1950s and 1960s.

In the United States, deregulation of financial markets has produced many effects, one of which has been the Savings and Loan scandal. For many years, Savings and Loan companies (S and Ls) were the epitome of cautious, conservative Middle America. Small savers deposited their money in the local S and L, which in turn lent the money to people to buy houses. Government regulations controlled very strictly how S and Ls could use the money deposited with them – effectively, it could be put only into low-risk assets. The managers of S and Ls were known as '3–6–3s', because of their alleged habits of borrowing at 3 per cent, lending at 6 per cent, and being on the golf course by 3 o'clock every afternoon.

In September 1981, the world of the S and Ls changed dramatically. Congress allowed them to buy and sell the entire portfolio of their higher returns. But more than that, complicated new accounting pro-3cedures were introduced which allowed any losses made over the previous ten years to be offset against tax. In other words, the American government, courtesy of the taxpayer, effectively agreed to underwrite any losses which S and Ls made, at the same time allowing them to trade in risky assets, which they proceeded to do on a grand scale. On a single day in 1985, for example, Twin City Federal Bank of Minneapolis traded no less than $1.3 billion of mortgage bonds.

Not surprisingly, deregulation of this kind, supposedly liberating S and Ls from old-fashioned restrictions, encouraged a massive squandering of money by S and L executives, and attracted sophisticated operators in organised crime like bees round a honeypot. Wall Street, too, in an entirely legal but morally reprehensible way, exploited the naivety of the S and L management by charging enormous fees to carry out their dealings, making billions of dollars in profit at the ultimate expense of the American taxpayer.

Far from promoting economic efficiency, this particular aspect of free-market policy will end up costing the American taxpayer literally hundreds of billions of dollars.

In a number of European countries, such as Italy, France, Spain and Sweden, the abolition of controls on the movement of capital on the foreign exchanges has removed a powerful weapon used by the authorities in defence of their currencies from the occasional speculative attack. Instead, they have been forced to rely upon interest rates to carry out this function. High interest rates might induce people to invest in a currency, so that not only will funds stay at home rather than flow abroad, but an inflow of capital from outside the country might even be attracted. But high interest rates also deter both consumers and companies from spending, so that the domestic economy is weakened and unemployment rises. In France, the absolute priority of economic policy during the past decade has been the preservation of the value of the franc abroad, the policy of '*le franc fort*'. To achieve this aim, interest rates have been very high. And unemployment has risen almost continuously throughout the 1980s to its current level of around 3 million.

In Sweden, the relaxation of controls on capital movements in the early 1990s had a more sudden effect. The ability of the banking sector to invest abroad had been constrained for many years by these regulations. Swedish banks lobbied hard to end this curtailment of their freedom to make money wherever they could. Their wish was granted, and they invested massively abroad, mainly in the European property market. Unfortunately, they bought at the very height of the property boom, so that, far from making money, the appalling losses sustained in a matter of a couple of years have effectively bankrupted the Swedish banks themselves.

These are just a few examples of the adverse effects which free-market policies can have in practice.

Most emphatically, all this is not to say that free-market policies are always wrong, but that the real world is far more complex than is allowed for in the economic model of Rational Man and competitive equilibrium.

As we saw in the previous chapter, the key factor used to describe the behaviour and motivation of individuals and companies is that of diminishing marginal returns. Consumers get smaller and smaller additional amounts of satisfaction – of utility, in the technical phrase – from each additional amount of any particular product or service which they buy. As a company gets bigger, production can always be expanded by increasing the amount of labour, materials, capital equipment and so forth – the inputs, again to use the technical phrase. But from any existing level of production, the extra amount which can be made from successive increases of a given amount of all the required inputs gets smaller and smaller.

In a famous passage in *Alice in Wonderland*, the Red Queen declares that she often believes six impossible things before breakfast. The model of competitive equilibrium appears to be requiring us to move into this kind of world. And especially so in the case of companies, where the evidence from over a hundred years of economic history provides powerful evidence against the validity of the theory as a description of reality.

The intellectual attraction and fascination of the model arise from two striking characteristics of the system as a whole, which follow logically from the assumptions on which it is based but which are not at all obvious from a purely verbal description of the behavioural precepts of marginal economics. Indeed, they are not obvious from even a mathematical description of the behaviour of individual people and companies in the model, and it is only when the behaviour of the system as a whole is described, by adding up the outcomes of all the individual decisions made, that the results can be demonstrated.

The logical proof of these two properties of competitive equilibrium requires pages of maths. But they can be described in words quite briefly. First, a free-market, competitive equilibrium is efficient, in the important sense that demand equals supply in every market, so that all the resources of an economy are fully utilised, and none lie idle.

Second, in such an equilibrium, no individual or company can be made better off by altering the allocation of resources in any way whatsoever, without making at least one person or company worse off. In other words, the distribution of income and wealth which emerges in the equilibrium cannot be altered by policies of taxation without making someone worse off. This property of competitive equilibrium is known in economics as a Pareto optimum, after Vilfredo Pareto, who quibbled and argued with Léon Walras over issues of social and applied economics, but whose 1909 book *Manuel d'économie politique* was an important extension and elaboration of Walras's original work on the theory of competitive equilibrium.

It was the demonstration of these two results which was the really exciting intellectual feature of the marginal revolution in economics, and that even today accounts for the fascination of the economics profession with the construct of competitive equilibrium. Adam Smith's concept of the benefit to the economy of people and companies pursuing their own self-interest appeared not just to have been proved formally by the use of mathematics, but to have been extended. And the extensions had strong ideological attractions.

In a pure, free-market economy, for example, demand would equal supply in every market. And since the market for labour is just the same in principle as the market for, say, bananas, the same conclusion holds. In the labour market, the number of people supplying their labour through being willing to work will equal the number of jobs which are demanded by employers. Supply equals demand, everyone who wants a job can have one, so that full employment prevails.

So, in an ideal world, since all markets clear by definition and there is no unemployment, the government does not need to intervene in the economy to balance supply and demand. Further, by Pareto's finding, any attempts to alter the allocation of resources which emerges can only be done by making at least one person or company worse off.

In short, either economic policy has no effects, or it hurts some group of citizens. Therefore there is no role for it. Governments in practice might make a mess of things quite frequently, but in the equilibrium model they should not even try to intervene.

One might observe that many academic economists around the world who teach these results almost daily see no harm whatsoever in governments having at least one particular economic policy – namely, the raising of taxes and the expenditure of this money on the salaries of economists and their institutions. Few and far between are calls by academic economists, particularly in Europe, for governments to take an important step in the direction of the competitive model by ending all funding for universities.

In the idealised world of competitive equilibrium, the role of government should be as small as possible. It is recognised that there are certain functions in an economy, such as defence of a country by its armed forces, which require collective provision, and which cannot be left to the decisions of self-interested individuals to provide. In principle, services such as education, health and pensions could all be provided in this latter way, but not defence. Either the United States has a nuclear strike capability, or it does not, and it is not possible for one group of Americans by their individual choices to enjoy such protection while the rest, by their individual choices, do not.

Without going into the technical details, it is possible to accommodate both the provision of services such as defence in the competitive equilibrium model and the ways in which taxes can be raised to finance them.

But the general implication of the theory of competitive equilibrium is that the role of government should be as small as possible, and a small public sector implies that the costs of maintaining it will be small, and so the levels of taxation needed to pay for it will be very low. As far as is possible, in this model the functions of the state should disappear. To best serve the interests of the people, the state should wither away.

This is of course very similar to the conclusion drawn by Karl Marx in his political writings: under socialism, the state would wither away. It may seem ironic that the free-market model of economics urges us that under free-market capitalism this phenomenon should also take place, but there are in fact more similarities between the theoretical economics of a pure socialist economy and those of a pure free enterprise economy than might be imagined. In the 1940s and 1950s, the concept of planning was far more fashionable in the West than it is now, and indeed of necessity many economies had actually been subject to rigorous controls and plans during the war. A number of academic articles at the time demonstrated that an omniscient socialist planner, by using the price mechanism as a way of deciding how resources should be allocated, could achieve results identical to those of an ideal, free-market economy, but with a more egalitarian distribution of income and wealth.

Socialist planning in theory could be just as efficient as free enterprise, and at the same time more equitable. Of course, the discrepancy between theory and practice in the planned economies of the Soviet bloc was plain, for all who chose to see, but there is a wide gap also between the principles on which the far more successful Western economies actually operate and the theoretical model of competitive equilibrium.

In a practical sense, leaving aside for one moment the theoretical world of competitive equilibrium, economists have actually made sensible use of Pareto's criterion in judging the overall desirability of many economic policies. If a policy could improve the overall welfare of one particular group of people or companies, but only at the expense of making another group worse off, there is a presumption that the losers should be compensated from the gains of the winners through the system of taxes and subsidies.

For example, the introduction of a new runway at an airport will add to the convenience of those who use it. Flights can be provided more frequently, and new destinations offered. But those living under the flight path will lose out through having to endure an increase in aircraft noise. Using Pareto's criterion, the economist's solution, in its simplest form, is to levy a tax on the use of the airport, and to hand over the proceeds to the nearby residents to compensate them for the reductions in their living standards brought about by the increase in noise.

Many problems arise in implementing this in practice, not least of which is the fact that different people have different levels of tolerance to noise. Ideally, those who suffer most should receive the most compensation. But if the government were to try to discover people's attitudes to increases in noise through a survey, everyone would have an incentive to exaggerate their dislike of noise in order to get more compensation. In practice, if such a measure were ever introduced, it would have to depart from the theoretical ideal and operate a rule of thumb, such as giving most to those who were closest to the airport itself, where noise is the highest, regardless of their alleged or actual tolerance to noise. But at least this would offer some compensation, if only of a rough and ready sort.

As a guide to the practical conduct of economic policy (quite separate from the fact that a Pareto optimum is a theoretical property of competitive equilibrium), the principle of compensating losers from the gains of the winners has much to recommend it. It is the basis for many policies put forward for dealing with environmental problems, on a wider scale than the example of aircraft noise given above. Such problems almost invariably arise as a byproduct of another activity. Aircraft produce noise, cars emit fumes, and fossil-fuel power stations give out carbon dioxide gas. But while the costs of these byproducts – externalities, to use the jargon of economics – are borne by a large number of people, they do not appear to their full extent in the prices of the goods and services whose consumption generates these costs.

Taxing such consumption more heavily to reflect its true social cost – in other words, adding the cost of externalities to the usual cost of the product – is seen as one way of dealing with such problems in practice. Such policies do not satisfy the more fundamental environmental criticisms which relate to the whole pattern of lifestyle and consumption in the West and to its ultimate sustainability, but they do offer an area in which economists can be of help to many people, it not all of them, who have environmental concerns.

The problems of applying economics to such practical questions begin to arise when the workings of the price mechanism are vested in real life with the power and authority they possess in the theoretical world of competitive equilibrium. It is one thing to use, as a practical guide to assessing the impact of any particular policy, a criterion based upon compensating losers from the gains of winners, and to influence prices by either taxation or subsidies as a way of trying to reallocate such gains and losses. But it can be dangerously misleading to believe that the price mechanism is an infallible solution to problems.

Staying with the issue of the environment, towards the end of Chapter 2 we came across an argument used by economists against the theses of the Limits to Growth studies in the 1970s. One such thesis was that the Earth was in danger of running out of key natural resources. Conservation measures were necessary to prevent this from happening.

Drawing on the price mechanism and the theorems of competitive equilibrium, the typical response of economists was to argue as follows: if a resource was beginning to run out, its supply relative to the demand for it would fall, and the price would rise. Demand would exceed supply. The price rise in turn would have two effects. First, there would be an incentive to search for further supplies of the resource, even in parts of the world where its extraction would not be profitable at the previous, lower price. If these searches were successful, the resource would not become exhausted after all. Second, the higher price of the resource would encourage the development of substitutes. If oil, say, really were running out, there would be a big incentive to develop wind and wave power as a means of supplying energy.

These two factors are undoubtedly a feature of the real world. When the countries of OPEC combined to raise the price of oil by three or four times in 1973–4, subsequent years saw both an increase in interest in alternative energy sources and, even more important, further exploration for, and extraction of, oil from difficult climates, such as the bleak and hostile North Sea.

But some economists looked much more deeply into the problem, and in the 1970s produced a number of important papers which addressed the question of whether the price mechanism could always be relied upon to save the world from running out of exhaustible resources. In a word, the answer was no.

In 1979, Partha Dasgupta of the London School of Economics and Geoffrey Heal, now of Columbia University, brought out a 500-page book entitled *Economic Theory and Exhaustible Resources*. A key sub-heading in one of their chapters reads: 'The impossibility of fully informative price systems'. In other words, it is not possible to prove the existence of a price system which will reflect all the information necessary to prevent a resource from becoming exhausted. Indeed, Dasgupta and Heal go further, and conclude their chapter by stating: 'We have noted several reasons why the market [i.e. the price mechanism] is likely to provide incorrect incentives for exploration activity.' In other words, the market is likely to fail!

The key reason why Dasgupta and Heal, among others, arrived at this conclusion was that in their theoretical models they allowed the future to exist. This may seem a bizarre statement to make, but it is not. The model of competitive equilibrium which has been discussed so far is set in a timeless environment. People and companies all operate in a world in which there is no future and hence no uncertainty.

Once uncertainty is introduced into the theoretical framework, many of the results obtained from the standard model of competitive equilibrium no longer hold. This is a point of the greatest importance, to which we return later in the chapter.

It is worth noting at this stage that the consequences of introducing uncertainty into the model are devastating. To follow on from our discussion above of competitive equilibrium and Pareto optimality, for example, in 1982 David Newbery of Cambridge and Joseph Stiglitz of Princeton proved that in an uncertain world a competitive equilibrium is in general *not* a Pareto optimum. In other words, except under conditions which even in their theoretical model the authors describe as being 'extremely restrictive', a very powerful and attractive property of the standard model of competitive equilibrium is simply not true.

Yet it is this standard, static model of equilibrium and its results which is taught as the core model of economics to students all over the world. Many economists have doubts about its validity as a description of reality. These doubts are held in varying degrees, some of them arising from the difficulties caused for the model by empirical evidence, and some from an awareness of theoretical results such as the ones discussed above. But despite such doubts, generations of students who are trained in economics at first-degree level accept its conclusions as the received wisdom, and its precepts pervade discussions of economic policy.

Remarkably, despite all the problems associated with it, the theory of competitive equilibrium retains a strong grip on the intellectual sympathies of academic economists themselves. In 1989, Darrell Duffie of Stanford and Hugo Sonnenschein of the University of Pennsylvania wrote an extensive review article on the theory of competitive equilibrium for the prestigious *Journal of Economic Literature*. The article began with the sentence: 'The greatest achievements of economic theory concern the determination of value in competitive markets and the extent to which competitive markets lead to an efficient allocation of resources.' The authors went on to say: 'Today, the general equilibrium model is not the exclusive province of the high-tech theorist; rather, it is a basic part of the professional economists's tool bag, and *one that is increasingly used* [my emphasis].' These sentiments are shared widely in the economics profession.

The profession in fact resembles the revellers in Edgar Allan Poe's chilling story 'The Masque of the Red Death'. Everyone is having a splendid time, indulging 'joyfully in virulently esoteric chat'. But some, at least, are aware of the existence of a presence among them that will ultimately cause the party to end in tears.

Perhaps the most devastating criticisms of the model of competitive general equilibrium have come from mathematicians and economists working within the profession itself. Two such examples have been mentioned already, the work of Dasgupta and Heal and that of Newbery and Stiglitz.

Economists feel able to dismiss sociological criticisms of their model of rational behaviour because sociologists have little or no mathematics. Economists are able to dismiss the conspicuous failure of certain policies designed to move the economy closer to the competitive ideal by pointing to flaws in the design of any particular policy.

Economists are even able to dismiss the vast weight of empirical evidence against the validity of their model, drawn from economic history, by the simple device of closing their eyes and chanting the 'as if' mantra, which goes as follows: it may appear that successful firms owe their success to the exercise of market power. It may appear that once a firm achieves dominance, it is very hard for competitors to break it down. It may appear that the long-standing success and dominance, and the ways in which such qualities are achieved, of companies such as Ford and Procter and Gamble contradict the assumptions of the theory. But, nevertheless, it is 'as if' competition in the sense of the competitive model, with its infinite number of firms, prevails. And very occasionally, as we saw at the end of the last chapter, a Microsoft does appear from nowhere to shake the dominance of an IBM, giving comfort and succour to the 'as if' believers.

But economists who can happily dismiss all these criticisms find it much harder to dismiss the mathematical critiques made from within the profession itself. These technical criticisms strike at the very heart of the theoretical model. For they take the model on its very own terms and ruthlessly expose its inadequacies.

Severe theoretical problems for the model of competitive equilibrium have in fact been known to exist for many years. For the important example to be discussed now, the original result was established no less than sixty years ago.

The theory of competitive equilibrium, as we have seen, is very much a theory of the behaviour of the economy at the micro-level. Each agent in the economy, whether a consumer or a producer, has at least one equation which describes his or her behaviour. The behaviour of the economy as a whole, at the aggregate, macro-level, is built up from the individual equations at the micro-level.

Even in a small economy, there will be a large number of equations describing the behaviour of each individual in it, whether the individual is a person or a company.

Competitive equilibrium requires that there exists a set of prices for all goods and services in the economy which ensures that demand in every single market is equal to supply. In other words, the price of each product must be such that the amount which producers are willing to supply at that price is equal to the amount which is demanded by consumers. If such a set of prices exists, all markets can clear and the potential existence of a competitive equilibrium for the economy, at least in a static world with no uncertainty, is established.

John von Neumann was an outstanding polymath, who made path-breaking contributions to subjects such as the mathematical theory of games and computing. He was perhaps the most brilliant of all the Central Europeans who thrived on and so much enriched the intellectual life of America in the middle decades of this century. In 1932, he gave some of his attention to the economic model of competitive equilibrium, and presented a paper at a mathematics seminar held at Princeton. Von Neumann asked a simple question: what mathematical assumptions are necessary in order to prove that a set of prices ensuring that supply equals demand in every market exists at all?

The question had been considered by Walras himself in his seminal contribution to the theory of competitive equilibrium in the early 1870s. Walras, and those such as Marshall who subsequently developed the theory even further, had the insight to realise that it was an important issue to address. But the treatment of it before von Neumann was rather rudimentary, and in any event the interest for economists was not in the mathematical proof of the existence of a solution, but in the consequences of a solution actually existing. In other words, in the consequences for economic policy which could be deduced from an idealised situation of competitive equilibrium.

Although the question itself was simple, von Neumann realised that the proof required a level of mathematics well above the capabilities of all but a small number of the world's economists in the 1930s, and which even now is normally taught only to economists in specialist classes at post-graduate level.

The essence of the problem is that there is a large number both of goods and services and of people and companies even in a small economy, each with an equation describing their economic behaviour. The ability to prove that a solution does exist for these myriad equations, that a set of prices exists at which demand equals supply in every market, requires some very special assumptions.

The problem is complicated by the fact that there are restrictions on the values which these prices can take, since otherwise the solution does not make sense in terms of its economics. To take the most obvious example, prices cannot be less than zero. A negative price means that the seller receives a negative amount for his or her product, or in other words pays the buyer to take the product away. So solutions in which prices are less than zero, while they might form a valid mathematical solution to the equations, are not permitted.

Von Neumann's problem was not to find an actual solution to any particular set of equations, but to find out what assumptions were needed to guarantee the existence of a permissible set of prices – for example, with no prices less than zero – in order to ensure that supply equalled demand in every market in *any* set of equations used to describe a competitive economy.

An analogy from high-school algebra might illustrate the point. The quadratic equation $x^2 - 7x + 12 = 0$ has two solutions, $x = 3$ and $x = 4$.* There are a number of ways of solving this particular equation.

*The mathematically challenged reader can check this easily. If $x = 3$, for example, x^2, which is x times x, equals 9, and 7 times x is 21. So we have $9 - 21 + 12 = 0$.

But it has been proved that a formula exists which can be used to solve *any* quadratic equation of this kind. The appropriate values can be fed into the formula, and the solution emerges. Von Neumann's problem can be thought of as analagous to the problem, not of solving any particular equation, but of proving whether or not such a general formula exists. If it does, solutions to any equations of this type are known to exist.

Von Neumann was able to prove that assumptions could indeed be made which would guarantee the existence of an equilibrium set of prices for any set of equations describing the behaviour of a competitive economy.* But it took more than a decade for the economic implications of his mathematical results to be appreciated.

Kenneth Arrow of Stanford University, subsequent winner of the Nobel Prize for economics and arguably the most fertile and productive economic theorist since the war, began work on the theory of competitive equilibrium in the early 1950s. It is really through his work that economists became aware of the stringency of the conditions that are required to guarantee the existence of competitive equilibrium.

The economic interpretation of the mathematical results can be stated essentially as follows, namely, that a sufficient range of goods and services should be produced to ensure there are very few gaps in the availability of markets in which consumers are able to participate. For the most part, this appears to be satisfied. But there is a very big gap in the provision of markets which concern *future* events. In financial markets and markets for many commodities, it is often possible to trade, not in the prices which obtain today, but in the prices which are expected to hold at particular dates in the future.

For example, it is possible for someone holding dollars to agree to exchange them for sterling, not today at the current exchange rate, but, say, in one month's time at a rate which is agreed today between the buyer and the seller. This latter rate will usually be different from today's rate, for currencies are expected to alter in value over time. Similarly, for many commodities, such as gold or copper or soyabean, markets exist in which contracts can be made to buy or sell fixed amounts of the commodity at specified dates in the future. Even more sophisticated markets exist, such as those which do not offer the direct ability to buy or sell in

*For interested readers, he used an extension of Brouwer's fixed point theorem, but readers to whom this means anything have probably guessed it already and are almost certainly better mathematicians than the present author.

the future at a price fixed today, but the option to buy a contract which would allow one to choose whether or not to buy or sell in the future at a price fixed today.

Outside such markets, the ability to trade in this way is extremely limited. Insurance can be obtained against certain contingencies, whereby a fee is paid today which guarantees the receipt of a larger sum in the future if a specific event takes place, such as damage to a car or the death of a partner. But in general people are unable to trade in future markets for the simple reason that these markets do not exist. It is not possible to go to the local supermarket and agree to buy a specific basket of goods in eleven months' time, say, at a price which is fixed today. It is not possible to agree to sell a house in twenty-three years' time at a price which is fixed today.

These examples may seem slightly odd, but they illustrate the point about the general lack of markets in which trade in the future can be carried out today. For most dates in the future, for most goods and services which are bought today, markets do not exist which enable contracts to be struck today about buying and selling in the future.

Yet according to the assumptions needed in the theoretical economic model to guarantee the existence of a competitive equilibrium, such markets must exist in proliferation. In other words, even given all the other assumptions of the competitive model – such as a large or even infinite number of consumers and companies, with no single company being able to exercise any control whatsoever over the market price of its product, nor any trade union able to exercise any influence over the pay and conditions of its members – it is still not possible to prove that a set of prices will exist which will permit demand to equal supply in all markets, without making the further assumption that there is a very large number of futures markets, transparently more than the number which exists in reality.

It is research such as the above that creates the most difficulties for orthodox defenders of the model of competitive equilibrium. By accepting, for the purposes of analysis, all the assumptions of the competitive model, and by refining them and making them more precise, it demonstrates the improbability of their existence in practice.

Economists are aware of this work, and some of the best minds in the profession have in recent years risen to the challenge, by constructing theoretical models which might be described as approximately competitive. In other words, models which examine how far one can deviate from the set of assumptions required to derive the model of competitive equilibrium, thus bringing it closer to the real world while still being able to retain most of its properties.

Much of such theory, particularly in the past decade, has focused on the problems caused either by firms having some degree of control over the price they can charge, or by workers having some control over wage levels through the influence of trade unions. Neither of these assumptions is permitted in the standard model of competitive equilibrium – they violate the basic mathematical assumptions which describe behaviour in the model. But even orthodox economists perceive that such influences may well exist in reality.

The concern of this recent theoretical work is to examine whether the existence of relatively minor degrees of control over prices enables a model to be generated which is similar to that of the pure competitive equilibrium construct. The research does not attempt to examine the consequences of a model in which large firms dominate markets, exercising power and influence through a broad range of strategies, such as pricing, advertising and promotions, research and development, and so on – in short a model which to many people seems a good description of reality – for it is recognised in economic theory that in such a world the propositions of competitive equilibrium certainly do not hold. Rather, the research is concerned with fairly small violations of the assumptions of the competitive model.

This literature is often motivated by a desire to save the equilibrium model from the challenge of empirical criticism. Joaquim Silvestre of the University of California, in a survey of such work in the *Journal of Economic Literature* in 1993, noted that 'most economists view [competitive equilibrium] as an idealisation. They accept that some agents have at least a minor price-setting capability that generates, they believe, an approximate Walrasian outcome.' But, as Silvestre shows, some of the more recent theoretical models have shown that even negligible violations of the assumption that no individual or group in the economy can exercise any influence over the prices at which any goods and services are bought and sold, lead to outcomes far removed from those of the standard model of competitive equilibrium.

The conclusions of this theoretical work are unsurprising. Almost forty years ago, an important contribution to the literature demonstrated that serious problems exist for the model of competitive equilibrium if any of its assumptions are breached. Richard Lipsey – the author, despite the implications of his paper, of a best-selling and highly lucrative textbook on economic theory – and Kelvin Lancaster, both based in London at the time, examined an important practical issue.

The authors were not dealing with the fundamental problem of whether a competitive equilibrium exists; they had a different concern. Supposing that, by some unspecified means, it was known that in the United States all the conditions required to satisfy the assumptions of the model of competitive equilibrium held in practice, except just two. For example, suppose that no firm could exercise any degree of control over its price, except, say, General Motors. And no trade union could influence the pay and conditions of its members, except, say, the Union of Automobile Workers. This actual example was not used in the Lipsey and Lancaster paper, whose language was mathematics, but it helps to illustrate their result.

If both the company and the union had their power taken away from them, all the conditions required for a competitive equilibrium to hold would be satisfied and, on the logic of the model, the whole economy would be better off. In such a situation, the guideline for economic policy would be clear: remove the power of both the firm and the union.

Lipsey and Lancaster effectively asked the question: what would happen if it were possible, for whatever reason, to take away the power of only one of these, leaving the other, whether the company or the union, to retain its power? Could it be shown theoretically that the economy would be better off than if both of them continued to hold their power? On the face of it, it seems logical that it should indeed be so. If a competitive equilibrium represents the most efficient allocation possible of the resources of an economy, a situation in which the UAW could influence wage levels but GM could not influence the price of cars ought by common sense to be more efficient than a situation in which both of them had their powers.

Unfortunately, common sense is not always a good guide to the truth. For Lipsey and Lancaster proved that such a statement is not necessarily true. In order to make an unequivocal statement, on the criterion of the equilibrium model itself, that an economy is better off if some of the violations of the assumptions required in the competitive model are removed, then *all* such violations need to be removed. If just one of many, or even just one of two, is removed, it is not possible to prejudge the outcome. The economy as a whole can theoretically be worse off if just one violation exists than it is when two such violations exist.

This is a result of great practical significance. For in reality, not just in

America but in every Western country, there are many breaches of the conditions required by the theoretical model of competitive equilibrium. There is a presumption, which as we have seen has been the driving force of policy in many Western countries in the past decade or so, that each single move towards the ideal competitive economy will improve the performance of the actual economy. Lipsey and Lancaster showed that no such general presumption can be made. And, despite subsequent papers on this topic, their basic finding has not been disproved. Namely, that each proposal to increase the degree of competition in an economy must be treated on its merits. Maybe it is sensible, or maybe it is not. Each policy must be examined carefully and judged empirically. It cannot be argued that increasing the degree of competition in an economy, when other obstacles to competition remain, will automatically improve the performance of that economy.

Mathematical economics has raised yet further difficulties for the construct of competitive equilibrium. Suppose, by some miracle, a competitive equilibrium does exist. There is a set of prices which if it were brought into being would ensure that all markets cleared. The question now becomes: how is this particular set of prices established?

Walras, over a century ago, realised this question posed potentially serious problems for his model. To overcome them, he assumed the existence of an auctioneer – or, rather, an Auctioneer, for this mythical creature has played an important role in theoretical economics ever since.

The role of the Auctioneer is to co-ordinate the exchange of information in the economy. A trial set of prices is issued by the Auctioneer to consumers and producers. They respond by providing information as to how much of each product they would buy or make if this set of prices existed. Except by a pure fluke, this initial trial set will not be the set which ensures that all markets clear.

The Auctioneer studies the responses of the agents in the economy, and issues another set of prices. People again respond by indicating how much they would buy or sell. The process continues until the set of prices which would clear all markets is arrived at by the Auctioneer. Producers and consumers are told that these are the prices which will exist. Only then is any actual buying and selling allowed to take place.

In practice, it might well be rather difficult for the Auctioneer to find the set of prices which would clear all markets. Indeed, there is no guarantee that it would be found at all. Recent theoretical work, which allows individual agents in the economy to search for themselves, always subject of course to the iron law of diminishing returns, faces exactly the same problem. The method of search we have described, in which a trial set is proposed and is then modified in the light of new information, is a familiar problem in applied mathematics. It has become well known in recent years as a method for finding practical solutions to systems of equations which cannot be solved directly.

In school algebra, a familiar problem is to find the value or values of the unknown variable, x, in order to satisfy an equation or equations described in the question. Although most readers will remember times when they despaired of ever being able to find the solution of a problem set for homework or in an exam, solutions do in fact exist to the sorts of equations used in problems for schoolchildren. Thinking back, for example, to the quadratic equation mentioned earlier in the chapter, we saw that there is a formula which can be used to solve any equation of this kind.

But there are sets of equations whose solutions, if they exist at all, cannot be found directly in these ways. An example is when there is a very large number of equations in the system, as is the case in the model of competitive equilibrium. In these circumstances, a variety of techniques is available, all based upon the principle used by the Auctioneer to find the values of the set of prices which will clear all markets.

An initial set of values is chosen, and fed into the system. The results are examined, and are used to alter the initial set of values to create a new set which hopefully comes closer to the desired solution. This new set is then fed into the system, and the whole process is repeated again and again.

Advances in computer technology have greatly facilitated the practical development of such techniques, which obviously require an enormous amount of number crunching. These developments have increased substantially our practical knowledge of the problems encountered in trying to find solutions to systems involving large numbers of equations.

It appears to be the case that the Auctioneer *can* guarantee to find the set of prices which clears all markets, but only by making some highly restrictive assumptions about the nature of the equations in the system. An analogy might help to illustrate the problem.

Imagine that an explorer, or, more likely, a participant in a television game show, is confronted by an enormous field. He or she is allowed to start from anywhere in the field. We might imagine the intrepid player being deposited by helicopter. The field has flat parts, but it is pitted with many craters, some small and some large, in the manner of a battlefield from the First World War. The task is to discover the deepest crater.

The difficulties, apart from the size of the field, are twofold. First, the game is played in pitch blackness and the only information permitted to the participant is to know whether he or she is on the flat, descending into a crater, or climbing out of one. Second, certain craters are so deep and their sides so steep that, once at the bottom, the player cannot escape from them. As can readily be imagined, the very deepest crater might never be found.

But suppose that there were only one crater in the field, and that from every point on the edge of the field the ground sloped downwards to its bottom. The discovery of the deepest part would then be an easy exercise.

Searching for solutions to sets of equations involves a process analogous to this. The only slight(!) complication is that the field exists not just in two or three dimensions, but in many dimensions!

The precise lay-out of the field will depend upon the equations which describe the behaviour of companies and individuals in the system, but there clearly can be no guarantee that in practice the topography will be sufficiently well-behaved to allow the Auctioneer to succeed in his task. In fact, scholars such as Richard Day of the University of California have recently constructed plausible examples involving a mere handful of equations in which it is not just difficult, but impossible, for the Auctioneers ever to discover a set of prices which ensures that demand equals supply in all markets.

The realisation that there might be many craters so deep that, once having got into one of them, our imaginary player can never get out has been of great concern to economic theorists in the past decade or so. The implication of such a situation is that there is not just one but many possible solutions to the equations which describe a competitive economy. In other words, there is not just one equilibrium in the economy, but many equilibria.* Many of the papers covered in the survey by Silvestre mentioned above address this problem.

Two problems in particular are raised for economic theory by the

*Economists could have learned from other disciplines, where it has been known for a long time that iterative techniques give no guarantee of finding the global optimum of a system of non-linear equations.

concept of multiple solutions. First, it appears to provide a rationale for government intervention in the economy after all. Even if the assumptions which are required for competitive equilibrium to exist all hold, a free-market economy is unable to co-ordinate the decision as to which of the many potential equilibrium situations will actually be called into existence.

Second, and even more important, the existence of multiple equilibria reduces considerably the generality of the policy implications which can be drawn from the competitive model. If there is a unique solution to the equations which describe a competitive economy, large changes can be analysed within this framework, since by definition the economy will always end up at the unique equilibrium position. But with many solutions, it is possible to make statements only about the consequences of small changes in the locality of any particular solution. Otherwise, the economy might not slide back into its original crater, but be shifted to a position in the field in which it goes into a different crater altogether. In this new solution, for example, the wages paid to different kinds of workers might be quite different relative to one another than they were in the initial solution. In other words, large changes around any particular solution might lead to important and unforeseen changes in the overall nature of the new solution at which the system ends up, and which the free-market system itself is quite unable to determine.*

But imagine now that a unique competitive equilibrium does exist, and that the Auctioneer is able to find it. We are already in a remarkable world, but what is in some ways even more remarkable is that no buying or selling is assumed to take place until the Auctioneer has found his Grail in the form of the set of prices which will clear all markets. No production is carried out, nor goods and services purchased, at prices which do not ensure that all markets clear.

But now suppose that, instead of simply informing the Auctioneer about the amounts they would buy and sell if the list of prices he announces existed, people were to buy and sell at prices which did not clear the market.

This is more than a mere supposition. It is an accurate description of what does happen in the real world. Even people who have the resources to assemble large amounts of information before buying and selling often

---

*Even this property of locally unique equilibria might not hold, for there is no guarantee in non-linear systems that even small changes might not lead to dramatically different outcomes.

trade at prices at which supply and demand are not equal. A good recent example of this is property companies in countries such as the United States, Japan and Britain. A vast over-supply of office properties exists in major cities, and even at rents which are set in desperation at close to zero there is insufficient demand to ensure they are occupied.

This phenomenon, of trading at false prices, to use the technical economic term, has serious implications for the model of competitive general equilibrium.

Once such trading has taken place, there can be no guarantee that, even if an equilibrium exists, the economy will ever converge to it. In fact, it is likely to move in cycles around the equilibrium, from one set of prices to another, at none of which are demand and supply equal in every market.

The final concept to be discussed in this chapter arising from mathematical work on the theory of competitive equilibrium brings us back to points raised earlier about the incorporation both of the future and of uncertainty into the model.

Uncertainty is an integral part of life, impinging on a whole range of issues, both trivial and important. Will it rain tomorrow when the children are being taken on a seaside treat? Will I have a job this time next year? Everyone deals with similar questions on a daily basis. As a cynic once remarked about economic forecasting, it seems to be very hard to get it right, particularly when forecasting the future and not the past. The future is inherently uncertain.

Yet this obvious and fundamental property of human existence was not analysed in any rigorous way in the competitive equilibrium model until the early 1950s, when Kenneth Arrow turned his attention to it, introducing uncertainty, albeit in a specific and restrictive way. (To put these qualifications on Arrow's work is not to detract in any way from the power of his analytical contribution. Rather, it is yet another illustration of how the absurdity of the competitive equilibrium approach has in many ways been best exposed by apparently esoteric work by mathematical economists.)

The task in the standard, timeless model of competitive equilibrium is to discover, if it exists, the set of prices which will ensure that supply and demand are equal, and that all markets clear. But once the future exists, a set of prices must be found which will clear all markets today; another set must be found for tomorrow, yet another for the day after, and so on, before any trading takes place.

In Arrow's version of the model, individuals and companies are permitted to be uncertain in the specific sense that they do not know for certain what the overall environment will be at any point in the future. For example, in a simple agricultural society, the set of prices which will clear all markets next year will obviously be different depending upon whether the harvest is good or bad. The task of the Auctioneer is multiplied many fold if the theorems of competitive equilibrium are to continue to hold.

Arrow demonstrated that, in order for a competitive equilibrium to exist, each person must prepare a complete list of all future states of the environment which might obtain. And everyone must hold absolutely identical and correct beliefs regarding the prices which would exist in each potential state of the world at every point in the future. This is a world which, transparently, bears no resemblance to reality.

Although the sheer intellectual power of Arrow's work captivated economists, the discrepancy between the world of theory and the world of reality, once the future was allowed to exist, did not escape attention. An important research task was to investigate whether the uncertain future could be introduced into the model of competitive equilibrium in a more realistic way.

Roy Radner, a distinguished American mathematical economist, was able to relax Arrow's assumptions in a brilliant paper in 1968. He proved the existence of competitive equilibrium, given all the usual assumptions needed in the single-period model, even if different people had different beliefs about the future state of the world.

This was in one sense a marked advance on Arrow's world, in which everyone had to have identical, correct beliefs. But there was a cost. For Radner also showed that, for his proof to be valid, everyone in the economy needs to have an infinite amount of computational capacity – not just access to a Cray super-computer, but literally an infinite amount of capacity.

All contracts in Radner's model are negotiated at the beginning of the history of the economy, and from then on all actions are determined by already chosen strategies. There is never any need for anyone to revise his or her behaviour, because the choice of strategy is predetermined from the outset, and contracts are negotiated for each market at each point in time in every possible state of the world before any actual trading takes place. In such a world, a competitive equilibrium might exist.

Radner's paper was rich in insights, for he explored the consequences of a world in which people had neither perfect foresight nor access to unlimited computational capacity. In other words, a world which begins to look something like everyday reality. (The stress in this last sentence is very much on the word 'begins', because all the other assumptions required in the competitive equilibrium model discussed earlier are retained.)

Radner's conclusion is stark. The model of competitive general equilibrium, in his words, 'is strained to the limit by the problem of choice of information. It breaks down completely in the face of limits on the ability of agents to compute optimal strategies.' In other words, once a realistic concept of uncertainty is introduced, the model ceases to be of value.

The research agenda of theoretical economics in recent years has contained an important item. Namely, to try to rescue the model of competitive equilibrium from the fundamental problems raised for it, not by mere sociologists, or by applied economists and economic historians who sully their hands with facts and evidence, but by members of the Imperial Guard itself, mathematical economic theorists. And the attempt has failed.

But to end the chapter on a positive note, perhaps the deepest insight in Radner's paper of twenty-five years ago pointed the way to a new analytical approach to micro-economics which even now has only just begun to be exploited.

As is often the case with penetrating insights, this one seems obvious once stated. If individuals and companies have infinite computational capacity, the entire future of the economy can be solved in a predestined way at the beginning of time. If not, individuals have to make decisions in a world in which there are two kinds of uncertainty. First, uncertainty about the future environment, with which the competitive model can cope. But second, uncertainty about the behaviour of others or about the outcome of as yet unperformed computations.

This latter point introduces a fundamentally different concept. The behaviour of any individual or company depends upon uncertain expectations about the future behaviour of the whole economy. But the future behaviour of the system as a whole is made up of the aggregation of the behaviour of all the individuals in the system. In other words, we have an economic system in which individuals at the micro-level are learning their own collective macro-behaviour, which latter is in turn the result of micro-behaviour.

Such systems have a property which might by now be familiar, for it is a recurring theme in the book. The behaviour of such systems at the aggregate, macro-level cannot be deduced from simple extrapolation of the behaviour of a single individual. The whole is different from the sum of the parts. There is such a thing as society.

Two hundred years ago, Adam Smith intuitively believed this to be true. Sociologists have long taken this proposition for granted. At the opposite pole to orthodox economics, with its focus on the rational, purposeful behaviour of individuals, sociology has been informed by the view that it is social and group norms rather than self-interest that drive behaviour. The mutual antagonism between the two disciplines is not helpful, for economists, once they abandon the intellectual structure of the competitive equilibrium model, might have a great deal to learn from sociologists. In fact, it is a sociologist, the American James Coleman, who has perhaps come closest to an attempt to blend the two disciplines, in his major work *Foundations of Social Theory*, published in 1990.

Unlike most sociologists, Coleman postulates the existence of rational individuals, and tries to base the derivation of social norms on rational individual behaviour. But although he does not set out his model in formal mathematics, Coleman is in no doubt about the fundamental importance of interactions between individuals, of how the behaviour of one person can influence the behaviour of others. His most scathing comment is reserved for the economist's model of competitive equilibrium based on the entirely independent behaviour of individuals, describing it as a 'broadly perpetrated fiction'.

The significance of Coleman's work from our perspective is that, while it is based on individual rationality, it shows quite clearly, from yet another intellectual perspective, that the behaviour of systems at the aggregate, macro-level is often very different from the behaviour patterns of its individual component parts.

Sociologists believe this to be true. Environmentalists regard it as an essential part of their analysis. And now support emerges for the proposition from that least expected of sources, mathematical economics.

CHAPTER 5

Mechanistic Modelling

Seventeenth-century Europe was a place of great religious ferment. Theological differences between the various Christian churches and sects were often magnified into issues involving life and death. A belief common to many of the protagonists was that their opponents either were, or had the potential to become, the Antichrist. Some very considerable intellects, along with many others of lesser calibre, applied themselves to the problem of identifying either whether Antichrist had actually appeared already, or was about to appear.

A technique which was used widely in this investigation was the so-called 'science' of numerology. Scholars would look carefully for coincidences in the appearance of sequences of numbers, searching for clues to identify Antichrist's appearance on Earth. Many predictions were made that he had in fact appeared. But since his appearance is prophesied to bring about a reign of dreadful terror and chaos, more thoughtful minds began to question whether this was in fact the case. Indeed, they began to wonder whether the discipline of numerology had any value whatsoever.

In 1690, John Owen, Chancellor of Oxford University, went so far as to state: 'Take heed of computation! How woefully and wretchedly we have been misled by it!'

This could serve as the epitaph for the discipline of economics in its current state. And an epitaph in particular for macro-economic modelling and forecasting, the theme of this chapter.

So far, most of our attention has been devoted to the micro-level, to the model of competitive equilibrium, because it is the core model of economic theory. Whatever nuances and qualifications they might make, orthodox economists ultimately subscribe to this model as a reasonable approximation of how the world operates. Its workings rarely, if ever, catch the attention of the media. And with good reason. For within standard economics the model is about as controversial as the fact that the Pope believes in God.

It is much more exciting, not to say amusing, for the media to feature disputes among economists as to how the economy operates at the aggregate, macro-level, and to ridicule the accuracy of macro-economic forecasts.

Almost every day, economists, particularly those employed by the publicity-conscious financial institutions, can be heard and seen pontificating and arguing with each other about the significance of the latest economic statistic to emerge, or pronouncing with great confidence on what the government should be doing about this or that problem. The remark of the Russian physicist Lev Landau, made in a different context, might almost have been designed as a perfect description of the gurus of Wall Street and the City of London: 'Cosmologists,' he wrote, 'are often in error but never in doubt.'

Whatever solution is offered, whatever prognostication is made, one quality above all is lacking from the various utterances. Namely, that of humility. For the record of economists in understanding and forecasting the economy at the macro-level is not especially impressive. Indeed, uncharitable writers might be inclined to describe it as appalling.

To be fair, economics is not a completely empty box in the way in which numerology was so clearly shown to be. Its status is similar to that of science before Newton. At the micro-level in particular, in certain well-defined circumstances, the discipline can offer useful insights into behaviour. But the contrast between the actual scientific achievements of the discipline and the confidence with which claims are made for it by its protagonists is striking.

A long-standing proposition in economics, for example, is the quantity theory of money. This asserts that inflation is always and everywhere caused by increases in the supply of money. At one level, the proposition is simply an accounting identity. It states that the amount of goods and services produced in an economy in any one period multiplied by the average price of the same goods and services by definition equals the amount of money in circulation multiplied by the 'velocity' of circulation of money.

It will be helpful to the subsequent discussion to write down this somewhat wordy proposition in the form of a simple equation. Using the symbol 'M' to denote the money supply, 'V' the velocity of circulation, 'P' the average price level and 'Q' the amount of goods and services produced in an economy, the quantity theory of money states that: $M \times V = P \times Q$. In other words, the amount of money in an economy, multiplied by the speed with which it circulates, equals the amount of goods and services produced multiplied by the price level.

One way in which this equation can be used is to measure V. The central bank of an economy knows how much money is in circulation, and governments make separate estimates of P and Q. So, given values for M, P and Q, V is measured as being that value which, when multiplied by M, is equal to P times Q. In fact, this is the only way in which V can be measured, for there is no independent way of doing so, unlike M, P and Q, for which well-defined and well-used procedures exist to estimate their values.

But it is not terribly interesting to use this equation simply to measure V, a rather esoteric factor which measures how fast money is circulating round any particular economy. And, indeed, the quantity theory of money does make much more imaginative use of it.

Suppose that the government or the central bank of an economy can control the amount of money in circulation, M. Suppose further that, ultimately, changes in the amount of money do not affect the amount of goods and services produced in an economy, Q. Temporarily, perhaps for as long a period as two or three years, increasing or decreasing the amount of money in an economy might lead to changes in how much is produced. But suppose that, eventually, changes in M have no effect on Q. Suppose, finally, that V does not change over time, but always keeps the same value. Rather more subtly, V can be allowed to change, but suppose that in some way these changes can always be predicted accurately.

If all these suppositions are correct, the quantity theory of money is valid, and there is a direct and predictable link between increases in the money supply and inflation. If M is increased by the government, and either V is constant or we know how it is going to change, we can compute how much the left-hand side of our equation, M times V, will change. And since eventually, on the right-hand side, Q will not change as a result of changes to M or V, P must rise by an amount equal to the change in M times V. The price level, P, rises, or in other words increasing the money supply has caused inflation.

The reader might reflect that an awful lot of supposing has to take place in order for the quantity theory of money to be true. But this has not stopped it from being of great practical importance, particularly over the past twenty years or so. The proselytising work of Milton Friedman, Nobel Prize winner in economics and a firm believer in the quantity theory, did much to push the theory forward into the policy-making domain. The conduct of economic policy in many countries has been strongly influenced by the view that inflation is a purely monetary pheno-menon. If the money supply is controlled, so is inflation.

For example, the Bundesbank monitors changes in the German money supply very closely, believing that if it can be kept under control, so can inflation. And given the dominant position of the Deutschmark in the European ERM in the 1980s and early 1990s, policies followed by the Bundesbank have had a powerful influence on policies in the other countries of the European Community. Latin American countries are repeatedly urged by the IMF to exercise monetary 'discipline' and control their money supplies in order to control the endemic inflation of that continent.

Staying with the theme of discipline, Mrs Thatcher, in her early years in power, was a great believer that inflation could only be caused by changes in the money supply. The sharp rise in inflation which took place in Britain in 1980 came as a complete surprise to her newly elected government, which had set strict new targets for the growth of the money supply. The fact that the government had also conceded enormous wage increases across the public sector and at the same time virtually doubled the rate of VAT – the tax rate on sales of goods and services – early in the same year could not, on the logic of the government and its advisers, affect inflation, for these policies did not involve an increase in the money supply. Unfortunately for the government and the theory, workers in the private sector demanded wage increases of a similar size, pushing up industry's costs, and companies simply raised their prices in line both with these higher costs and with the new spending-tax rate. Inflation soared towards 20 per cent.

There are circumstances in which increases in the money supply do trigger increases in inflation. In the middle of the third century AD, for example, the Roman Empire experienced a tremendous crisis which almost destroyed it. In the space of fifty years, there were no fewer than twenty emperors: eighteen of them died violent deaths, one was held captive abroad, and the other was a victim of the plague. There was constant debasement of the currency, and the price of corn rose to well over a hundred times its previous levels. But such inflation was modest in comparison to the dramatic hyper-inflations of our own century, as, for example, in Germany in the 1920s; in Central European countries, most notably Hungary, at the end of the Second World War; and at present in the newly formed countries of the former Soviet bloc. Inflation in some of these examples far exceeded an annual rate of 1 million per cent. In the single month of July 1946, prices in Hungary rose at an annualised percentage rate of more than 1 followed by sixteen zeros, and in August 1993 a similar calculation for Serbia produced a percentage rate of more than 3 followed by seventeen zeros.

But the claim that inflation is always and everywhere purely caused by increases in the money supply, and that the rate of inflation bears a stable, predictable relationship to increases in the money supply is ridiculous.

At a purely practical level, there is no unique definition of what constitutes the money supply. A range of indicators is used and appears in the financial press. The various definitions are, by convention, denoted by the capital letter 'M' followed by a number. So we have, for example, M0, M1 and so on, usually up to M5, although there can be subtle variants such as M1A. The rule is, the bigger the number, the more factors are included in the definition of money.

At a narrow level, money might be defined simply as the total value of notes and coins circulating in the economy. But one could argue that money which is held in bank accounts and which can be withdrawn on demand is virtually the same thing as cash, so this, too, should be included in the definition. A case can be made for including the money held in other bank accounts. For example, a deposit account which requires one month's notice before it can be withdrawn is not as accessible as a pile of banknotes in the back pocket, but it is money which the owner can obtain.

The differences would not matter if all definitions of money tended to move together, but throughout the Western world at any point in time there are often large differences between the rates of growth of the various definitions of M. Simply by looking at the statistics published by the IMF for the growth in M1 and M2 – two measures which are close together in terms of what is and what is not included in their definitions, and so might be expected to move together quite closely – it is easy to pick out examples. Between 1985 and 1987, money as measured by M1 in the United States grew by 15 per cent, but by 25 per cent on its neighbouring definition given by M2. Between 1987 and 1990, M1 grew by 14 per cent, and M2 by only 8 per cent. In Britain, in the two years from 1988, M2 money grew by 23 per cent, but M1 grew by no less than 37 per cent. The list of examples could go on for a long time.

Virulent debates rage over the exact definition of M which should be used for the monetary theory to work. But the problems with the quantity theory of money run even deeper. The assumption of the theory that the velocity of circulation of money is constant simply does not hold. In other words, increases or decreases in the money supply are often accompanied, even over a period of years, by changes in the speed with which money circulates. Since the right-hand side of the equation in the quantity theory of money is the amount of money in circulation multiplied by the speed with which it circulates, it follows that if both of these factors change, the direct link between money and prices is broken.

In most Western countries during the past decade, the velocity of circulation of money, on all definitions, has altered with the impact of financial deregulation. Just taking evidence for the velocity of M2 published by the IMF illustrates the point. In America, velocity fell by 12 per cent between 1981 and 1986, and then rose by some 6 per cent by the early 1990s. In Australia, velocity fell 13 per cent between 1981 and 1988, and has since risen by no less than 30 per cent. In France, from the early 1980s to the early 1990s, it rose 14 per cent, but in neighbouring Germany it fell 13 per cent. The most conspicuous fall was in Britain, where over the decade the velocity of M2 fell by 48 per cent. In Britain, in fact, despite the fact that during this period the money supply rose fourfold, prices barely doubled, the potential link between monetary growth and inflation being broken by the collapse in the measure of velocity.

Of course, as we noted above, the velocity of circulation does not have to be strictly constant for the theory to have any chance of success. It is rather that any changes in it have to be predictable. But the deregulation of financial markets in many countries in the 1980s is just one example of a range of factors which has prevented velocity from being predicted with any degree of accuracy. Such events change the rules of the game, as it were, and disrupt any established relationships which might exist.

Perhaps the only example in history of completely successful predictions being made with M occurred in Thomas Middleton's Jacobean play *The Changeling*. One of the characters possesses a magic elixir in a phial marked, quite simply, 'M'. He is able to predict repeatedly and with great accuracy the impact on others of consuming the potion. How unlike the economic forecasts of today! The forecasting problems encountered with the quantity theory of money extend to other aspects of macroeconomics. The media highlight the differences between monetarist and Keynesian economists, and this is not unreasonable, for they can make a lively story. But in many ways, the juxtaposition of monetarist and

Keynesian positions is a false one. Importantly, both approaches share the same Victorian, mechanistic view of the world.

Many of the differences can in fact be understood from the quantity theory of money equation discussed above. In essence, and with some but not a great deal of risk of simplification, the key distinction between a monetarist position and a Keynesian one is that the former holds that changes in M, however defined, can ultimately have no impact on Q, while the latter believes that they can.

This is a very important practical difference for macro-economic policy. Either such policy has no influence on how much is produced in the economy as a whole, or it does have some. The reader may feel, in the words of a catch-phrase fashionable in Britain: 'I think we should be told.' But macro-economics cannot give a clear-cut answer.

Governments have a whole range of macro-economic policy measures which they can take, and changes in many of these measures will have implications for the growth of the money supply in the economy. For example, in the United States there is a gap of hundreds of millions of dollars each year between the amount which the federal government spends and the amount of income it receives from taxes. In Japan, in response to the deepest recession since the war, the government has recently decided to increase the level of its expenditure without raising taxes to pay for the increase. Increased spending on public transport and on housing, for example, is part of the Japanese measures.

But these differences between government spending and its income from taxation have to be financed in some way. At its simplest, unlike the rest of us when we go into debt, the government can simply print some more money to pay for its extra spending. Or it can try to persuade – by, for example, offering high interest rates – both individuals and institutions such as pension funds to lend it the money instead.

In practice, the links between changes in the amount which the government needs to pay for its spending and changes in the money supply can be considerably more complex and circuitous than the basic textbook examples mentioned directly above, and a substantial proportion of the differences between the various schools of thought in macro-economics arises from differences in their technical accounts of these imperfectly understood mechanisms.

But whether governments increase spending without raising taxes, or cut taxes without reducing spending, the resulting need to pay for the gap in the government's budget has implications for the money supply.

Monetarists maintain that such policies, however they are financed, cannot influence the total amount of goods and services which are produced, while Keynesians believe that they can. But just as the monetarist camp is split as to the precise measure of M which is relevant for their theory of inflation, Keynesians are divided on the exact strength of the impact of government macro-economic policy on output as a whole.

Theoretical macro-economics has developed in recent years to produce what effectively amounts to a synthesis of the various schools of thought. And it is this synthesis which is taught the world over on courses in macro-economics. What might be termed pure monetarist or pure Keynesian positions can be regarded simply as special cases of this more general, synthesised model of macro-economics. If certain links in the model are activated with a certain strength, results which are more inclined to the monetarist position are obtained, while the activation of other links gives the model varying degrees of Keynesianism.

An analogy with a railway signalbox which controls a complicated and busy junction might help to illustrate the point. Economists and politicians often speak of the 'levers' of economic policy, even if in the high-tech world of today it is buttons which are pressed rather than levers which are pulled. All the people who draw up the plans for which train is to be routed where share a great deal in common about the operation of the railway. They all agree that the railway has engines and carriages, and that they run on rails. This might seem obvious, but if the signalbox were controlled by someone who imagined he was supervising a horse race such as the Grand National or Kentucky Derby instead, all sorts of problems might ensue. With this common background, the task of the particular signalman on duty is to pull various levers, which activate certain signals and certain patterns on the track, and which in turn choose the direction the train will take. One set of levers will activate the equipment to send the train in one direction, and a different set will ensure that the train ends up on a different track. Similarly, the choice of which connections are activated will decide the direction in which a particular theoretical specification of a macro-economic model goes, towards monetarism or Keynesianism.

The role of the signalman in applied macro-economics is played by people with statistical training, known as econometricians. Their job is to analyse macro-economic data using statistical techniques, to try to decide which links in the system are the appropriate ones to activate. But this is a rather humdrum description of what can be an intricate and intellectually challenging task. Econometricians working with macro-data may often see themselves in the much grander role of arbitrating the disputes between the various schools of macro-theorists.

I should know, for I spent most of the 1970s and early 1980s as an applied macro-economist, before the gradual accumulation of evidence forced me to the conclusion that, despite intensive effort, econometrics had not succeeded in resolving the various theoretical disputes – nor has it done in the succeeding decade. The weight of evidence may some-times point very clearly in one particular direction, but it is never quite convincing enough to persuade someone who really does not want to believe the result.

Despite the problems, there is a large number of macro-economic models in regular use around the world, in treasuries, central banks and in large commercial companies, almost all of which are based upon the general, shared theoretical framework of macro-economic behaviour. The models differ in the strengths of their various linkages, which are still the source of endless discussion among applied econometricians, but the underlying approach is common to all.

It is in these models that the theory of macro-economics is applied and confronted with empirical data on a regular basis. Despite the potential importance of this in adjudicating between theoretical arguments, the activity of building and using these macro-models is rather looked down on by the academic profession. An important reason for this is that the interest of most academics is in micro-economics, in the implications of the model of competitive equilibrium.

A secondary reason, perhaps, is that those who get involved in using data are thought by some to be not quite gentlemen, almost as if they were involved in trade, or as if, Heaven forbid, they got their hands dirty. An experience early in my career illustrated the point to me clearly. An aspiring economist and close contemporary of mine, while still a very young man, was highly regarded by the mainstream academic theorists in Britain. Within just a couple of years of taking his first degree, before obtaining a doctorate, he was elected to the economics faculty in the University of Oxford. He proceeded to consolidate his reputation, but after only a few years he decided to abandon academic life and to try and make money as a macro-economic forecaster in business. Great was the consternation among Oxford theorists, and eloquent were the pleas for him to see the error of his ways. The phrase 'prostituting himself', if not used openly, was hinted at strongly. But to no avail.

As it happens, there is an amusing sequel to this story. Several years later the young economist, then prospering, was approached by a drinks company to see if he could do some lucrative consultancy work for them in a dispute they were having with the European Commission on sales of one of their products. They had, they said, already commissioned another economist to work on this, but they would bring him along. An appointment was made and, on the due day, the management team from the drinks company entered the economist's office. Following them, at least having the grace to look sheepish, was the other economist, the author of their econometric study of the drinks market in the European Community, at last identified as being none other than one of the highest of Oxford's theoretical high priests!

The main practical uses of macro-economic models are not so much to adjudicate between rival theories as to act as a source of advice to governments and to business. A substantial amount of resources has been devoted in the past twenty years to developing and refining these models. In Europe, this has been mainly at the expense of the taxpayer, although in the United States commercial funding of the models has become the norm. But despite this effort and attention, the performance of the models is sadly lacking.

The nature of the advice the models are supposed to be able to provide is twofold. First, to assess the likely consequences, across the economy as a whole, of changes in government policy. The various linkages within the models discussed above trace and monitor, in complicated ways, the implications of changes in one part of the model as they feed through into other parts of the model, often taking time for the full consequences of the various connections in the model to take effect. Second, the models are used to assist in the production of forecasts of factors such as the growth of national output, unemployment, interest rates, inflation, and so on.

As an example of their use to assess the impact of policy changes, VAT is levied on most items of consumer spending in the countries of the European Community. Macro-models can be used to supply answers to the question: what would happen if the rate of VAT were changed? This very question was actually asked of the six leading macro-models in Britain in an exercise to compare their structures carried out in the summer of 1993. For the purposes of the exercise, VAT was assumed to be reduced by one percentage point.

In the first instance, it seems logical that a reduction in the rate of tax on spending would lead to some reduction in the average price at which goods and services across the economy are sold. Indeed, all six models agreed that initially this would happen, but in varying degrees. A couple of models thought that average prices would fall at once by 0.6 per cent, while at the other extreme another model considered that prices would hardly fall at all, by just 0.1 per cent. One reason for the variations is the different ways in which the models represent the links between taxes on consumer spending and the way in which companies set their prices. If VAT changes, companies have a choice of either passing the change on to the consumer through changes in prices, or absorbing the change themselves through their profit margins, leaving prices to the consumer unchanged. The more companies pass changes in tax on to consumers, the more will prices change in response to a change in tax rates.

So the six models differed in their account of what would happen to prices as soon as the rate of VAT was changed. But at least they all agreed that prices would fall. An even bigger disagreement arises when the models trace through the consequences of a change in VAT over a period of three or four years. After four years, two of the models continued to give the answer that prices would fall, and by amounts greater than the initial impact. But one model said that, by then, prices would not have altered at all, while the other three answered that a reduction in VAT now would actually lead to higher prices in four years' time!

In other words, a finance minister trying to decide whether or not actually to change VAT, or a managing director trying to understand the consequences for his or her business of such a change, would be given quite different answers depending on which particular model was selected to tackle the question. In the immortal words of the salesman: 'You pays your money, and you takes your choice.'

Such disagreements between models about the empirical consequences of practical policy changes are widespread, and other examples could readily be supplied, from models both of the British and of other economies. The differences in the answers arise from the cumulative effect of what are often small and apparently insignificant differences in the various linkages within the models. Providing a full account of the reasons for such differences can be a challenging job for the model operators, in the same way that, for example, tracing connections on a complicated electrical switchboard requires skill.

But a flavour can be given of the connections which are activated when the impact of even such a simple policy as changing the rate of VAT is examined. Prices change, and so then do wages, for wage bargainers, whether in trade unions or not, do take account of what is happening to prices. Changes in wages imply changes in industry's costs, which in turn have further implications for prices. A reduction in VAT reduces the amount of income which the government receives from tax, so that the gap between government expenditure and income widens; this gap has to be financed in some way or other, so the money supply has to expand and/or interest rates increase. As prices and wages change, the purchasing power of consumers changes. If the net impact of the changes in prices and wages is to make consumers better off, for example, they will spend more, and some of this spending goes on imports. So the country's trade balance worsens, which again has to be financed in some way, which may have implications for the exchange rate of the country's currency, changes that may feed through into changes in the costs of imported materials, which in turn has implications for prices.

The above paragraph may seem complicated. And so it is, for these models have grown and grown in size. A single model may now be made up of literally hundreds of equations, each purporting to represent some aspect of economic behaviour, and each connected to other equations in the system.

The models may seem impressive and intimidating when their mathematical specifications are set down on paper, but when it comes to their use in forecasting they are so unreliable that virtually no model operator in the world dares allow his or her (although almost invariably his) model loose on its own.

Just after the last world war, the mysterious Howard Hughes had an aeroplane built of truly enormous size. By far the largest in the world, it looked wonderful on the drawing board, and even more marvellous once it was built. The only slight problem was that it could barely get off the ground. It had to be scrapped.

In the same way, the macro-economic models are unable to produce forecasts on their own. The proprietors of the models interfere with their output before it is allowed to see the light of day. These 'judgmental adjustments' can be, and often are, extensive. Every model builder and model operator knows about the process of altering the output of a model, but this remains something of a twilight world, and is not well documented in the literature. One of the few academics to take an interest is Mike Artis of Manchester University, a former forecaster himself, and his study carried out for the Bank of England in 1982 showed definitively that the forecasting record of models, without such human intervention, would have been distinctly worse than it has been with the help of the adjustments, a finding which has been confirmed by subsequent studies.

The importance of adjusting the output of such models was brought home to me at an early stage. At the end of 1975 I was employed at the National Institute of Economic and Social Research in London, then as now one of Britain's most prestigious macro-economic modelling and forecasting institutions. Purely by coincidence, a number of senior people left more or less at the same time, and I found myself, at the age of twenty-five, in charge of producing the forecast with the Institute's model of the British economy.

At the time, the British economy was in dire straits. Inflation was high, the pound was falling and the balance of payments was in deficit. But there was a glimmer of hope, for the extraction of oil from the North Sea was beginning to come on stream. By the simple process of adding several billion pounds of oil exports to the model's forecast of total British exports and subtracting a similar figure from the forecast of Britain's import bill to represent savings on imports of oil, I was able to produce a forecast for Britain in 1976 and 1977 which, by the standards of the time, was very optimistic. To my amazement and trepidation, the media seized on this sliver of potential good news, and the Institute's forecasts, for the first and probably the last time, were headline news in the mass-circulation, tabloid press. Fortunately for me, this was one adjustment of a model's output which turned out well, although every forecaster will have his or her own personal horror story to tell, over which a veil will be discreetly drawn.

In many ways, the models are like tarantula spiders. Careful handling of both is required, but in the case of the spiders this is not just for the obvious reason. For if their handlers lose control and drop them, they explode. These interesting creatures use hydraulic pressure to extend their legs, and the fluid splatters on impact. In the same way, macro-models have a particular fascination of their own, and a tendency to explode.

In recent years, even the combination of models supported by the judgments of their operators have produced forecasts which have been seriously misleading. During 1992 and early 1993 alone, big errors have been made in forecasts. We have seen that the Japanese recession, by far the deepest since the war, was not predicted. Neither the strength of the recovery in America in the second half of 1992 nor the slow-down in the first half of 1993 was really anticipated. And in Europe, neither the turmoil in the ERM nor the depth of the recession in Germany was foreseen by the models.

A survey published by the Paris-based international body, the Organisation for Economic Co-operation and Development (OECD) in June 1993, illustrates the problem quite clearly.

The forecasting records of the two major publicly funded international bodies, the forecasts of the OECD itself and the IMF, and of the national governments were compared. For the major seven world economies, the forecasts for the next year ahead for output growth and inflation were examined.

The benchmark used by the survey for comparison was a naive projection that next year's growth of output or inflation would simply be equal to this year's. In other words, this benchmark required no knowledge of economics to produce, and a forecast could be made with it by anyone who understood the elementary arithmetic of percentage changes.

Over the 1987–92 period, this extremely simple rule performed at least as well as the professional forecasters in projecting next year's economic growth rate. And in terms of inflation, the rule performed as well as the OECD and IMF, and slightly better than the national governments. In other words, the combined might of the macroeconomic models and the intellectual power of their operators, whether based in national governments or installed in tax-free splendour at public expense in Paris or in the IMF in Washington, could not perform any better than the simplest possible rule which could be used to make a forecast.

The record of forecasting is poor whatever the theoretical nuance of the model concerned, whether it leans towards monetarist or towards Keynesian properties. A survey of the accuracy of British economic forecasts, for example, carried out by the London Business School in 1993, concluded that differences over time between the predictions from the various schools of thought are very small. But the most striking fact to emerge from this study is that errors in forecasts are much greater than differences between apparently contending schools of thought. This is by no means a new discovery, but it represents valuable confirmation of previous studies over the years which have come to the same conclusion.

The best recipe for forecasting success, conclude the London Business School researchers, displaying a degree of irony as welcome as it is rare among economists, is to 'forecast often and forecast late'. In other words, the more forecasts made during the course of the year, the greater the chance that, purely at random, one of them will prove to be reasonably accurate. And by forecasting as close as possible in time to the actual period being forecast, much more information becomes available about what is likely to happen. Of course, this information is not confined by some secret code to economic forecasters. It is information in the public domain, available to anyone wishing to make an informed guess about the prospects in the immediate future.

Occasionally a forecaster will get things broadly right for a couple of years, and be lionised as a hero. But there is no guarantee that next year's forecast will not be the worst of the lot. Indeed, this is not merely a supposition. It has actually happened a number of times, as I once learned to my cost, back in the late 1970s.

All the problems of macro-economic models – the contradictory answers different models give to the same question, the poor forecasting record, the inability to trust a model on its own – exist despite the effort devoted to their maintenance and construction. This is despite the fact that model builders and operators, particularly in Europe, where a greater proportion of their work is funded by grants from the taxpayer than it is in America, pride themselves on incorporating the latest nuances of macro-economic theory into the specification of their models.

The overwhelmingly dominant fashion in macro-economic theory in the past fifteen years or so has been the concept of 'rational expectations'. Such is its hold on the profession that it has been scarcely possible in recent years to publish articles in many journals, either on theoretical or applied macro-economics, without using it.

The idea, which has been incorporated extensively in the applied macro-economic models discussed above, has a powerful attraction for economists. As we have seen in previous chapters, economic theory at the micro-level is based upon the concept of the rational, self-interested individual, and the properties of the model as a whole are built up by adding together the equations which describe the behaviour of people and companies.

Macro-economists had a long-standing concern that their own theoretical models, intended to describe behaviour of the economy at the aggregate level, were not founded so clearly on the principle of individual rationality. Spending by individual consumers, for example, is perhaps the single most important feature of any developed economy, accounting for well over half the total amount of spending in every Western country. From the very beginnings of macro-economic models in the late 1940s and early 1950s, equations have been built to try to describe the behaviour of consumer spending. Various factors are thought to influence the total amount consumers spend. Their incomes, for example, are obviously important, and possibly their wealth, the amount of debt they hold, the level of unemployment, interest rates and so on. Econometricians, using statistical techniques, have worked hard to discover both which factors really do influence consumer spending, and how strong each influence actually is.

But leaving aside the fact that there is still no agreement on the best set of factors to use when trying to account for the total amount which consumers spend in this way, the process of simply searching the data with econometric techniques leaves many economists uneasy, for such results could be seen as mere descriptions of fluctuations in economic series at the aggregate level, giving no account of why individuals behaved as they did, in ways which led to these movements in the data series for spending as a whole.

Rational expectations appeared to offer a solution which would place macro-economic theory on what, for economists, was a much more secure foundation. Expectations are obviously important in a range of economic decisions, such as the income which an individual expects to receive over the next few years, or the rate of return expected on an investment. But it is not usually possible to observe or measure expectations directly, apart from in certain specialised areas of financial markets where, as we mentioned in the previous chapter, deals can be struck about prices which are expected to obtain in the future. There are also surveys of spending plans by companies, or of the degree of optimism felt by consumers, but in general data on expectations are fairly sparse.

The idea of rational expectations is that 'rational' economic agents – in other words, people and companies – will not just learn from their mistakes in forming expectations, but that the learning process will enable them to identify the true model determining the behaviour of the economy. They will then use this model in order to form expectations. It is as if (that favourite phrase of economists) everyone not only has his or her own personal macro-model of the economy, but everyone has the same model and, to stretch credibility even further, a model which happens to be a true and correct representation of how the economy behaves. This model will then be used to form expectations. By definition, economic agents are 'rational', so they should use this rational method of forming expectations.

Apart from its logical attraction for economists, the concept had the added bonus, at both the theoretical and applied levels, of creating lots of opportunities to indulge in fascinating intellectual exercises, replete with mathematical manipulation in the differential calculus. But even a moment's reflection might lead one to believe that many individuals have very little grasp of many of the true models which govern their everyday lives, let alone a personal copy of the correct macro-model of the economy.

In the present day, for example, at the very end of the twentieth century, surveys appear from time to time in all Western countries which show that many adults think the Sun revolves around the Earth. On a more trivial level, a survey published in Britain in the spring of 1993 revealed that dog owners attributed a level of intelligence to their pets which was on average that of a nine-year-old child. A substantial minority believed their animals to be more intelligent than university students.

An orthodox economist would dismiss these examples as frivolous, since it is not necessary to know either how the solar system operates or how intelligence in different species can or cannot be compared in order to maximise one's individual economic welfare. They equally dismiss another serious problem for rational expectations – the fact that, while ordinary consumers are presumed to know the true model of the economy as they go about their daily business, economists themselves in their professional capacities clearly do not know the 'true' model which governs the economy. This particular problem is again dismissed by invoking the trusty phrase 'as if'.

Baseball players or cricketers do not need to be able to solve explicitly the non-linear differential equations which govern the flight of the ball. They just catch it. So it is always possible to argue that people act 'as if' they knew the true structure of any particular system, without necessarily being able to articulate it.

However, a curious form of schizophrenia is invoked by this argument. A team of applied mathematicians playing baseball or cricket could solve the equations governing the flight of the ball. So a group of economists who, in their roles as consumers and employees are assumed to act rationally and act as if they know the true structure of the economy, ought to be able to articulate this in their professional capacity. This, as we have seen, they are singularly unable to do.

It is not surprising that the economist's concept of rationality does not bear scrutiny at the aggregate level. Given its crucial importance, the amount of empirical work which has been done to test its validity is ridiculously small, but some interesting work has at last been done in the past decade.

In the mid-1980s, several studies in Britain and the United States examined data from surveys of economic expectations to see if they stood up to the tenets of rationality. As mentioned above, such surveys cover factors such as the expectations of business about investment and inflation, and the overall confidence of consumers. Careful examination of the evidence by researchers such as Lovell in America and Ken Holden and David Peel of Liverpool University in Britain concluded that, in the detached language of science, 'the hypothesis of rational expectations did not appear to be consistent with the data'. In other words, it was wrong.

These studies seem conclusive. But this is to reckon without the intellectual dexterity of the orthodox, who with an incisiveness rivalling that of Perry Mason or Columbo, argued that surveys of business opinion could not be used to provide evidence either for or against the hypothesis of rationality. Companies which are asked to complete a survey questionnaire have no economic incentive to make accurate forecasts in it. Since they are not paid, they do not need to make accurate responses.

To argue that, because no money is at stake, companies might not transcribe their genuine views into surveys carried out by government bodies and by their own business and trade associations is to ignore the fact that companies have every incentive to construct accurate forecasts for their own business decisions.

More recent work in the United States has examined data generated by groups who *do* have a direct incentive to get things right – namely, economic forecasters. As we have noted already, their forecasts are financed almost entirely on a commercial basis, and yet several studies using this data conclude that even forecasts generated by professional economic forecasters do not support the hypothesis of rational expectations. For example, in 1993 Baghestani and Kianian of Colorado published a paper which examined American macro-economic forecasts over the 1981–91 period. They concluded that, out of seventy-five forecast series examined, only two satisfied the conditions of rationality. In other words, no fewer than seventy-three of them failed to support the concept of rational expectations.

The techniques of behavioural science have also begun to be used to test the concept of rationality from a number of perspectives, with some devastating results. We saw in Chapter 2 that a recent study from Cornell University, the latest of an increasing number of such papers, showed quite clearly that people, except those whose minds had been scrambled by the study of micro-economic theory, are far more co-operative and less competitive than the postulates of economic theory assert rational individuals should be.

A paper published as long ago as 1982 by Joël Huber illustrated yet another dimension of apparent irrationality in consumer behaviour. A group of students was asked to choose between two apartments, one close to college but expensive, the other further away but cheap. The distance and rents were calibrated so that each apartment was chosen by roughly half the students in the experiment. A second group was then asked to compare the two, but this time a third apartment was on offer. This was both the furthest away from college of all three, and more expensive than the one further away in the original experiment. The addition of this third choice increased dramatically the proportion of students choosing the second apartment. In other words, instead of dividing equally between the first two apartments on offer, many more now chose, for no apparent logical reason, the second one. According to the economic concept of rationality, this should not happen.

To take yet another example, theory requires that because, by definition, individuals are rational, the preferences of any individual must be internally consistent. For example, if a consumer prefers Coca-Cola to Pepsi-Cola, and Pepsi-Cola to lemonade, then he or she is deemed to prefer Coca-Cola to lemonade. This characteristic of preferences is known technically as transitivity, and must hold if an individual is to have consistent preferences. If product A is preferred to product B, and product B to product C, then, for consistency, A must be preferred to C.

A paper by Graham Loomes and colleagues at the Centre for Experimental Economics at the University of York was published in 1991, to the credit of the journal, in *Econometrica*, one of the world's leading technical economic journals. The paper provides strong evidence against the view that consumer preferences are transitive. Loomes approached the question using the methodology of behavioural science, constructing games which people played under controlled conditions, and analysing their behaviour. A number of papers in the 1980s had used the same methodology and had also rejected the concept of transitive preferences, but their exact approaches had been the subject of detailed criticism. Loomes and his collaborators designed their experiments to meet these specific objections, and still their results rejected transitivity.

The implications of the non-transitivity of individual consumer preferences are profound.

Economists believe that consumers reveal their true preferences through their actual purchasing decisions. Indeed, the phrase 'revealed preferences' is used in theoretical models of consumer behaviour to describe this activity. Firms observe the revealed preferences of consumers, and the market mechanism, the Invisible Hand of Adam Smith, comes into play to ensure that these preferences are met. The concept of revealed preference is essential to the view that 'the market knows best'. By acting in their individual self-interest in a competitive environment, companies are able to satisfy the true preferences of consumers.

The axiomatic claim that the market mechanism is satisfying the true preferences of consumers is undermined if these preferences themselves are non-transitive. For the signals sent by revealed preference are then potentially contradictory. Companies receive conflicting messages about the range of goods and services which should be provided to satisfy consumer needs.

The soft drinks example used above illustrates the point. Suppose a small neighbourhood shop has space on its shelves to stock only two types of soft drink, Pepsi and lemonade. Sales of Pepsi heavily outsell those of lemonade. The proprietor, a firm believer in the free market, is anxious to please his customers by offering them a choice, so he stops buying lemonade and puts Coca-Cola on his shelves instead. He notices that most people switch to this, and it is the sales of Pepsi which languish. But one week the delivery van has no more Pepsi available, so the shop-owner has some lemonade put back on his shelves, alongside the Coca-Cola. To his bewilderment, lemonade sales are much higher than those of Coca-Cola. When the delivery van calls next week, what should the poor man do to satisfy his non-transitive customers? The market has given him contradictory signals.

The appropriation of the word 'rational' to describe the basic postulates of orthodox economic theory was a propaganda coup of the highest order. The world's most expensive public-relations firms could not have done better. It carries the implication that any criticisms of it, or any alternatives put forward, are by definition irrational, and hence not worthy of serious contemplation.

But those economists bold enough, along with colleagues from other disciplines, to test and challenge the traditional view of rationality find it seriously wanting.

And the large-scale macro-economic models, the meeting place of macro-theory and empirical data, fully equipped as they have been with the economist's concept of rationality, have made little or no progress in improving our ability to understand and predict the world.

By any reasonable criteria, the discipline of economics as a whole, in its present state, is sadly lacking. Encouragingly, more and more attention is being given to alternative approaches which offer hope of escape from the present impasse. In the words of St Paul's Epistle to the Corinthians: 'When I was a child, I understood as a child, I thought as a child. But when I became a man I put away childish things. For now we see through a glass darkly; but then face to face.' The exciting possibility is opening up that one day we will be able to see the workings of the economy 'face to face', and the focus of this book now moves to the articulation of ways by which we might indeed obtain a better understanding of the behaviour of economies at the macro-level.

PART II

TOWARDS THE FUTURE OF ECONOMICS

CHAPTER 6

Unemployment and Inflation

The economic concepts of rationality and equilibrium pervade discussions of one of the major targets of policy for Western governments, the rate of inflation. And it is inflation and its links with another target of policy, the rate of unemployment, which are the themes of this chapter.

For a long period after the Second World War, the primary aim of economic policy was not to control inflation, but to maintain a low level of unemployment. Memories of the high unemployment and poverty of the 1930s ran deep, and the attitude of the millions of ex-servicemen and women who had risked their lives for their countries in order that the bad old days should be banished for ever was a powerful electoral force.

In the early 1940s, many economists believed that Keynes's insights developed during the previous decade made possible the creation of full employment on a permanent basis. Governments had the power in times of recession to boost the economy by increasing their own spending, creating jobs and reducing unemployment. As we saw in the previous chapter, the question as to whether or not the economy works in such a way as to give governments this power is still an unresolved macro-economic dispute between monetarists and Keynesians.

Even in the 1940s, Keynes did not lack his academic critics, but governments liked the practical nature of his message. The New Deal in the United States in the 1930s was an inspiration as to what governments appeared to be able to do to rescue their economies from deep depressions. In most of Europe, a new social settlement in which governments were committed to maintaining low levels of unemployment was not put into place until after the war. The war itself, a struggle of life and death, obliged governments to take control of their economies and to mobilise all available resources for the war effort, so that unemployment was very low. But the degree of physical control and direction which this involved would be unacceptable in peace-time Western democracies. So during the war itself, economists thought hard about how the low levels of unemployment were to be preserved once the war had ended.

The most notable expression of the post-war social settlement was the 1944 Beveridge Report in the UK, which laid the foundations of the welfare state, not just in Britain but elsewhere in Europe.

One worry which economists had was that full employment would lead quite rapidly to upward pressure on money wage increases, with consequent increases in industry's costs and in inflation. Economic theory suggests that if there is strong demand for a product in relation to the available supply of a product, the price will rise. In conditions of full employment, by definition there is a high level of demand for labour. So there will tend to be upward pressure on the price of labour. In other words, on wage rates. And since wages are the single most important item of costs in the economy as a whole, higher wages put pressure on companies to increase prices.

The favoured solution of the distinguished generation of economists involved in the construction of the post-war social settlement was that of incomes policy, often referred to at the time as wages policy. Such a policy would regulate the increase in money wages, and would thereby break the presumed link between full employment and inflation.

One of the very first lectures I attended at Cambridge in the autumn of 1968, never having studied economics previously, was given by Lord Kahn, revered as the closest collaborator of Keynes and, indeed, credited in the oral tradition of Cambridge as having had the original insights which led to Keynes's theories. The lecture was virtually incomprehensible.

This was not necessarily due to the intellectual difficulty of Lord Kahn's topic. For the lecture was almost inaudible. The great man mumbled into the lectern, occasionally raising his head, clearing his throat, and pronouncing the phrase 'wages policy'.

A fashionable communications consultant to whom I related this anecdote over twenty years later remarked that this showed what an outstandingly successful lecturer Lord Kahn had been. Most people, he declared, tried to put across too many points in a presentation. The fact that I had been able to remember the key point of the lecture at this distance in time showed how effective it had been.

In the event, the prophecies of Lord Kahn and his colleagues in the 1940s appeared for many years after the war to be wrong. Full employment co-existed with low levels of inflation for a quarter of a century. Figure 1 presents annual average rates of unemployment and inflation in eleven Western countries for various periods during the forty-odd years from the early 1950s to the present day. As a flavour of the evidence, over the 1951–73 period inflation averaged only 2.7 per cent a year in America and unemployment 4.6 per cent. In Japan, inflation was 5.1 per cent a year and unemployment only 1.6 per cent. In Britain and Germany, the average rate of inflation was, respectively, 4.1 and 2.7 per cent, and the respective unemployment rates 1.8 and 2.6 per cent. Across a range of Western countries, the average rate of inflation over this long period varied between just under 3 per cent a year for those countries with the lowest inflation, to Japan's 5 per cent, which was the highest rate. And everywhere, employment was high and unemployment low.

By the standards of world history, the inflation rates over this period were of course very high. A rate of inflation of 4 per cent, for example, implies a doubling of the level of prices every eighteen years. On the biblical measure of three score years and ten, prices would rise around eight times during the lifetime of an individual.

In contrast, the century preceding the Second World War had been one of unusual price stability. Prices had risen during economic booms, but they had actually fallen during recessions. So in 1932, for example, the average level of wholesale prices in the United States was precisely the same as it had been exactly a century previously, in 1832.

Over a still wider span of history, in so far as meaningful comparisons can be made, price levels have in fact risen, but not as quickly as in our own post-war period. The price of basic consumables – cereals, meat, cheese, drink and clothing – in England, for example, rose sixfold between 1250 and 1750, an average annual rise of less than 0.5 per cent a year, which was also the average from 1750 until the outbreak of the Second World War.*

But the rise in real living standards during the quarter-century after the Second World War was quite unprecedented, as was the preservation of such low levels of unemployment over such a long period of time. The rate of inflation which accompanied these successes seemed a small price to pay, and in any event it was much lower than economists in the 1940s feared it might be if full employment were maintained.

One possible explanation for this is that in many countries, particularly on the continent of Europe, rapid advances in the efficiency of agricultural production released millions of workers from the land, and made them available for employment in both industry and the service sector of the economy. In the large economies of continental Western Europe – Germany, France and Italy – those employed in agriculture as a

---

*The outstanding piece of historical investigation compiling a price index from the thirteenth century until the early 1950s was carried out by Phelps-Brown and Hopkins, *Economica*, 1956.

FIGURE I   Average annual rates of inflation (p) and unemployment (u)

Country	Period								
		1951–60	61–7	68–73	74–9	80–86	87–92	51–73	74–92
Germany	p	1.9	2.7	4.2	5.5	3.5	2.4	2.7	3.8
	u	4.3	0.8	0.9	3.4	6.5	6.7	2.3	5.6
France	p	5.5	3.4	5.7	10.1	8.7	3.0	4.9	7.4
	u	2.1	1.4	2.5	4.5	8.6	9.7	2.0	7.7
Italy	p	3.0	4.2	4.9	15.1	12.7	5.5	3.9	11.2
	u	7.7	4.5	5.8	6.6	8.9	10.6	6.2	8.7
Belgium	p	1.9	2.8	4.4	8.1	5.9	2.5	2.8	5.5
	u	4.8	2.3	2.6	6.3	11.3	8.5	3.5	8.8
Netherlands	p	3.0	3.6	6.1	7.0	4.1	1.8	4.0	4.3
	u	2.4	1.2	2.1	4.9	10.0	8.1	2.0	7.8
UK	p	3.4	3.2	6.4	14.4	7.6	5.5	4.1	9.3
	u	1.4	1.7	2.6	4.4	10.6	9.0	1.8	8.0
Sweden	p	4.6	4.0	5.1	9.3	8.6	6.2	4.6	8.0
	u	1.8	1.6	2.2	1.9	2.8	2.5	1.8	2.4
US	p	2.1	1.7	4.8	7.8	5.9	4.1	2.7	5.9
	u	4.4	4.9	4.7	6.7	7.8	6.0	4.6	6.9
Canada	p	2.1	2.1	4.4	8.7	6.7	3.7	2.7	6.4
	u	4.4	4.7	5.4	7.2	9.8	9.0	4.8	8.7
Australia	p	5.8	2.1	5.0	11.4	8.4	5.3	4.4	8.4
	u	2.1	1.8	2.0	5.0	7.6	8.1	1.9	7.0
Japan	p	3.8	5.6	6.5	9.5	3.1	1.8	5.1	4.7
	u	2.0	1.3	1.2	1.9	2.5	2.3	1.6	2.3

percentage of the total labour force fell by around 15 percentage points between the early 1950s and the mid-1960s. So although the demand for labour was high, the effective supply of labour to industry was rising rapidly, which might have relieved pressure to push up money wages.

But countries where agriculture was already very efficient at the end of the war, and where only a small proportion of the labour force worked on the land, and so did not flood into urban areas and industry, also experienced low inflation. In Britain, for example, agriculture accounted for barely 5 per cent of the total number in employment even in 1950, and in Canada the percentage was less than 4. In the United States, agricultural employment fell by 2 million between the mid-1950s and mid-1960s, but relative to the size of the working population this was a small figure, being only some 4 percentage points.

The average rate of inflation remained surprisingly low in the buoyant economic circumstances which prevailed. Around this unexpectedly low average, inflation did seem to fluctuate with unemployment in the way in which economic theory suggested it should. The fluctuations were small, but mild recessions in which unemployment rose seemed to moderate the inflation rate, and mild booms had the opposite effect on both variables.

The early and mid-1960s, for example, saw a period of strong up-turn in growth in many Western countries, and the average rate of unemployment fell below that which had obtained for most of the 1950s. And inflation was on average higher in this later period than in the previous decade. Again, full details of average unemployment and inflation rates for the periods 1951–60 and 1961–7 are given in Figure 1. But as examples, in Japan unemployment was, in the two periods respectively, 2 and 1.3 per cent, and inflation 3.8 and 5.6 per cent. In Germany, the respective unemployment rates were 4.3 and only 0.8 per cent, and inflation 1.9 and 2.7 per cent.

In contrast to most of the rest of the world, unemployment in the United States was slightly higher in the 1961–7 period, being 4.9 per cent compared to 4.4 per cent in the 1950s. But even the American experience appeared to support the idea of a negative relationship between inflation and unemployment, for inflation was slightly lower in the later period than in the 1950s, at 1.7 per cent compared to 2.1 per cent.

Given the rudimentary computer technology of the immediate post-war period, statistical analysis of any degree of complexity to quantify this theoretical relationship between inflation and unemployment was difficult to carry out. Nevertheless, interest grew in quantifying the relationship between inflation and unemployment in any given country by the use of statistical techniques.

In an innovative paper in 1958, Bill Phillips, a British engineer turned economist (whose marvellous machine featured in Chapter 2), produced a statistical relationship which demonstrated a negative relationship between money wage changes and unemployment, using British historical data from 1861 to 1913. In other words, when unemployment rose, the rate of increase of money wages fell, and vice versa. This relationship became famous in economics, known in the literature, not surprisingly, as the Phillips curve. Following Phillips's paper, researchers looked for, and found, similar kinds of relationships in the data for the period after the Second World War, both in Britain and in other countries.

The most influential contribution here came from two American economists, the Nobel Prize winner Paul Samuelson and his colleague Robert Solow, in 1960. Phillips's work had linked wage increases to unemployment. Although wages are by far the biggest single component of costs across the economy as a whole, and higher costs usually mean higher prices, Phillips had not made an explicit link between inflation and unemployment. Samuelson and Solow, at the annual meeting of the American Economic Association, surveyed the various explanations which had been given for fluctuations in the rate of inflation in the United States since the war. Arcane disputes existed on whether it was a high level of demand which pulled prices up, or pressures from supply which pushed them up. The two eminent economists cut through the tangle of arguments, pointing out that in practice many of the different theories then current could never be distinguished from each other, for they had an identical implication: when unemployment was high, inflation would be low, and vice versa. After discussing Phillips's work, they noted that no study existed which examined the link between inflation and unemployment in America, and proceeded to fill the gap.

Samuelson and Solow's conclusions were hedged with appropriate cautions about margins of error around their estimates, but they provided two clear guidelines for American policy makers. First, to have zero inflation in the United States, an unemployment rate of between 5 and 6 per cent was required. Second, at unemployment of 3 per cent, which broadly corresponded to most people's definition of full employment in America, inflation would be in the range of between 4 and 5 per cent a year.

Economic policy makers now appeared to have a strong degree of control over the economy at the macro-level. Within the prevailing Keynesian framework, they already believed that by manipulating policy instruments such as tax rates, interest rates and public spending, the level of unemployment could be decided by the government. With Phillips's relationship, extended by Samuelson and Solow, the rate of inflation also seemed to be within the power of government to choose. The Phillips curve appeared to describe a relationship, on a known scale, between inflation and unemployment. So if, for example, a government decided to set a target for unemployment, it could use the Phillips relationship for its particular economy to read off the rate of inflation implied by the desired rate of unemployment. If it thought that the former was too high, the choice of a somewhat higher rate of unemployment would enable a lower rate of inflation to emerge. In short, governments thought they could pick-'n'-mix.

However, a number of economists at the time, most notably Milton Friedman, remained troubled by the idea that governments could influence the economy in any way, for good or for ill, except by either interfering with or promoting the workings of the market. As we have seen, according to the model of competitive equilibrium it was not just an article of faith that governments should not attempt to interfere with the workings of the economy; it had been 'proved' that they should not.

Towards the end of the 1960s, with the Phillips curve having been the received wisdom among policy makers for less than a decade, events moved in such a way as to present the critics with a great opportunity. This they seized ruthlessly, proceeding to subject the Phillips curve to an intellectual colonisation, whereby it became integrated within the traditional orthodoxy of economics; in the process, its implications became safely neutered.

Using data from the 1950s and 1960s, reasonably successful models linking inflation and unemployment could be constructed for most Western economies. But at the end of the 1960s, things appeared to go wrong. In the United States, Britain and France, for example, between 1967 and 1970 inflation doubled.

During the years either side of 1970, Phillips curves broke down all over the West. Comparing the average rates of inflation and unemployment in the years 1968–73 with those of 1961–7, for example, in nine out of the eleven major countries for which evidence is presented in Figure 1, both unemployment *and* inflation were clearly higher on average in 1968–73 than they had been in 1961–7. An even clearer break took place around 1974, with both inflation and unemployment being distinctly higher in the 1974–9 period than even the 1968–73 period in ten out of the eleven major countries.

It was this emerging instability of Phillips curve relationships that Friedman and others, who wished to reassert at the macro-level the implications of the micro-level theoretical model of competitive equilibrium, that governments should not interfere in the economy, used to attack the idea that governments could exercise a choice between different combinations of inflation and unemployment. And they went further, to argue that the breakdown of the Phillips curve discredited Keynesian economics in general – that it discredited, in other words, the idea that governments by manipulating tax rates and spending decisions could control the level of unemployment.

The key to the attack was expectations about the future, and the presumed rationality of individuals and companies in forming such expectations – the idea which we discussed in the previous chapter. The argument went as follows. Inflation had existed for most of the post-war period, and people, as rational individuals, had gradually learned from this experience. They had learned not only to expect that inflation would continue in the future, but also about the Phillips curve relationships which appeared to exist.

In other words, the critics argued that people and companies had learned that if, say, unemployment began to fall, inflation would rise. And with this new knowledge, their behaviour altered. As soon as unemployment began to fall, they expected that inflation would eventually rise, and instead of waiting for it to happen as they had done in the 1950s and early 1960s, they anticipated such a rise in, for example, their pay bargaining behaviour. People asked for higher wages as soon as unemployment fell because they took this fall to be a signal that inflation would rise at some stage in the future. It was because of this changed behaviour that Phillips curves, which described behaviour as it had been in the past, were breaking down.

Keynesianism, the free-market economists argued, might have appeared to have worked in the 1950s and for much of the 1960s; governments might have been able to influence the level of output and employment in the economy by changing their spending levels or by varying tax rates – but now people had learned that such policies, when used to stimulate the economy, would eventually lead to inflation.

The serious challenge presented to free-market orthodoxy by the combination of Keynesian control of output and unemployment and Phillips-type choices between inflation and unemployment seemed to be removed, and the orthodox felt vindicated.

Perhaps, temporarily, governments could still give a boost to the economy, but the rational expectations of people and companies meant that eventually this would simply dissipate itself in higher inflation, rather than be translated into higher levels of output and employment. Eventually, not only was there no trade-off available to governments between the two economic policy targets of inflation and unemployment, but governments could not control the rate of unemployment by their spending and taxation decisions.

*

In terms of economic theory, by combining the Phillips curve with the concept of rational expectations, the curve, once so threatening to free market economic orthodoxy, was safely absorbed by it.

The arguments did not stay purely in the realms of theory, but passed rapidly into political discourse. For example, in Britain in 1976, the administration was controlled by the Labour Party, a notionally left-wing party of democratic socialism. The then prime minister, James Callaghan, chose the occasion of his own party's annual conference to introduce his comrades to the idea of the rational expectations Phillips curve. He did not quite put it in those terms, and used rather more demotic phrases, but his message was unequivocal: 'We used to think you could spend your way out of a recession,' he told delegates in a country where unemployment had just doubled in eighteen months, 'but I have to tell you in all sincerity that this is no longer the case.'

The rational expectations Phillips curve implies that, for any particular economy at any point in time, there is a unique level of unemployment at which inflation will neither accelerate nor decelerate. This sets the constraint on the level of unemployment which is sustainable. Around this unique level, a Phillips-type link between inflation and unemployment might well exist, but deviations from this unique rate of unemployment would be purely temporary.

The phrase 'Non-Accelerating Inflation Rate of Unemployment' – or NAIRU for short – is often used in economics to describe this supposed unique level of unemployment. But, showing the usual terrifying propaganda skill of the economics profession, the impersonal acronym of NAIRU is often translated into the phrase 'the natural rate of unemployment'. What could be more natural? Anyone arguing against the concept is, by clear implication, defying the forces of nature itself.

This theoretical concept still plays a central role in contemporary macro-economics. The hypothesis of the NAIRU has been and continues to be very influential, not just in academic circles, but also with financial journalists and policy makers. The 'natural rate' of unemployment, it is argued, cannot be affected by government policies designed to alter the level of spending in an economy, for the reasons discussed above. It is determined instead by 'supply-side' forces. In an economy in which imperfections and obstacles to the workings of the free market were removed, the 'natural rate' of unemployment would be very low. In accordance with the model of competitive equilibrium, the resources of such an economy would be allocated efficiently, so everyone who wanted to could get a job.

As yet another illustration of the power of economic ideas on the conduct of practical policy, the concept of the 'natural rate', far from remaining confined to esoteric discussions among theorists, has motivated an intense debate, both at the level of the European Commission in Brussels and within the member countries of the European Community themselves, about whether the present high levels of unemployment in Europe are due to too much regulation of, and a lack of flexibility in, the labour market. In other words, whether Western European labour markets have become too far removed from the ideal of a competitive market to function properly, so that the 'natural rate' of unemployment is high.

The idea is not confined to the countries of the European Community. The IMF, for example, staffed by bureaucrats on tax-free salaries and inflation-proof pensions, regularly calls for greater flexibility of labour markets as being the only policy which will reduce unemployment, by reducing the 'natural rate'. John Flemming, then chief economist of the European Bank for Reconstruction and Development, which is notorious for spending more on furnishing its own offices and on chartering private jets for its directors than it gives out in loans, recently urged the economies of Eastern Europe to avoid the errors of their Western cousins, and to ensure that their labour markets stay flexible.

Unemployment itself is the topic of subsequent chapters, but two remarks might be permitted at this stage. First, that the rapid move from planned to free-market economies in the former Soviet bloc, with no intermediate stage, has already resulted in unemployment rates of 20 or 30 per cent – or even higher – in a number of these countries, making remarks about the need for flexibility seem a little out of place. And second, as we noted in Chapter 4, in Western Europe it is the British government which has led the way on deregulation of the labour market throughout the 1980s and early 1990s. Yet at the time of writing unemployment is around 3 million in deregulated Britain, in regulated France, and in regulation-choked Italy, three countries of very similar populations. To the casual observer, if not to the economist, these similar levels of unemployment might well suggest that labour market flexibility, or the lack of it, is not tremendously important in determining unemployment in these three large European economies, with their quite different experiences of flexibility.

Measures to reduce the 'natural rate' of unemployment through increased labour market flexibility take a variety of forms. Laws which weaken the power of trade unions – a policy followed by the British government in a series of measures in the 1980s – are often an integral part of any such proposals. A further dimension, prominent in the current debate within the European Commission, is whether those costs to companies of employing workers which are additional to the normal wage or salary are too high. For example, the entitlement to maternity leave at the company's expense, the right to redundancy payments when a worker is dismissed, and so on.

Yet another theme which has persisted for many years is the argument that the provision of unemployment benefits is too generous, so that the unemployed are encouraged to remain at leisure, choosing to keep their unemployed status in preference to the discipline of work. For example, two British academics, Richard Layard of the London School of Economics and Stephen Nickell of Oxford, have been influential in arguing that the length of time for which people are allowed to draw benefit is 'crucial' in determining the present high levels of unemployment in Western Europe.

This last argument seems on the face of things to be a difficult one to sustain, since the regulations on this aspect of unemployment benefit have changed only slowly, if at all, in the various EC countries during the past twenty years. If anything, regulations have been tightened against the recipients of benefit, making it more difficult for them to draw it for long periods. Yet unemployment now is typically four times higher in European countries than it was two decades ago. Despite this seemingly intractable empirical difficulty for the argument that tightening the rules for drawing unemployment benefit is crucial to reducing unemployment, the idea persists and has influence with policy makers.

But it is evidence such as this which has led to criticism even within the economics profession of the concept of the 'natural rate', and of its implication that only 'supply-side' measures can solve the problem of unemployment. The 'natural rate' idea holds a dominant intellectual position within economics, but it does not lack its critics.

For example, Robert Solow, formaliser of the Phillips curve link between inflation and unemployment over thirty years ago, has been prominent in drawing attention to the fact that estimates of the 'natural rate', both in America and in Europe, correspond closely with the actual levels of unemployment experienced in the recent past. Since unemployment in the West has been higher in most countries in the past twenty years than in the previous twenty, estimates of the 'natural rate' have also risen.

This in itself raises doubts about the validity of the concept. Whatever the actual rate of unemployment happens to have been in the recent past, the policy conclusion of free-market economists is always the same: permanent reductions in unemployment can only be achieved by 'supply-side' measures of flexibility and deregulation.

Of more general concern is the fact that many of the factors which are supposed to contribute to the lack of flexibility of labour markets, particularly in Europe, and to impede the workings of free-market forces, have not changed a great deal over the years. We gave the example above of the duration of entitlement to benefit, but the argument can be extended to most, if not all, of the so-called supply-side factors which are presumed to have worsened over the years and to have led to a sharp rise in the 'natural rate' of unemployment.

Actual unemployment in Europe has risen fourfold in the past twenty years, and most estimates of the 'natural rate' in the various countries have risen by a similar amount. Yet flexibility of labour markets, however defined, has not changed markedly over this period. This is not to say that such factors have no influence at all over unemployment, but the magnitude of their changes over time has simply not been sufficient to account for the enormous rise in unemployment which Europe has experienced – and in Britain, on any conceivable definition, labour market flexibility has increased since the election of Mrs Thatcher, yet unemployment is now also very high, close to the European average.

Despite such evidence, the concept of the 'natural rate' remains a powerful one, in both the practical debate over, and the conduct of, economic policy, and within the discipline of orthodox economics. It was reached by incorporating rational expectations into the Phillips curve and, as we have seen in previous chapters, the idea of rationality is intellectually attractive to economists. Further, according to the theory, at any point in time the 'natural rate' is an equilibrium rate, in the sense that the economy has a natural tendency to settle at that rate, and the equilibrium itself is unique. In other words, there is only one rate of unemployment in a particular country at a particular point in time which corresponds to the 'natural rate'. Rationality, equilibrium and uniqueness of equilibrium – the 'natural rate' and the rational expectations Phillips curve embody all these concepts which are so beloved of orthodox economists.

An examination of the data on inflation and unemployment in a wide range of Western countries over the past forty years tells a story which is different from the Phillips curve, both in its original form and in its current guise, augmented with rational expectations. Analysing the data with none of the orthodox preconceptions of equilibrium and uniqueness of equilibrium allows us to identify the true relationship between inflation and unemployment. It is a relationship which has different policy implications from either of the specifications of the Phillips curve, old or new, in the literature of economics.

The experience of the United States provides a good illustration of this theme. Figure 2 plots the rate of inflation in the United States over the period 1953–92 against the rate of unemployment in the previous year.* Each of the points in the chart marks the rate of inflation, and the rate of unemployment associated with it. Reading across from the left-hand axis shows the rate of inflation at any particular point, and reading down from this to the bottom axis shows the unemployment rate linked with this.

For example, in the bottom left of the chart, there are two points marked at which inflation was very low, just above zero in fact. These happen to be the years 1953 and 1954. Reading down from these points tells us that in the previous years, 1952 and 1953, unemployment was very low, at under 3 per cent. Another example is the highest point in the chart, reading across from the inflation scale. This point corresponds to 1980, when inflation in America was at a post-war high of almost 13 per cent. Tracing down from this point to the unemployment axis tells us that in the previous year, 1979, unemployment had been around 6 per cent.

This type of chart is known as a scatter diagram – perhaps, one might think, looking at the way in which the points are scattered around in it in a seemingly random fashion, not surprisingly. The purpose of such charts is to convey information graphically about the strength of the link between two variables – in this case, inflation and unemployment. In

*The general points which can be made from this chart would not be affected if the current year's unemployment rate were used instead. The previous year is chosen because the statistical correlation of this with inflation is slightly stronger.

FIGURE 2 Scatter plot of American inflation
and unemployment, 1953–92

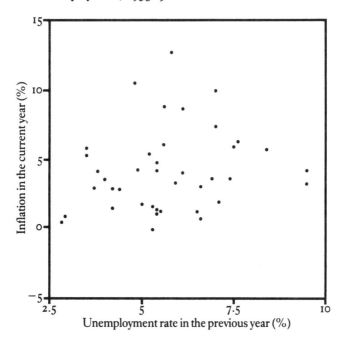

Figure 2, there is little apparent pattern in the way in which the points are distributed. But suppose there were a pattern. Suppose, for example, the points tended to slope downwards, from left to right, across the chart. This would tell us that a Phillips curve of some kind existed, with high levels of inflation appearing towards the top left of the chart, and low levels towards the bottom right. And reading down to the unemployment axis, we would then see that points of high inflation in the top left were associated with points of low unemployment, and points of low inflation in the bottom right with high unemployment.

Figure 2 tells us quite clearly, without carrying out any statistical analysis, that a single Phillips curve has not existed in America over the post-war period, and hence that there is not a clear relationship between inflation and unemployment. In fact, formal statistical methods indicate that, if anything, there has been a very weak *positive* relationship between the two over this data period. In other words, the evidence for the past forty years indicates that, on average, a rise in unemployment seems to have been associated not with a fall, but with a rise in inflation.

Figure 3 presents the same data, with added information. Different observations are corralled into three different groups. Not every single observation is organised in this way – the observations for 1953 and 1954 which we discussed earlier remain outside a group, for example, and 1972 and 1973 are difficult to classify. Within each of these groups, the points do slope downwards from left to right, exactly as a Phillips curve would expect. The slopes are not identical, and the observations in each group do not lie on a neat, straight line. But the general, downward slope is clear.

FIGURE 3 Scatter plot of American
inflation and unemployment, 1953–92

The important point about the groupings is that there is a very definite pattern determining which observations fall into which grouping. The bottom left group contains all the years 1955–71. The middle group includes 1985–92. And the group furthest away from the axes of the chart includes the years 1974–84.

Looked at in this way, the data suggest that three different Phillips curves have existed in the US in the last forty years or so. And it suggests that, quite suddenly, at certain times, they shifted their position quite markedly.

A more formal statistical analysis in fact points to the possible existence of as many as five groups. Sub-divisions of the two biggest groups can potentially be made, so that data from 1974–9 and 1980–4, for example, are in two different groups.

In other words, the evidence from America since the early 1950s points to at least three and perhaps as many as five different Phillips curves, and thus to as many as five different levels of the 'natural rate' of unemployment. Moreover, on each occasion that the Phillips curve, and hence the 'natural rate' implied by it, has shifted, it has done so quite suddenly.

This has not gone unnoticed. In 1988, for example, two economists prominent in America, Oliveer Blanchard and Larry Summers – the latter now part of the Clinton administration – were the first to move away from the idea of a unique equilibrium 'natural rate' of unemployment, admitting the possibility of multiple equilibria.

During the post-war period, the American economy has moved through time on paths linking inflation and unemployment, on which the traditional relationship between the rate of inflation and the level of unemployment appears to operate. But the economy has been shocked at periodic intervals on to a path which gives an inflation rate which is permanently either higher or lower for any given rate of unemployment than that implied by the previous path. In other words, it appears as if Phillips-type relationships hold, but that they are not stable over time. This is what one might conclude from the American data presented in the charts so far.

But such an interpretation conceals the underlying law which describes the link between unemployment and inflation.

In most Western economies, the general relationship is not in fact between the rate of inflation and the level of unemployment, but between the *rate of change* of inflation and the *rate of change* of unemployment.

We need not be concerned here with the statistical tests which establish this point. A condensed summary is provided for the interested reader at the end of the book, along with a reference to the published proceedings of the conference held at Cambridge University in 1993 in which I give full technical details of the work. But the flavour of the results can be seen quite readily from the American data as presented below.

Figure 4 is another scatter diagram linking inflation and unemployment in the United States over the post-war period, but with one

FIGURE 4 Scatter plot of changes in
American inflation and unemployment, 1953–92

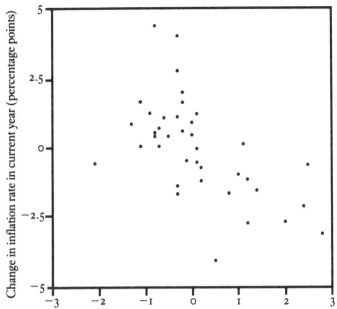

Change in unemployment rate in the previous year (percentage points)

important difference. It is the *changes* in both the rates of inflation and unemployment which are plotted, instead of the rates themselves.

A striking feature of the chart is that, unlike the data in Figure 2, there is a distinct pattern to the plot. Although the points do not lie on a perfect curve, the scatter of data slopes down unmistakably from the top left to the bottom right. Increases in the rate of inflation tend to be linked to falls in unemployment, and vice versa.

There are a few points which lie away from the general pattern. In particular, there are two years at the top of the change in inflation scale in which the rate of inflation rose by around 4 percentage points. These two years are in fact 1974 and 1980, the years of two major inflationary shocks in the Western world, when world oil prices rose dramatically.

Unlike the data in Figure 2, it is not possible to group the data in Figure 4 in a way which corresponds to continuous sequences of years, to blocks of time. For example, at the bottom right of the chart there are four years in which the rate of unemployment rose by 2 percentage points or more. These are 1954, 1958, 1975 and 1982, points which are by no means close in time.

In other words, the downward sloping relationship between the change in the rate of inflation and the change in the unemployment rate is valid over the *whole* of the period examined in the chart.

All three schools of thought on the link between inflation and unemployment – the original Phillips approach, the rational expectations Phillips model, and the model described above – agree on one point. At any moment in time, a Phillips curve exists which describes a negative relationship betwen inflation and unemployment. If unemployment falls, for example, and the economy moves along the curve, inflation will rise.

In the original Phillips curve, the economy can be moved to, and can stay on, any point of the curve. In the rational expectations model, this is not possible. There is a unique point on any such curve, corresponding to the 'natural rate' of unemployment, at which the economy will settle naturally. Attempts to move the economy up or down the curve on a permanent basis by government spending policies are doomed to failure. The economy can only move away from the natural rate temporarily. But believers in both the old-style Phillips curve and in the rational expectations 'natural rate' curve have to invoke shifts in the relationship – perhaps as many as five in the post-war period for American data, for example – in order to extract the theoretically expected negative relationships between the levels of inflation and unemployment. Taking the period as a whole, as we have seen, gives a relationship between the two which if anything is positive.

By approaching the data without the theoretical baggage of the 'natural rate' concept, and seeing what the data tell us, what hypothesis is consistent with the data, we can establish a clear negative relationship between *changes* in inflation and unemployment over a forty-year period without having to invoke shifts of behaviour in any way. But the fact that the apparent relationship between the levels of inflation and unemployment shifts all over the place does not surprise us in any way, because at any given *level* of unemployment, the rate of inflation is indeterminate.*

One way of visualising this is as follows. It is as if, at any point in time, an economy can either move *along* an existing curve linking the levels of inflation and unemployment, or the curve itself can move, whether in

---

*The clearest way to express this, for readers who understand basic calculus, is as follows. The true relationship is between the first derivatives of inflation and unemployment, so by simple integration the relationship between the levels of the two variables is indeterminate up to an arbitrary constant.

response to deliberate policy actions by the government, or in response to an external shock to the economy. If unemployment, say, rose, the process of the economy moving along the curve would of itself lead to lower inflation. If, at the same time, the position of the curve itself shifts, inflation may still end up falling, but equally, if the curve shifts far enough, it may even rise.

The 'natural rate' hypothesis also admits movements of the curve, but only in response to specific supply-side events which either improve or handicap the workings of market forces in the economy. And, as we have seen, shifts in curves which link the levels of inflation and unemployment are far too abrupt to be explained by slow-moving supply-side factors.

We noted above two particular periods when the phenomenon of unemployment and inflation both rising at the same time was observed in many Western countries. Orthodox economics, with its model of equilibrium, finds it hard to accept that specific historical events and the reactions to them can determine the paths which economies take over long periods of time. But one of these periods in particular has been of great importance to the economies of Europe over the past twenty years.

At the end of 1973 and early in 1974, the West experienced the first and most serious oil-price shock, when the price of oil quadrupled virtually overnight. The rest of the 1970s was taken up by the absorption of and reaction to the oil-price shock. And over the 1974–9 period as a whole, in almost every country, both inflation and unemployment were higher on average than they had been in 1968–73.

Dramatic differences within Europe arose immediately following the oil-price shock of 1973–4. Countries were placed very rapidly on different inflation paths. And the process of restoring broad international convergence has involved very high rates of unemployment in those countries where inflation rose the most following the shock. In other words, specific reactions to the events of 1974 produced specific consequences whose effects are still with us today.

The German domination of European economic policy, for example, owes a great deal to the particular response of the Germans to the oil-price shock. In the post-war years to 1974, Germany built a reputation as a low-inflation economy. The international agreement of Bretton Woods, shortly after the war, had committed the developed economies to maintaining fixed exchange rates between their currencies. Apart from occasional adjustments here and there, they succeeded in doing this for the best part of a quarter of a century. But by the early 1970s the system was breaking down under pressure. The German mark, for example, because of the country's reputation for low inflation, was revalued upwards against most other currencies. But the gap in percentage point terms between German inflation and elsewhere in Europe was not large.

After the oil-price increase, the position changed rapidly and dramatically.

In 1973, inflation was very similar in a number of European countries. In Germany it was 6.7 per cent, in France 7.1 per cent, in Belgium 6.7 per cent and in the Netherlands 7.7 per cent. The initial reaction to the oil-price shock was also very similar, with inflation averaging 10–12 per cent in 1974. But by as early as 1975, the shock had moved the economies on to different inflation/unemployment paths. Inflation in Germany fell back to only 4.3 per cent, but stayed in the 10–12 per cent range in France, Belgium and Netherlands. Even more diverse shifts occurred in Italy and Britain, where inflation rose in the space of barely twelve months from a rate of 10 per cent a year to one of over 20 per cent.

This experience by itself is sufficient to show the emptiness and implausibility of the 'natural rate' hypothesis, which requires us to believe that, in the space of twelve to eighteen months in the mid-1970s, market imperfections in European countries, which had been broadly similar for twenty years, suddenly became dramatically different.

Inflation rates, at any given level of unemployment, did change rapidly, but because of the particular circumstances and responses which prevailed in each country, rather than in response to fundamental shifts in the supply-side behaviour of the various economies. The key factor, common to all European economies, was that the oil-price rise led to a shift in real incomes from these countries to OPEC. The higher oil price meant the OPEC countries became better off, and the Europeans worse off. The degree to which this was perceived by the workforces in the various European economies was crucial to the path which inflation took. Higher oil prices meant higher inflation – the cost of energy had risen.

In Germany, the workforce recognised very quickly that this meant their living standards had to fall. The nation as a whole had lost part of its income to OPEC, so workers could not regain their real living standards by putting in claims for higher money wages. An inflationary spiral of higher prices leading to higher wages, leading in turn to higher costs and still higher prices, was avoided. This was a triumph for the German concept of the social market, deliberately created after the war to aid recovery. In Germany, private companies got on with their business with minimum interference from government, but did so within a social framework which emphasised the rights and responsibilities of both sides of industry. For example, workers had the right to be consulted about a whole range of factors affecting their lives, and indeed the right to be involved in the process of decision making, in a way which is still unheard of in countries like Britain today. But in return, they had a responsibility to act reasonably which, at their first major test, they did.

In contrast, in varying degrees, the workforces elsewhere in Europe failed to realise that living standards had to fall. In Britain, for example, the situation could hardly have been better designed to produce an explosion in inflation. In the autumn of 1973, the then Conservative government agreed a formula with the trade unions whose aim was to reduce inflation during the coming year. Unions were asked to take a smaller pay rise than they wanted, but with the legal guarantee that, if inflation rose faster than expected, everyone's pay would be increased immediately by an agreed amount, rather than people having to wait for the bargaining process in the next annual pay round to see if they could claw back their losses. It says much for the accuracy of economic forecasting even then that, within a matter of weeks of this agreement being concluded, the oil-price shock happened, and the inflationary outlook worsened. A policy, known as the threshold agreement, whose intention was to slow down pay increases, now acted as a powerful force pushing them up.

But worse was to come. In the spring of 1974, the Conservatives were rather surprisingly defeated at a general election. But the incoming Labour government did not have a majority in Parliament, so another election was bound to be held soon. In the circumstances, it was probably too much to ask of any government that it should do the sensible thing and cancel the threshold agreement, pleading *force majeure*. It was certainly too much to ask of the Labour government of that time, which was predisposed to give the trade unions anything they wanted. And they wanted a lot. In early 1975, the railwaymen turned down an offer of a 27.5 per cent increase on the grounds that it was not enough.* It was only the rapid rise in unemployment, doubling during 1975, which frightened the workforce into moderating their demands dramatically, which

---

*Rather like the Walrus with the oysters, I deeply sympathised. Despite the fact that I had been working for barely a year, an increase of 53 per cent had been stuffed into my own pay packet.

brought inflation back towards even 10 per cent a year.

A great deal of Europe's subsequent economic experience can be traced back directly to the events of 1974 and early 1975. As a result of the specific reactions in Germany to the oil-price shock, the German economy emerged on a much more favourable inflation/unemployment path than most of the rest of Europe. For any given level of unemployment, the level of inflation in Germany was lower than elsewhere. This consolidated strongly the German image of a low-inflation country, and enabled the central bank of Germany, the Bundesbank, to become powerful throughout Western Europe.

Further, during the late 1970s and early 1980s, most of the EC economies decided to construct their own version of the Bretton Woods agreement, whereby their currencies would be fixed in value against each other. This mechanism, the European Exchange Rate Mechanism (ERM for short), required inflation rates in the member countries to be reasonably close together if it was to survive. For if one country's inflation rate was, say, 10 per cent and another's only 2 or 3 per cent, a fixed exchange rate between the two currencies would mean that the goods and services produced in the high-inflation country would become more and more uncompetitive on price. But with the European economies having been shifted on to different inflation/unemployment paths in the mid-1970s, as Figure 1 shows, similar inflation rates in European countries towards the end of the 1980s implied quite different rates of unemployment. As it happens, the recent shock of reunification may well have moved Germany to a less favourable inflation/unemployment path, so its continent-wide influence on the conduct of economic policy has probably peaked.

The economic concepts of rationality and of equilibrium, of the 'natural rate' of unemployment, continue to occupy the dominant position within the discipline of economics in discussions of inflation and unemployment. Through this position, they exercise a powerful influence on the discussion and conduct of economic policy.

The conventional view that the underlying relationship is one between the levels of inflation and unemployment is not supported by the data. And it seriously misleads policy makers.

The prime aim of anti-inflation policy should be to shift the economy from one inflation/unemployment path to another – to shift the curve, rather than try to move along it: in other words, to administer a favourable shock to the underlying relationship between the rate of change of inflation and the rate of change of unemployment.

One possibility is to shock the system by draconian measures. In recent European experience, this could have been one potential outcome of the ERM, although it is now transparent to all but the most ardent European federalists and believers in complete European monetary union that this particular experiment has failed.

An alternative is to try to create a set of values in which a system of social consensus and cohesion prevails. This is a task which ranges far beyond the narrow confines of conventional economic policy. Economic policy is far too important to be left to economists.

Given the experience of the 1980s, the creation of such a framework of behaviour is a challenging task. But it is one of which Adam Smith would have approved most heartily.

And it is one where the incentive to succeed is high. Once the true relationship between inflation and unemployment is understood, with luck and skill, a free lunch *is* possible.

CHAPTER 7

Attractor Points

At present, many Western economies are bedevilled by high levels of unemployment. The supply of labour – those in work and those who are unemployed – is transparently greater than the demand for labour, the number of jobs available. As I write, in mid-1993, almost 9 million people are unemployed in the United States, and in the European Community the number is around 17 million, and rising. Measuring unemployment as a percentage of the total of those in employment plus the unemployed – the unemployment rate – gives a mid-1993 figure of 7 per cent for America and approaching 12 per cent for the European Community.

High levels of unemployment are not a recent phenomenon. They have happened before and, what is more, can persist over long periods of time.

In the peace-time years of this century, unemployment in the United States has averaged over 6 per cent of the labour force, with a maximum of no less than 22 per cent. In today's terms, this average amounts to 8 million people. In Britain in peace-time, unemployment has averaged almost 6 per cent, with a maximum of 15 per cent. Indeed, over the whole of the last 140 years (the longest time-span for which data of any remote degree of reliability exist), unemployment in Britain has averaged 5 per cent – almost 1.5 million people in today's terms. Even in Germany, the most successful economy in Europe, in the peace-time years since 1920 unemployment has averaged over 4 per cent – well over 1 million in present-day terms.

Even in the intellectual framework of orthodox economics it is not expected that unemployment is everywhere and always zero. For example, there will be people in the process of changing jobs, either voluntarily or involuntarily. Some may be unemployed because of the seasonal nature of their work, and so on. But the long-run averages of over a million in each of the main European economies might be considered rather a large number of people to be in the process of changing jobs.

More subtly, as mentioned briefly in the previous chapter, it is argued that the apparent existence of large numbers of unemployed does not mean that the labour market is not in equilibrium. For example, many of the unemployed may have chosen that status, and not be seeking work. They are not therefore part of the supply of labour, since they prefer the leisure of unemployment to the discipline of work. In the jargon, these individuals have carried out the 'rational, self-interested analysis of utility maximisation', and have concluded that benefits plus leisure are better than wages plus work.

This argument ignores the fact that most states have, and have had over time, rather strict laws which prevent the voluntarily unemployed from drawing benefit at all. A substantial apparatus exists to enforce not only these laws, but also the laws which prevent those drawing benefit from working at the same time in the black economy. Of course, this is not to say that ingenious individuals cannot circumvent the regulations, but the problem is not widespread.

The concept of extensive voluntary unemployment has existed for many years. But rather less is being heard of it at present than even, say, ten years ago, for the current wave of unemployment is now sweeping over many members of the middle class, who had previously thought themselves virtually immune from the problem. Suburban forty-somethings, whose lives have been a caricature of devotion to work, now find themselves unemployed. When the man next door loses his job, it is rather hard to persuade many people that the unemployed are simply a bunch of idle scroungers.

The solutions offered by orthodox economics at present to the problem of high unemployment focus on removing what are seen to be obstacles to the workings of the free market. As we saw in the previous chapter, the emphasis is on deregulation and creating flexibility in the labour market. Economics has a strong faith that if the market economies of the developed world can be moved closer to the ideal world described by the model of competitive equilibrium, unemployment will fall.

In the 1930s, the previous period of high unemployment, the orthodox had a stronger belief that the self-adjusting tendencies of market econ-omies were already sufficiently powerful to guarantee that full employ-ment would eventually be restored.

Keynes addressed this question in his magnum opus, *The General Theory of Employment, Interest and Money*, published in 1936, attempting to demonstrate, while retaining as many of the precepts of orthodox economics as possible, how high levels of unemployment could persist for long periods of time. In other words, within the context of the model of competitive equilibrium, to show that a violation of just one or two of its many assumptions would lead to outcomes quite different from those of competitive equilibrium, in which supply and demand are equal in every market and all resources are fully utilised.

As mentioned in the early chapters, Keynes believed that the whole corpus of orthodox economic theory offered a view of the world which was seriously misleading, and that attempts to use it as a guide to the conduct of economic policy often had disastrous results. His aim in setting up a model which contained many of the postulates of orthodox theory was to try to carry along with him as many people as possible from the economics profession. The more his model was able to encompass the precepts of existing orthodoxy, the narrower the scope for disagreement, and the greater the hope which Keynes had that his fellow economists would be persuaded by his analysis.

It was by no means a foolish strategy to follow, but it was not without risks. For, as we shall see, by conducting the debate as far as possible within the framework of orthodoxy, Keynes allowed the orthodox a response which would not have been available to them if he had put forward a model which was fundamentally different to that of standard economics. Essentially, in reply, Keynes's critics argued that, although he claimed to have written a 'general' theory, it was no more than a particular case of the even more general theory of orthodox economics. Keynes's model, they claimed, could be contained within the received wisdom.

Keynes tried to show that market economies could settle in equilibrium states in which the labour market did not clear, and in which the level of unemployment was high. He believed that this was due to a particular example of market failure, developed in his concept of effective demand.

In a situation where, for whatever reason, substantial unemployment exists, the potential demand for goods and services in the economy is higher than actual demand – or, in other words, the level of demand which would exist if unemployed resources were put to work is higher than the actual level.

To illustrate this point, imagine a town in the rust belt of America or in the declining industrial areas of Europe in which a large factory such as a steelworks has been closed down, and people are unemployed. The high-street baker, for example, might want to buy a new suit from the local tailor's shop, but is not able to afford it because he is no longer selling enough bread and cakes in his shop. The tailor might long to spend more money on cakes, but not enough people are now buying his suits and jackets. Both the baker and the tailor may be forced to make some of their staff redundant, because their takings are too low to meet the costs of employing them. The unemployed themselves want to spend more money with both the baker and the tailor, but simply cannot afford to do so. The amount which people would like to spend, if unemployment fell, on the products of the baker and the tailor is high, but the actual demand is low. If the unemployed could suddenly be put back into work, the actual level of demand would rise, and a virtuous circle would be created in the town. More would be spent at the baker's and the tailor's, who could in turn not only spend more money themselves, but employ more staff to help them cope with the increased customer demand.

Keynes believed that the market system could not communicate efficiently this potential level of demand to companies and individuals in the economy. The system can only inform people about the actual level of demand, and it is on this actual level that decisions are made as to how much to produce, how many people to employ, what to spend, and so on. If in some way the market economy could function so that decisions were taken on the basis of the potential level of demand, more goods and services would be produced, more people employed, and more would be spent.

Of course, companies and individuals might be aware in principle that the potential level of demand is higher than the actual level. In our example of the old industrial town, the local baker and tailor know that if unemployment were to fall their takings would rise. But no single company has an incentive to act on this basis. For if it does, alone, the result will simply be that its increased production remains unsold. The baker might bake more cakes, but if he does they will just go stale in the shop. If all the companies in the town could signal to each other that they were each about to increase production, they would have a real incentive to do so. But the market system cannot communicate such an intention effectively.

Keynes's remedy was for the government to intervene to overcome such examples of market failure. If the government took action to stimulate spending in the economy, by cutting taxes to make those in work better off or by increasing its own spending, decisions on increased spending by companies and individuals would have a basis warranted in fact rather than in theory. The economy as a whole could enter a virtuous circle and move towards its potential, full employment level of demand.

This analysis attracted a barrage of intellectual criticism, and, as we noted in Chapter 5, it is one which has persisted in various forms to the present day. The most effective attack at the time was led by another Cambridge academic, A. C. Pigou,* and in the decade of life left to him after writing the General Theory, Keynes effectively conceded the theoretical point made by Pigou.

The argument centred on the concept known as the real balance effect, which remains an important idea in macro-economics. We pointed out in Chapter 5 that modern-day macro-economics has developed what is effectively a synthesis of the various schools of thought, and that the precise properties of any particular macro-model, theoretical or applied, will depend upon whether or not various linkages are activated within the model. One such linkage is the real balance effect. The modern macro-model will give results which are more or less strongly inclined to the original views of either Keynes or Pigou, depending upon whether this particular link is activated, and upon the strength of the connection. This shows the weakness, not of Keynes's arguments, but of his strategy of persuasion. By deliberately retaining as many as possible of the precepts of orthodox economics, Keynes permitted the development of Keynes*ian* economics, which could be comfortably absorbed as a special case within the more general model of theoretical macro-economics.

The idea underlying the real balance effect is that a level of unemployment which is sufficiently high will lead not only to inflation being eliminated, but to the price level falling, or in other words to negative inflation.

A substantial part of people's wealth is held in assets (balances) which are denominated in money terms. In other words, a saver may have £10,000 in a bank or building society. Regardless of the rate of interest

---

*Somewhat bizarrely, the name of this ardent believer in market-clearing equilibrium has been linked posthumously with the high-level Soviet penetration of the Cambridge élite which took place in the 1930s and 1940s. While it is true that Keynes believed he could save capitalism from what many of his contemporaries regarded as its terminal crisis, so that a devotee of the Soviet system would have had every reason to discredit Keynes's ideas, Pigou's disguise could hardly have been bettered – so much so that the whole idea appears preposterous to many people.

or the rate of inflation, this capital sum remains the same in nominal terms – £10,000. A falling price level would increase the real value of this capital sum. In other words, if prices fall, the same amount in terms of money, £10,000, can buy more goods and services. People who hold such assets, or balances, will have become richer. This increase in wealth not only enables people to buy more products, but gives them the confidence to spend. And so, eventually, spending will rise. The actual level of demand in the economy will increase, and a virtuous circle will be created which, without the help of government intervention, will lead the economy back to full employment.

This argument was conducted at a purely theoretical level, with virtually no reference to empirical evidence. The time-scale, for example, over which such an effect might have an impact was not quantified, prompting Keynes's famous remark that 'in the long-run we are all dead'. Nowadays, this is widely misunderstood as the sort of cynical remark which a clever Cambridge chap might make.

But the statement Keynes was making was in fact a very positive, practical one. Although he accepted the logic of Pigou's real balance effect, in the 1930s, with unemployment running to tens of millions in both America and Europe, he saw little point in waiting for the workings of a theoretical device which might at some distant time in the future restore full employment. Action was required immediately.

At the time, a few economists, such as Irving Fisher in America, queried whether the real balance effect would be sufficient to restore full employment. They did so in terms which are particularly relevant today. Fisher, for example, was concerned that the behaviour of debtors might not be symmetrical with those of creditors. Just as assets are denominated in nominal terms, so too are debts. A falling price level does increase the real value of assets. But it also increases the real value of debts. This meant that, theoretically, the real balance effect could work in both directions, encouraging those with savings to spend more, and those who are borrowers and in debt to spend less. If debtors cut back on spending more than creditors increase it, the economy will continue to spiral down, with ever-rising levels of unemployment.

Keynes himself, in a paragraph in one of the concluding chapters of the *General Theory*, recognised the importance of fluctuations in the value of stockmarkets on consumer spending, particularly at the time in the United States. He argued that, especially if people had borrowed to buy shares, falling stockmarkets could intensify a recession. But he did not use this argument with sufficient strength in the debate over the Pigovian real balance effect.

The American economist James Tobin revived this idea ten years or so ago, and Edmond Malinvaud, a distinguished French economist, has recently warned the European Commission of the practical dangers of such an effect in the current circumstances. But in general, theoretical economics has ignored this point, despite its relevance to current circumstances, and in particular to those economies in which debt levels are high relative to incomes. Japan, America and Britain are the major examples.

The lower the rate of inflation, the worse is the situation for debtors. If inflation becomes negative and the general level of prices falls, the problem becomes even more acute. And it is potentially exacerbated even further in the present day by the fact that the prices of many of the assets which people and companies hold are not, like bank deposits, fixed in money terms. Compared to the 1930s, for example, many more people own houses, the prices of which can go down as well as up.

A large number of individuals and companies who bought property in the price booms of the late 1980s now find that the value of such properties has fallen while the size of their debt is fixed in money terms, and has therefore stayed the same. In other words, they are suffering from 'negative equity'.

In such circumstances, a policy obsession with securing very low inflation, and even with eliminating it altogether, can be extremely dangerous. Apart from the likely short-term impact on unemployment of such a policy stance, very low inflation means that the real value of debt is eroded very slowly. Debtors will be constrained in their behaviour for a long period of time.

It is important here to emphasise, once again, that the debate nowadays is conducted within the shared framework of orthodox macroeconomics, in which the properties of the model as a whole depend upon the activation and strength of various key linkages. Keynes, in the form in which he has been absorbed by modern macro-theory, plus a negative real balance effect which outweighs Pigou's positive real balance effect, begins to look like the original Keynes, even though the policy implications are different. For in such a world the most effective way to revive confidence and stimulate spending is for governments directly to underwrite private sector debt. This suggestion is not a mere flight of fancy. The Japanese government has supported its fragile banking system, and even the British government, which is in general hostile to state intervention, has made some money available for the purchase of empty homes from individuals.

For all the theoretical debate in macro-economics, Keynes's original position has had an enormous influence on Western policy making since the Second World War. By regulating the level of spending in the economy and the rate at which it grows – through changes in tax rates, public spending and interest rates – governments believed they could control the level of unemployment.

As we have seen, in the past two decades or so, macro-economics has emphasised those linkages in its general theoretical model which give results which are more monetarist and free-market than they are Keynesian and government-intervention oriented. And this intellectual fashion has dominated the world of policy making. But there are signs now that the special case of Keynesianism in the general macro-model is coming back into fashion. The crisis in unemployment has finally begun to attract the attention of the world's political leaders.

In June 1993, Jacques Delors, president of the European Commission, commissioned a series of studies into the problem of unemployment, culminating in the Commission's white paper on employment, published at the end of 1993. On a still wider scale, at the July 1993 Tokyo summit of the world's leading economies, on the initiative of President Clinton, a new emphasis was placed on job creation as a policy priority.

Newly fashionable policies designed to improve the quality of the labour force through education and training form part of every government's plans. But Keynesian demand-management, through a public-spending and interest-rate policy, is becoming respectable once again.

Whether by making the economy more competitive through a better quality of labour, or by acting directly on the level of demand, the intention is to stimulate economic growth. By promoting the growth of output, it is widely believed that employment will grow, and that unemployment will fall. But will higher levels of output, achieved by whatever means, prove any more effective in creating jobs and reducing unemployment than the policies of the past twenty years have done?

Let us first clear our minds of all existing macro-economic theory – an easier task for some than for others, whose thought processes might have become distorted by years spent wrestling with the real balance effect and the intricacies of monetary theory.

Let us examine the data and see what broad conclusions might be drawn. Instead of starting from abstract economic theory and trying to manipulate the facts around it, here and in the following chapter we shall be trying to answer the following questions: what are the key characteristics of unemployment which are observed? What kind of model will contain and explain these characteristics?

The first question is to examine the link between economic growth and unemployment.

Contrary to received wisdom, both of policy makers and of macroeconomic models, there is little connection over time between the rate of economic growth and either the growth in employment or the level of unemployment. The Clinton administration in the autumn of 1993 raised the spectre of jobless growth in the recovery taking place in the American economy. But many Western economies have experienced this for the past two decades.

With broadly similar patterns of economic growth, Western economies over the past twenty years have shown enormous diversity in the rates both of job creation and of unemployment levels. Between 1970 and 1992, the American economy grew in real terms by some 76 per cent, and the economies of the European Community by 73 per cent – in other words, by almost identical amounts. Yet employment in the United States rose over the same period by 45 per cent, compared to only 7 per cent in the EC.

The low rate of employment growth in Europe does not mean that new jobs are not being created, even during recessions and even in Europe. These figures refer to the net increase in employment, subtracting numbers of jobs lost from the number created.

As we shall see, cycles of recession followed by boom are an integral feature of the behaviour of developed economies. In the upswing of the cycle, during the expansionary phase when output rises quickly, the number of new jobs created relative to the number of jobs lost increases, and employment expands. The opposite holds during the recessionary phase of the cycle.

But the connection between movements in output and employment over the course of the economic cycle – which is usually anything between four and eight years' duration – misleads people into believing that this relationship necessarily persists over the course of several cycles. In Europe in particular, it is a purely short-term phenomenon, and the correlation which is observed *during* the economic cycle between growth and employment is not valid in the longer term.

In most European countries, the proceeds of economic growth in the past twenty years have not been used to generate new jobs but have been appropriated by those who have remained in employment. Over this period, the real incomes of Europeans who have remained in work have grown substantially, while the unemployed have been excluded from sharing in the benefits of growth.

The Spanish economy provides a striking example of this. At one level, Spain has been a success story. Between 1970 and 1992, the Spanish economy virtually doubled in size in real terms, growing by 93 per cent. But in 1992, employment was actually 2 per cent less than it had been in 1970.

The other economies in the EC show very similar patterns. Figure 5 shows the total growth in a number of economies over the 1970–92 period, and the corresponding percentage change in employment. The chart shows that in the major European economies during the past quarter of a century, real output has grown by at least 50 per cent, and in most cases by around 75 per cent, but that there has been virtually no net job creation. In some of the smaller European countries, such as Austria and Norway, however, employment has expanded, not on the same scale as in the United States, but by appreciably larger amounts than in most of Europe.

Similarly, there seems to be no connection between economic growth and unemployment. The experience of the twenty-odd years immediately following the Second World War misled people into believing that a rapid rate of growth is necessary to bring about low unemployment.

The rates of growth experienced in a number of countries were very rapid during this period. From the early 1950s, once more normal, peace-time conditions had been restored, to the early 1970s, the average annual rate of growth in many countries in continental Europe was of the order of 5 per cent. And unemployment was low, averaging some 2 per cent, with the exception of Italy, where the regional problem of the Mezzogiorno kept the average level higher.

But even during this period, very low unemployment was preserved with markedly different growth rates in a number of countries.

Unemployment averaged just under 2 per cent in Germany, Norway and Britain, while the average growth rates were, respectively, 5.5, 3.9 and 3 per cent. In other words, Britain maintained low unemployment with a rate of growth barely half that achieved in Germany. Over the same period, despite a growth rate of 3.5 per cent, America experienced an average unemployment rate of almost 5 per cent.

FIGURE 5 Real GDP and employment growth, 1970–92

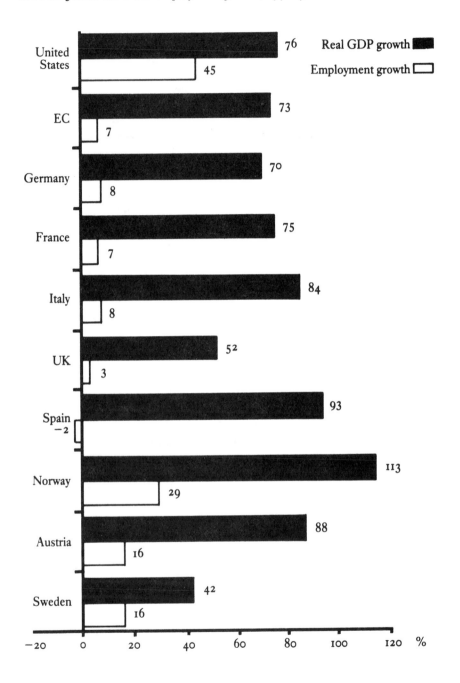

The growth rates of many Western economies from the late 1970s, once the initial impact of the oil-price shock had been absorbed, have been similar to each other, at an average of around 2 per cent a year in real terms. Yet against this background of similar growth rates over a period of some fifteen years, unemployment rates vary substantially across countries. Figure 6 shows annual average growth and the average rate of unemployment in a range of countries over the 1978–92 period. To give a flavour of the evidence, Austria, Germany and Spain all grew by an average of 2.3 per cent a year. Yet unemployment averaged 3 per cent in Austria, 6 per cent in Germany and 16 per cent in Spain.

On an international basis, there has been no correlation over the past fifteen to twenty years between the rate of economic growth and either the growth in employment or the average level of unemployment.

Existing macro-economic models, of whatever theoretical nuance and of whatever developed economy, contain a link between the level of output in an economy and the level of employment. According to the models, the faster output grows, the more rapidly employment grows. And the more jobs which are created, the lower is unemployment.

But for any given path of economic growth, on the basis of international experience over the past twenty years, the rate of unemployment is indeterminate. In other words, a wide range of unemployment rates appears to be compatible with any particular average rate of economic growth over time.

We have already seen similar empirical objections to orthodox theory concerning the rate of inflation. For any given rate of unemployment, or path of unemployment over time, the rate of inflation is indeterminate. In other words, a wide range of inflation rates appears to be compatible with any particular path for unemployment over time.

This ability of economies to move on, and switch between, different paths over time, raises serious problems for the concept of equilibrium in economics. And, as we saw in Chapter 4, economic theorists have been forced in recent years to admit the possibility of the existence of multiple equilibria in their models. The empirical data tells us that this concept is not merely a theoretical possibility, but a reality.

Think back to our old friend of Chapter 4, the Auctioneer, carrying out his task of searching for the set of prices which will clear all markets. The challenge set for him, as he wanders blindfold over the multi-cratered terrain, is sufficient to daunt even the most resolute hero of classical Greece. He may never find his desired solution, even if he

FIGURE 6 Annual real GDP growth and average
unemployment rates, 1978–92

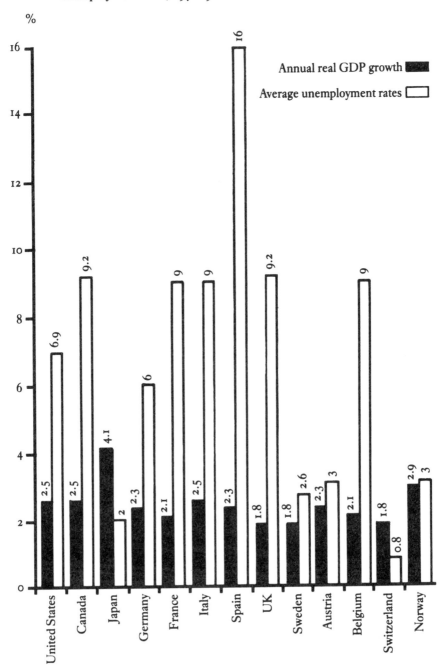

searches to eternity. Or there may be many such solutions.

Orthodoxy regards the economy as a complex, but nevertheless ulti-mately explicable and controllable, machine. There is an equilibrium path which the machine will follow, once the various component parts are serviced and in full working order. But on examination of the facts, this concept is not supported in the context of two key postulated relationships of macro-economics – between economic growth and employment/unemployment, and between unemployment and inflation.

There is not just one but many paths which an economy might follow over time. The one it does actually follow depends upon specific reac-tions to specific events at critical points in time.

We need to abandon the economist's notion of the economy as a machine, with its attendant concept of equilibrium. A more helpful way of thinking about the economy is to imagine it as a living organism. The economy has the ability, when prodded or stimulated, not simply to wobble around a fixed position, but to jump to a different position altogether. In other words, the economy may not move simply up and down a curve held in a fixed position, such as a Phillips curve, but it may shift rapidly from one curve to another.

As we saw in the previous chapter, in terms of the relationship between inflation and unemployment, we can think of the economy as if at any point in time a Phillips-type relationship existed, along which the economy is able to move. But it is as if the economy is also able to leap from one Phillips curve to another, so that the relationship between the *levels* of inflation and unemployment is indeterminate.

Similarly, at any point in time, it is as if a relationship exists between the growth of output and employment (or unemployment). Such a con-nection may stay in the same position over the course of a single economic cycle, or even over the course of many cycles. Faster growth will create more jobs, if the economy simply moves up and down a curve which links output and employment. But if the economy jumps from curve to curve, the relationship between growth and employment becomes indeterminate, for the actual path which an economy follows over time is then a mixture of movements along a fixed relationship between growth and employment, and movements of the relationship itself.

Any model attempting to explain the level of employment and/or unemployment should have this property, which as we have seen is supported strongly by the empirical data – namely, that changes in the rate of economic growth need not automatically lead to changes in employment or unemployment.

Further, any model should have the additional property that when shifts in the established behaviour patterns of employment and/or unemployment take place, they do so rapidly, with no tendency for the economy to revert to the previous pattern of behaviour. The presumption of economic theory that self-equilibrating forces exist which, after a shock, will restore the previously existing position of the economy is simply not supported by the evidence of the actual behaviour of unemployment.

The usual way of presenting graphically the movement of a factor such as unemployment over time is in a simple plot of the data. The movements are traced out on a chart. Figure 7, for example, plots the rate of unemployment in the United States over the period from 1974, when the first oil-price shock hit the West, to 1993. As can be seen, unemployment rose sharply in 1975, then fell, before rising again in the early 1980s. In the mid- to late 1980s, American unemployment fell

FIGURE 7 American unemployment rate, 1974–93

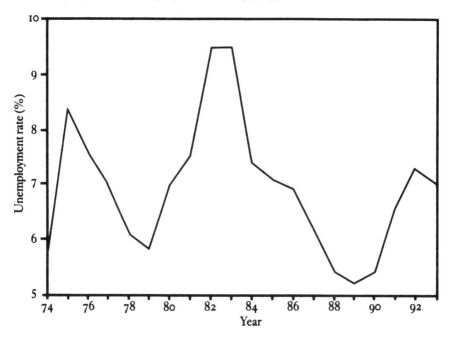

again, rising in the most recent recession, and beginning to fall as the economic recovery gathered pace in 1993.

An alternative method of presenting these data is to use the scatter diagram technique discussed in the previous chapter. There, the rate of inflation was plotted in a scatter against the rate of unemployment. In this case, we simply use the rate of unemployment and construct a scatter diagram, plotting the rate in any particular year against the rate in the year previous to it. The resulting points in the scatter diagram are then connected together. Figure 8 plots the data of Figure 7 in this way – in what is sometimes described as a phase portrait and sometimes as a directed scatter plot, but which we will term, to give it a literal description, a connected scatter plot (CSP for short).

FIGURE 8 Connected scatter plot of
American unemployment rate, 1974–93

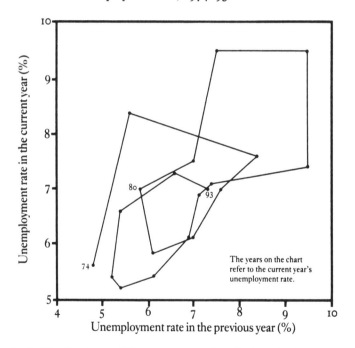

The years on the chart refer to the current year's unemployment rate.

The individual points of the scatter are labelled with the current year. Thus, the chart begins in 1974. In this year, reading across from the left-hand axis, we can see that unemployment was around 5.5 per cent. Reading down from this to the axis at the bottom, the chart tells us that unemployment in 1973 was just under 5 per cent. Unemployment rose sharply in 1975, to over 8 per cent, and the level for this year is similarly identified by reading across from the left-hand axis. Reading down from the point labelled 1975 to the bottom axis, unemployment in 1974 reappears, but this time as the rate prevailing in the previous year. The points in the diagram are then connected together in sequence.

Although there are considerable swings in the connected scatter plot, the data do appear to be cycling around a rate of unemployment of somewhere between 6 and 7 per cent. In the early 1980s unemployment moved higher, but then came back. In the late 1980s the rate was lower, but in the past few years it has swung back into a cycle centred on a point somewhere between 6 and 7 per cent. The connected points trace out somewhat irregular but nevertheless recognisable ellipses around this point.

Plotting data in this way can provide four pieces of information. First, it can show whether the series tends to move in reasonably regular cycles, or indeed whether or not it moves in cycles at all. A data series, for example, which simply rose in value at a constant rate over time would appear as a straight line when set out in a connected scatter plot. A series which, in contrast, exhibited perfectly regular cycles would appear in a connected scatter plot as a perfect ellipse. Second, a connected scatter plot can show the average value of the series around which the series fluctuates, if reasonably regular fluctuations exist. This is the point at the centre of the ellipses traced out in such a plot. Applying technical jargon, we can call this point the 'attractor point' of the data. It is as if the data in the series are attracted around this point.* Third, CSPs can illustrate the magnitude of cycles around the attractor point. An ellipse which, for example, was very tightly drawn around an attractor would imply that the data, when plotted over time, showed only small fluctuations. And finally, the chart can convey information on what we might term the strength or

---

*A cautionary note must be entered immediately. The concept of attractors has a rather precise meaning, and the detection of such points in a rigorous way can be a difficult task involving some advanced mathematics. Such techniques have wide applications to data from the physical and biological sciences, where data series with large numbers of observations are usually available. Such data, too, tend to be very pure, in the sense that there are few errors of measurement and few purely random fluctuations with which to contend. The similar task of detection in economics is made very difficult both by the relatively small number of observations available, and by the rather noisy nature of much economic data. But both the graphical technique and the concept of an attractor point can be illuminating, as long as we remember that the rigorous standards of the applied mathematician are here operating, out of necessity, in a rather relaxed way.

power of the attractor point – in other words, the tendency of the data to move back into cycles around the attractor from points which might be quite far away. A strong attractor will pull the data back towards it even from quite distant points, while a weak one will easily lose its grip. In the latter case, a shock to the system will move the data series completely out of the control of the attractor.

From Figure 8, it seems that over the past twenty years or so the American economy has moved around quite a strong attractor point for unemployment, corresponding to a rate of between 6 and 7 per cent. In the absence of a major shock, we can suppose that unemployment in the United States will continue to fluctuate around this level.

The experience of the European economies has been quite different. To illustrate this point, connected scatter plots of unemployment in the current and previous year are drawn up, but this time over a slightly longer period, from 1960 to 1993.

The four charts that make up Figure 9 illustrate the range of patterns which unemployment has followed in Europe over the past thirty to thirty-five years; Figure 10 gives the same information for Japan.

Figure 9a shows the development of unemployment in Germany, using data for the former West Germany throughout in order to retain consistency over time. The cluster of points at the bottom left of the chart covers the pre-oil-shock period, from 1960 to 1973. Unemployment was low, moving around an average rate of around 1.5 per cent. The first oil shock, as in the rest of Europe, increased unemployment rapidly, but the German economy quickly found a new attractor point of some 3.5–4 per cent unemployment. We discussed in the previous chapter the way in which the German workforce perceived the true implications of the oil shock more quickly than did workforces elsewhere in Europe. Following the second oil shock, in 1980, unemployment again rose rapidly. But again, the economy settled quickly into a new, feasible solution path of around 7 per cent unemployment.

The impact of reunification represents a shock of considerable magnitude which is in the first instance particular to the German economy. The cost of rebuilding the economy of the former German Democratic Republic far exceeds the most pessimistic estimates made prior to reunification, and this knowledge has undoubtedly damaged confidence in Germany. In 1991 and 1992, for example, the costs averaged some 200 billion DM in each year, or no less than 6 per cent of West Germany's total national output. Despite this, the economy appears to have

FIGURE 9A Connected scatter plot of
West German unemployment rate, 1960–93

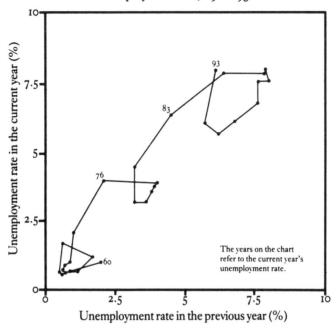

FIGURE 9B Connected scatter plot of French
unemployment rate, 1960–93

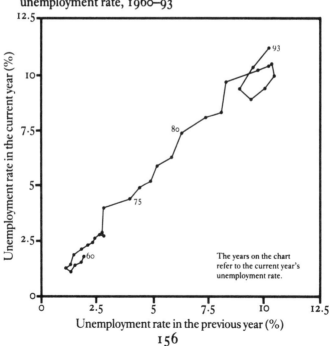

FIGURE 9C Connected scatter plot of British
    unemployment rate, 1960–93

FIGURE 9D Connected scatter plot of Swedish
    unemployment rate, 1960–93

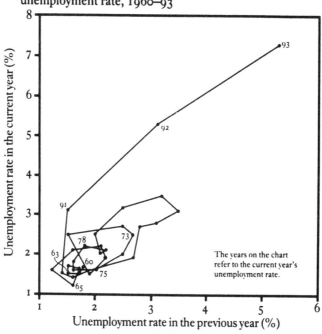

FIGURE 10 Connected scatter plot of unemployment
in Japan, 1960–93

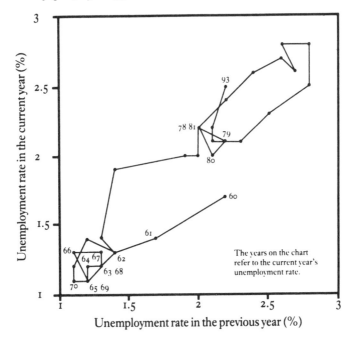

remained linked to its current attractor point as far as unemployment
itself is concerned, although, as we mentioned in the previous chapter,
it is far more likely that the inflation/unemployment relationship has
shifted, so that in order to achieve any given level of inflation in future,
a higher rate of unemployment will be required.

To sum up, we can see from Figure 9*a* that unemployment in Germany has moved around a series of attractor points. When serious
shocks have been administered to the economy, the attractor point has
moved, but unemployment has settled quickly into the new pattern of
cycles.

France presents an altogether different picture. Unemployment in
France since 1960 has not for the most part settled into a path around
an attractor point. The first few years of the 1960s do exhibit a cycle,
shown in the tiny cluster of points at the bottom left of Figure 9*b*. But
since the mid-1960s unemployment has risen almost inexorably in
France. There are now signs, from the mid-1980s, that an attractor
point for unemployment is beginning to emerge. But it is at a high rate,
of around 10 per cent, and with a fairly large ellipse around this point.

In other words, unemployment in France seems set to fluctuate quite substantially around a high average rate of some 10 per cent.

The pattern in both Italy and Spain is qualitatively similar to that of France, although in the case of Spain the level of the attractor point for unemployment which is starting to emerge is close to 20 per cent.

In Britain, a strong and stable attractor existed in the 1960s and early 1970s – indeed, back into the 1950s as well – around a low level of unemployment. Following the oil shock of 1973–74, the economy was thrown off this path, experiencing a rapid rise in unemployment. Figure 9c shows a new attractor point beginning to emerge tentatively around 1980, but this economy was slower than Germany's economy to find a new, potentially stable, path. In fact, almost as soon as it had begun to settle, the second oil shock hit the economy. But since the mid-1980s the path of unemployment has begun to follow a new ellipse, which moves widely around a high level of unemployment.

The experience of Britain is the template for countries such as Belgium and the Netherlands, and also for Australia.

Most economies in Europe appear now to be on paths which will generate substantial fluctuations in unemployment, around historically very high levels.

The economies which cause the most difficulties of interpretation at present are the group of small economies which have experienced very low levels of unemployment throughout the 1970s and 1980s, such as Austria and the Scandinavian countries.

Sweden, whose unemployment is charted in Figure 9d, presents the most difficult example. A very strong attractor point existed for a long period of time at a low level of unemployment. Even when unemployment moved temporarily to rates almost double that of the attractor point, it was drawn back into the pattern of ellipses around the point. But a dramatic change came in the early 1990s, coinciding with the financial liberalisation of the economy, which we discussed in Chapter 4. The Swedish economy experienced a very severe shock. Any short-term, or even medium-term, projection of unemployment in Sweden is highly uncertain. The economy has been shocked away from a stable and powerful attractor point, and a new attractor point has not yet emerged.

In contrast to the substantial shifts in patterns of behaviour exhibited by most European and North American economies, Figure 10 shows how well the Japanese economy has ridden any shocks, either generated within the domestic economy, or abroad. There are two attractor points over the 1960–93 period, but even around the higher of the two unemployment moves in a very low range of between 2 and 3 per cent. Japan is, of course, in a deep recession at present, and the existing social and economic relationships within the country, which have preserved low unemployment for a long period of time, are undergoing great strain. But, so far, they have survived.

Conventional macro-economic policy is essentially concerned with trying to speed up or slow down the movement of an economy around the ellipse it follows when locked around a stable attractor point. These movements correspond to the fluctuations of the economic cycle. In the expansionary phase of the cycle, unemployment falls. In other words, unemployment in the current year is less than unemployment in the previous year, while during the recession years of the cycle unemployment rises, so that when such movements are plotted on a connected scatter plot they trace out an ellipse.

Different versions of the general theoretical macro-model of contemporary economics, with their own particular nuances and linkages between the various sectors of the economy, may offer, as we have seen, different policy prescriptions. For example, in the world of Keynes's arch-critic, Pigou, the government need do nothing during a recession. The workings of the market economy will themselves be sufficient to revive confidence. In Keynes's own world, during the recessionary phase, cuts in taxes, increases in public spending and reductions in interest rates are the conventional way of stimulating the economy. And at the peak of the cycle, movements in policy in the opposite direction are required in order to slow the economy down.

Each cycle around an attractor point will have its own particular characteristics. Economies do not follow the Platonic ideal of perfect ellipses around any given attractor point, so that it may be possible to make improvements to the performance of an economy as it moves around its attractor point. Britain and Japan, for example, are the most prominent examples of economies in which negative real balance effects seem to be strong, so that a programme of socialising a certain amount of private debt would be effective.

But unemployment cannot in general be dealt with permanently by the conventional instruments of economic policy. At best, these simply move the economy around a solution path centred on a particular attractor point corresponding to a particular rate of unemployment. And much of the present policy discourse on unemployment is underpinned by the misleading premise of an underlying link between economic growth and unemployment, by the mistaken belief that any short-run relationship between the two which exists persists over time. It is also based upon a notion of equilibrium arising from the economist's mechanical view of the world, a view at an ever-increasing variance with reality.

By approaching the data without the theoretical baggage of macro-economics and seeing what the data tell us, just as in the previous chapter, a quite different picture begins to emerge.

What policy makers should be aiming for is a more ambitious solution. The real challenge, especially in Europe, is not to move the economy around the present attractor points of unemployment. It is to shift the attractor points themselves sharply downwards.

Whether concerning the relationship between inflation and unemployment, or the forces which govern unemployment itself, specific events and specific reactions to these events can determine the paths which economies take over long periods of time. Shocks persist, and economies show no natural tendency to revert to solution paths on which markets clear and full employment is restored.

CHAPTER 8

The Dynamics of Unemployment

The linear, mechanistic view of the world which pervades orthodox economics is simply not capable of capturing the richness and complexity of the rhythms and fluctuations of developed economies. As we have seen, in order to understand the patterns of behaviour exhibited by unemployment over the years, we must discard the orthodox economic concepts of equilibrium and rationality. We need instead to develop a new approach.

The aim of analysing data series on unemployment is to characterise the general pattern of behaviour underlying the growth and fluctuations of developed economies. The pattern observed in any individual economy over any particular period will obviously be affected by specific events which lie outside the domain of any general description of behaviour.

A more descriptive approach, which takes account of the specific conjuncture of economic, institutional, social and cultural factors, is required to understand these particular events. For example, the years immediately following financial deregulation in the Anglo-Saxon economies in the 1980s were clearly influenced by the culture of conspicuous consumption associated with deregulation and the boom in financial markets. Our aim in this chapter is not to capture the precise shape and timing of every economic cycle in great detail, but rather to construct a model which is an approximation of the underlying behaviour of the system which generates the data observed. As an analogy, imagine the problem of drawing a good map of the world, or any particular country or region within the world. By definition, the best map is of identical size to the area being mapped, and contains exactly the same features on exactly the same scale. Of course, even at the level of a village or an individual mountain, say, such a map is not in the least practical.

A good map must represent the key features of the required area, but in so doing it must necessarily omit a great deal of minor detail. Naturally, the amount of detail left out will vary tremendously with the purpose to which the map is being put. The key features of the geography of the world can be conveyed successfully on a couple of sides of paper. But such a map would be of little value to a mountaineer negotiating a tricky path in the Alps or Himalayas. A good map necessarily simplifies, seeking to portray the key features of interest to the task in hand. In the same way, a model which attempts to represent the behaviour of a series of data over time should not usually try to account for every single detail.

The task we have in mind here is to produce the framework for a model which will account for the key features observed in the data series for unemployment in developed market economies. (The word 'model' here means a series of statements, usually but not necessarily in mathematical format.) The exercise is by no means motivated by pure intellectual interest. A model which is able to account for the essential characteristics observed in the movements of unemployment gives us a base from which both to address current orthodox economic precepts on unemployment, and develop ideas as to how policy should best be conducted in order to reduce it.

We have already noted two such essential features in the previous chapter.

First, in the long run the relationship between unemployment and economic growth is indeterminate. A relationship can exist in the short run, over the course of an economic cycle or even several cycles, but in the longer term it is not necessarily the case that faster growth brings lower unemployment. This important point, which is quite contrary to the received wisdom of economic policy, is simply noted again at this stage; it will be revisited in the next chapter when we develop the economic content of our model of unemployment. At this stage, our concern is to try to identify the sort of mathematical model which is likely to be of most use in approximating the characteristics observed in the movements of unemployment.

The second feature already noted is that an economy can be shifted off an established path, away from an established pattern of behaviour. And when this occurs, the change is rapid and dramatic, with no in-built tendency for the economy to revert to its previous path. An example of this is the response of many Western economies to the oil-price shock of 1973–74. Further, following such a shock, the behaviour of the economic system is irregular for a number of years. In other words, it shows no systematic, regular pattern for some years, before it begins to settle again.

The patterns observed in unemployment in the post-war world can be seen equally well in data series stretching much further back in time. A particular challenge for economic historians in constructing such series arises from the fact that the concept of unemployment changes over time. For example, in the early days of industrial capitalism in Britain in the early nineteenth century, there was almost no provision made by the state for the welfare of the general population. Very young children were expected to crawl up chimneys, or to work among the machinery of factories; we might remember here Dickens's graphic representation of the young David Copperfield working in the Murdstone bottling factory. We have observed, in Chapter 2, that old people were expected to work until they dropped, or be packed off to the workhouse to die. In definitions of unemployment in the West in the 1990s, children without work are no longer counted as being unemployed. They are in education. Men and women in their seventies who are without work are no longer counted as being unemployed. They are retired.

Many complaints are made nowadays in Europe and the United States about the working conditions which prevail in the rapidly developing economies of the world. Our indigenous workforces are felt to be facing unfair competition from the low-wage sweatshops of these economies. In fact, parts of the Far East are now approaching Western levels of prosperity, so that these complaints no longer apply to these particular economies. But conditions in the rest of the rapidly developing countries are certainly no worse, and probably better in many respects, than the conditions which prevailed when the foundations of the West's current prosperity were being laid in the early years of industrialisation.

Definitions of unemployment do therefore change over time. The problem is further complicated in many Western countries by the size of the agricultural workforce before the present century. Relatively primitive agricultural societies are classic examples of the tenets of Parkinson's Law: work expands to fill the time available in which to do it. At harvest time, everyone is extremely busy. But for large parts of the year, the workforce, rather than being unemployed, is under-employed.

The country for which the longest data series for unemployment of any degree of reliability exists is Britain, the first country to industrialise, and these data appear to be typical of the experiences of other developed economies. The precise pattern of unemployment over time varies from country to country, but qualitatively the movements of the series have similar properties. Figure 11, for example, plots the rate of unemployment in both America and Britain in normal peace-time years from 1900 to 1993, and shows quite clearly the similarity of the long-run data in both countries.

FIGURE 11 Peace-time unemployment rates in
America and Britain, 1900–93

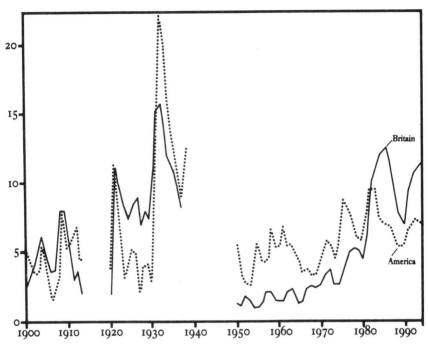

In both countries, for example, unemployment rose very rapidly in the early 1930s. After the Second World War, unemployment exhibited fairly regular fluctuations around low average levels for at least a quarter of a century. In both countries, unemployment rose noticeably in the mid-1970s, but as we saw in the previous chapter, in the United States it settled quickly into a new series of fluctuations around a slightly higher average level than in the previous two decades, whereas in Britain it took longer to settle, and eventually did so around a considerably higher level. Although the precise, quantitative experience of both countries has been different recently, qualitatively it has been similar: the attractor point was shocked to a higher level.

In short, an approach which is successful in giving insights into unemployment in Britain is likely, with some adjustments, to be applicable to the United States as well. Indeed, the evidence from Europe and Japan charted in the previous chapter, albeit over much shorter time-spans, suggests that there are broad similarities in the patterns of fluctuations in unemployment across a wide range of countries.

Figure 12 plots the British unemployment rate over the period 1855–1993. What initial suppositions might one reasonably make about such a series? There seem to be at least five distinct behaviour patterns. First, data over the 1855–1913 period follows fairly regular cycles. The length of time between each peak and trough of the data is roughly equal: that is, the time gap between the low points of each cycle is roughly the same, and so is the gap between the succession of high points in the series. But although the cycles are regular, they are big, with large fluctuations from peak to trough. In the jargon, they have a high amplitude. In other words, the changes in unemployment over the course of any particular cycle in this period are large.

FIGURE 12 British unemployment rate, 1855–1993

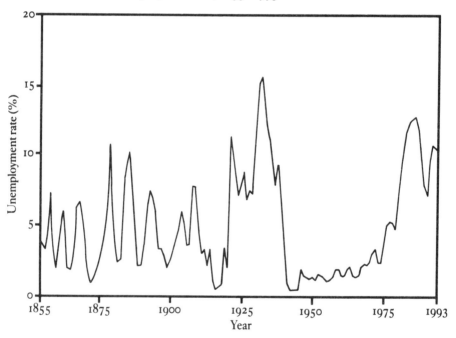

Although the period is now rather distant in time, it does have relevance to the current debate on deregulation and flexibility of the labour market. Pre-First World War Britain was a society much closer to free-market ideals than Western European economies have been in general for the past fifty years. Workers had very few rights, there was extensive casualisation of labour, and the alleged burden on companies of present-day factors such as maternity leave and redundancy payments was almost non-existent. Yet despite this, unemployment was not at all low, averaging almost 5 per cent of the workforce over the period as a whole, and quite frequently rising to 8 or even 10 per cent, or some 2.5 million in today's terms.

The second point to note from Figure 12 is that there are two short periods, in the mid-1910s and again in the early to mid-1940s, when the series shows very little fluctuation and takes values which are very close to zero. These are, of course, the periods of the world wars, when society both needed and was willing to operate under different values, with everyone contributing to the war effort, and with all available labour resources being used.

Third, one would probably identify the period from the late 1940s to the early 1970s as a distinct period. Although there is a slight upward trend over this period, the average value is very low. The period also seems to contain its own, fairly regular cycles, as we saw in the connected scatter plot for British unemployment in the previous chapter. But the size of the fluctuations – the amplitude – is far smaller than in the pre-First World War period.

The data in the periods 1920–38 and from the mid-1970s to the present day are harder to characterise so cleanly. The first period has an average level which is very much higher than anything which went before. Even the data of the 1920s take high average values, which are made to seem small only by the record levels reached by the series in the early 1930s. The period overall has large fluctuations, but of an irregular kind.

The observations in and immediately following the mid-1970s also lack regularity in the fluctuations, although, as we saw in the previous chapter, a regular cyclical pattern seems to have developed over the most recent decade, with large fluctuations of the kind seen in the nineteenth century, around a very high average level.

Pulling these points together, we can see from the data that any model which attempts to approximate and account for the behaviour of unemployment must show a number of key characteristics.

First, the economic system is capable of settling into long periods in which behaviour is reasonably regular. In any one of these periods, fluctuations occur in the data, each separated by similar, but not identical, lengths of time, and showing similar, but again not identical, movements up and down during a complete cycle. For as many as 100 of the 140 years of data plotted in the chart, this is a broad general description of the properties of the data.

Second, as we have already noted, the data are sensitive to shocks, and the path they follow at any particular time, the mode of behaviour into which they have settled, can shift markedly and rapidly. The behaviour of unemployment following such a shock can be, as for example in the inter-war period, irregular for a number of years before it begins to settle into a pattern once again. As we saw in the previous chapter, the length of time needed to establish a new pattern of regularity can vary. Following the 1973–74 oil-price increase, the German economy began to settle into a new pattern as early as 1977–78, but the French economy took until the mid-1980s for regularity to emerge.

The third point to observe is that both the average level of unemployment and the size of the fluctuations over the cycle differ between the different periods which do have regular cycles.

In short, the data show regular patterns of fluctuations, but the size of the fluctuations, and the average level of unemployment around which such movements take place, varies in different periods. Established patterns of behaviour can, when shocked, shift rapidly, and following such a shock behaviour is irregular for some years.

The key characteristics of the behaviour of unemployment are seen in many of the data series studied in a different discipline, namely that of biology. In epidemiology, for example, epidemics such as measles and rubella come in fairly regular cycles, of varying amplitude at different periods of time, which are interspersed with fluctuations of a more irregular kind.

The populations of many animal and insect species show similar kinds of behaviour over time. The sheep blowfly, for example, is a pest whose behaviour in Australia is important in sheep farming, which is significant to the Australian economy overall. Careful studies have been carried out to obtain data on the fluctuations in the blowfly population, and the resulting series has been well studied by biologists. Cycles of approximately 35–40 days' duration dominate the data, but the period of each cycle is not exactly the same, and the maximum number of blowfly observed in successive cycles varies over time. Yet another data series in biology records the number of lynx trapped each year on the MacKenzie river in Canada over the period 1821–1934. Although the economic importance of lynx is far less than that of the blowfly pest, the series has become a classic, studied alike by biologists and statisticians, because of the intellectual challenge involved in obtaining a good mathematical approximation of its behaviour.

Data series like these, mixtures of reasonably regular cycles, of different amplitudes, with periods of apparently irregular behaviour, can be seen far more widely than in economics and biology. In a subject like physiology, for example, where the initial symptoms of many acute diseases show themselves in marked changes and irregularities in previously regular rhythms and fluctuations of behaviour, such as patterns of breathing. And in a completely different area, Howell Tong at the University of Kent in Britain, a leading mathematical statistician, has pointed out that some of the earliest civil servants to appear in world history were in China, where their task was to supervise waterworks and compile records about the height and flow of rivers. This highlights the importance of river flows in ancient China, where the ability to produce food in sufficient quantities was crucially dependent upon irrigation systems and, ultimately, upon the amount of water in the rivers. Even today, this is a vital factor, in China and in many other countries around the world. And the data generated by river flows over time show the pattern of mixtures of regular and irregular fluctuations.

The number of sunspots seen each year has been recorded since at least 1700. The physical processes which govern fluctuations – of which spots are one manifestation – in the behaviour of the Sun are still not well understood by scientists. Yet these fluctuations are seen to have more and more importance for the Earth's climate, so that it is important to obtain a mathematical model which can be used for prediction. For interest, the series for the annual average number of sunspots from 1700 to 1988 is plotted in Figure 13. There is rather more regularity in terms of length of cycle over the whole of the period than there is with the unemployment data, but the patterns in terms of the size of the cycles from peak to trough, with groups of cycles sometimes showing only modest peaks, and others showing very high ones, are similar.

More generally in climatology, scholars are beginning to realise that marked changes in the behaviour of the Earth's climate can take place very rapidly, and not simply at times when the planet is subjected to a major shock through being hit by a large extra-terrestrial object. Increasingly, careful reconstructions of the Earth's climate are showing a history which exhibits the by now familiar pattern of periods of stable behaviour, with fluctuations of reasonably regularity, punctuated by irregularities before a new stable pattern emerges.

Thus, we can see that an enormous number of data series from widely different disciplines exhibit the same qualitative characteristics as

FIGURE 13 Mean annual sunspot data, 1770–1987

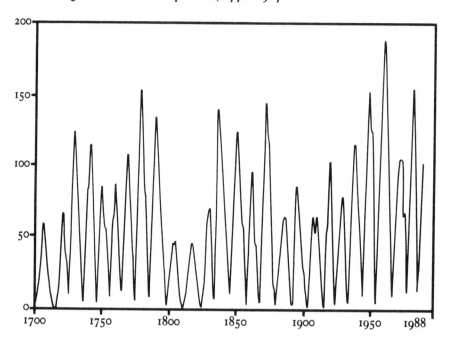

unemployment in developed economies. Researchers from the biological and physical sciences have struggled to understand the movements of their objects of study. An important motivation for this research is that the true processes which determine the behaviour of such series over time are rarely understood completely, and in some cases, such as the sunspots example, the description 'imperfect' might well be an overstatement of our level of understanding.

The aim is therefore to develop models which give a reasonable approximation to the complete set of factors, and their various interactions, responsible for generating the data. In this way, the process of building knowledge through observation, of constructing models which from the outset are compatible with the empirical characteristics of the observed data, can contribute directly to a better theoretical understanding of the behaviour of a series. As we saw in the first chapters of the book, classical economists such as Adam Smith were very much of the same frame of mind. The economies which they observed had certain key characteristics, for which their theories tried to account: data and theory were intertwined. It was only with the onset of the marginal revolution that the habit of deducing logically, from a set of rational principles, how the world *ought* to behave, with little or no reference to how it did in reality, began to permeate economics.

Once a reasonable model is obtained, the end-use to which it can be put is twofold. First, it can be used as a means of predicting what will happen to the series in the future. Second, it is a means of understanding the effects of policies designed to alter the patterns of behaviour in a series, such as a programme of inoculation against a disease.

We gave an example of such questions being asked of models in Chapter 5, when we discussed orthodox macro-economic models and the way their proprietors used them to answer questions such as what would happen if public expenditure were increased, or taxes reduced. But since, as we saw, such models are not good approximations of the behaviour of the economy, there is little to be learned from them.

The understanding of data series of the kind discussed above has been improved considerably in many disciplines in the past ten to fifteen years through the use of what is known as non-linear mathematics in the specification of models designed to approximate their behaviour.

The phrase 'non-linear mathematics' may appear intimidating, and it may help to give a particular illustration of what is involved by taking a look at models which generate chaotic behaviour.

The concept, if not the detail, of chaos theory has to some extent penetrated popular culture, and has seized the imagination. There is even a Chaotician among the characters of *Jurassic Park*.

It is important to note from the outset of this discussion that chaotic systems are in fact special cases of the more general class of systems which are non-linear. In other words, all chaotic systems are non-linear, but not all non-linear systems are chaotic. But, given that many people have at least heard of the concept of chaos, a discussion of chaos will help to clarify some important points, without at the same time introducing the much less familiar idea of non-linearity.

The idea most closely associated with chaotic systems is that a tiny change in one part of a system, such as the Earth's climate, can eventually lead to large changes throughout the entire system. Perhaps the most famous example is that of the wings of the butterfly. The beating of the wings of this creature in the rain forests of Borneo or South America can in principle create major changes in the weather patterns experienced throughout the world. The butterfly could equally well beat its wings in a less exotic place, such as, say, the rather barren North London suburb of

Neasden, and have the same effect. But it is perhaps more in keeping with the striking originality of the concept that a remote and impenetrable location should be the presumed scene of the action.

The idea was formulated in its modern guise in two outstanding papers by the meteorologist Edward Lorenz in the early 1960s, working at the Massachusetts Institute of Technology. He proposed a mathematical model, containing in fact only three variables, to account for thermal convection in the circulation of the atmosphere and of the oceans. Such circulation in turn determines to a large extent changes in the Earth's climate. In the same way that a map of the world can inform us of the main outlines of geography in a couple of pages, so a good model of some of the key factors which determine the world's weather can be constructed in terms of only three factors.

It might be hard, indeed extremely difficult, to carry out this latter exercise successfully. But it is only our long-standing familiarity with maps of the world which causes us to forget what a major intellectual achievement this was when it was first done successfully centuries ago.

Unfortunately, Lorenz published his findings in obscure meteorological journals, where the results lurked virtually unrecognised for a decade. But what he had in fact discovered was a system which generated chaotic properties. The precise nature of the mathematical definition of such properties need not concern us here. What is important to us is the fact that in chaotic systems, practical long-range forecasting becomes impossible. Models which are virtually identical, except for very small differences, will eventually, when solved over many time periods, produce solutions which are completely different.

Models can differ in a number of respects, for example in the factors which are included in them, or in the precise way in which the same set of factors is designed in the model to interact with each other. Lorenz's original discovery related to a rather subtler potential difference, known in the jargon as the initial conditions. He took his three-equation model of convection, and produced two solutions, using exactly the same model in each case, over time, into the hypothesised future. The only difference between the solutions was that the values of the factors in his model which he fed in to start the system running were slightly different.

An analogy might illustrate the point. Suppose the flight of a jumbo jet is determined by a series of factors which, when combined together, make up a chaotic system. Fortunately, this is not the case in reality, but let us suppose that it is. Imagine now this hypothetical jumbo on the runway at

New York's Kennedy Airport. Just behind it is another jumbo, exactly identical in every possible respect in terms of its construction, fuel load and so on. Each jumbo contains the same number of passengers, of the same weights, sitting in identical places, with identical luggage.

All this information is needed in order to predict where the imaginary jumbo will end up at the end of its chaotic flight (we might think of the passengers as having subscribed to a superior form of mystery tour). Everything has now been specified in terms of the factors which will determine the flight paths of the two aircraft, except the weather at the point of take-off. The first jumbo takes off in windless calm. The next one follows it, on an identical runway, taking off at an identical point. The only difference is that a zephyr of a breeze springs up after the first one takes off. In a chaotic system, this tiny difference in the conditions in which the aircraft take off can have an enormous effect on their flight paths and on where they eventually end up. One could arrive at Heathrow in London, and the other in Tokyo's Narita Airport, all because of the puff of breeze at take-off – because of a tiny difference in the initial conditions of the flight paths.

Similarly, in Lorenz's weather model on his computer, tiny differences in the starting conditions of a model otherwise identical in every respect, over all of the solution paths which were generated with it, led to large differences in the eventual outcomes.

All this may seem a long way from unemployment, but it is not. Data series for unemployment in developed economies appear as if the true underlying relationships which generate such observed patterns of behaviour are sensitive in this way. Perhaps the simplest way of illustrating this graphically is by reference to the connected scatter plots of the previous chapter. The shape of the various ellipses in these diagrams, each of which describes the fluctuations in unemployment during a stable period of behaviour, varies depending upon the precise point in the diagram at which such stable periods begin. In other words, the behaviour of unemployment in terms of the regularity and size of its fluctuations, when it settles into a stable pattern, appears to depend upon the conditions which exist at the start of such patterns.*

*Of course, strictly speaking, the diagrams illustrate a hypothesis rather than prove a point, but since non-linear models with limit cycles are in fact necessary for a proper understanding of unemployment, no harm is done by referring to them in this way. It is these models which are the focus of our interest, and which are developed in the next chapter. Such models are not sensitive to initial conditions in the strict sense, since the data generated by them do not have a positive Lyapunov exponent, but the periodicity and amplitude of such data are sensitive in this way.

It is important to note that the behaviour of a system which is sensitive to its initial conditions does not mean that the data series which it generates are random. A genuinely random series of data cannot really be understood or predicted in any meaningful way. It might be possible to set limits within which the values of the series will usually fluctuate, but that is all. An everyday example of this is shaking dice. Provided that the game is a completely fair one, successive shakes of a single die will produce a truly random series. It is not possible to discover a rule which will enable consistently successful predictions to be made about the next number to appear, no matter how much information is available about previous shakes, and no matter what the previous sequence of shakes has been. The chance of any particular number appearing on the next shake is simply one in six.

In terms of the sequence of numbers obtained from shaking a die, we can obviously say that the values observed all lie between one and six. We can also say that, eventually, it is almost certain that each single number will have been shaken an equal number of times. But 'eventually' may be a very long time indeed. It might need just 200 shakes, or 2 million, or even 2 billion. This knowledge is of no value in predicting the exact number or numbers that will appear on the next shake or sequence of shakes.

Chaotic data series appear in many respects to be identical to random series. To the human eye, when plotted on a graph, they appear to have similar characteristics. Both types of data series appear to lack any sort of pattern of behaviour. But there is a crucial difference between the two. A chaotic data series is generated by a mathematical expression which can in principle be discovered. If we knew with absolute precision – to the billionth decimal place if necessary – the structure of this expression and the values of all the factors in the system at the start of any solution path, the series could in principle be forecast with complete accuracy as far ahead into the future as we wished, despite the fact that the series is chaotic. In practice, of course, researchers can only approximate the structure of the model which generates the data. And this is where the problem of forecasting such systems lies.

Even with a very good approximation, the fact that the true structure is not known perfectly will mean that eventually, because of the great sensitivity of chaotic systems to their overall specification, forecasts generated by the approximation will develop serious errors. In the short-term, before the errors begin to cumulate, perfectly reasonable forecasts can be made. In other words, knowledge that the data being examined are chaotic rather than random can be of great benefit in improving short-term forecasting accuracy; there has already been a distinct improvement in the practical, everyday understanding that physical and biological scientists have of the phenomena they investigate.

The superior understanding of the underlying processes which generated the data does not simply improve short-term forecasting, but it can also give invaluable insights into the key factors which drive the system, and the way in which they operate.

One practical issue at present concerns whether prices in financial markets – shares, exchange rates and so on – are either random or chaotic series. Research over the years, often very sophisticated but nevertheless using standard techniques, suggests that they are in fact random series. It is not possible to devise a rule which will enable consistently profitable decisions to be made.

A great deal of this research has been carried out by economists. Financial markets, as we saw in Chapter 4, conform far more closely to the theoretical ideal of markets in the model of competitive equilibrium than do markets in any other area of economic activity. It is therefore important for the discipline of economics that financial markets should allocate resources efficiently, for if the concept of market efficiency is not valid in this area, it will certainly fail throughout the rest of the economy.

The concept of market efficiency in financial markets has a narrow, but precise, definition. Efficiency does not mean that these markets, for equities, currencies and so on, are allocating resources in a way that increases the productive efficiency of the economy as a whole, ensuring that funds go to the best companies, for example, to invest in their businesses. In America and Britain, industrial companies obtain only a tiny fraction of the money they need for business investment from the stockmarkets; most of it comes from profits or from borrowing.

What efficiency in financial markets means is that prices, which are the means of balancing supply and demand, are efficient, in the sense that they reflect all available information about the assets which are traded.* The price of shares in General Motors, for example, reflects all the information which is available about GM at any point in time. Only

---

*Technically, there are three versions of market efficiency – weak, semi-strong and strong – but they all imply that it is impossible to predict the future price of a financial asset on the basis of its price in the past.

unpredictable news about GM can cause its share price to change, and since unpredictable news is by definition unpredictable, so changes in the GM share price are unpredictable. No rule can be discovered, as is the case with a fair dice, which will enable consistent profits to be made from trading in GM's shares.

Test after test appears to confirm the theory of market efficiency – one implication of which, incidentally, is that the expensive advice about investing which financial institutions offer to their clients is of no value whatsoever. But an interesting exception is beginning to emerge. Using a variety of techniques based on the principles of non-linear mathematics, it seems that it is possible to derive profitable rules for trading in financial markets, or at least in some of them. A number of companies, such as Fujitsu, Japan's largest computer firm, and Fidelty, a large Boston-based fund manager, are using non-linear techniques either to manage funds directly or to advise on how funds should be managed, and they are getting results. Even in financial markets, the concept of market efficiency does not hold.

Both chaotic and non-linear systems more generally have the potential to offer deeper insights into how the world operates than does the standard linear model of science. Until ten or fifteen years ago, most science – not just economics, but physics and engineering as well – was carried out using linear techniques of analysis. Scientists were well aware of non-linearity, but tended to avoid the problem by substituting complicated linear approximations to it whenever it arose.

The linear view of the world is a very powerful one. In many instances it gives an extremely good account of how the world operates, and most of the practical examples of the success of science on which our society is built are derived using linear analytical techniques. Such techniques are often very intricate, requiring the use of difficult mathematics. Linearity is by no means always the same thing as simplicity. As we saw in Chapter 3, it was the very success of scientists using linear techniques that motivated the economists of the marginal revolution to emulate them, and to seek to bring the same degree of rigour and precision to the study of economics.

But linear techniques, no matter how sophisticated, are not very good at understanding data series which have the characteristics we discussed earlier in the chapter – that is, series which often appear to be moving in fairly regular cycles, in terms both of the duration of each cycle and of the size of the fluctuations in the data over the course of the cycle, but which suddenly exhibit patterns of irregular behaviour, before settling into a new pattern of near-regularity.

An important reason for the comparative failure of linear techniques in analysing such data is as follows. If a data series is generated by an underlying system which is non-linear, the impact on the system as a whole of a small change in the value of one of its variables can depend upon the values which all the variables in the system take at the time when the change is made. This is the same idea as the concept of sensitivity to initial conditions discussed above, which is often but not always true with non-linear systems (in the special case of non-linearity which is described by chaos, it is always true). But it is *never* true with linear systems.

So, techniques which rely solely upon linearity will give results which can be seriously misleading whenever this sensitivity exists. Sometimes the linear approach will give a reasonable approximation to the behaviour of non-linear data. At other times, it will perform badly. To paraphrase the old nursery rhyme about the behaviour of the little girl: when it is good, it is reasonably good, but when it is bad it is horrid.

The Oxford biologist Robert May, who has had perhaps some of the most valuable insights on non-linearity over the past fifteen years, discovered an example of a policy change whose initial consequences could seriously mislead policy makers relying on advice from a linear view of the world.

As discussed above, the pattern of many diseases such as measles or rubella is best understood by non-linear models. May asked the question: What would happen in such models if a programme of inoculation were carried out? One would intuit that the incidence of the disease would fall away as the programme began to work. Instead, May found that often, although the models predicted that eventually this would happen, the path by which the new low levels were reached was highly irregular – so irregular, in fact, that there might even be short-term increases in the incidence of the disease after the programme began, leading policy makers to conclude that their policy had failed. May's findings were by no means purely theoretical, for data from actual examples of inoculation programmes, such as one against rubella in Britain, showed exactly the kind of responses predicted by his models.

Good economists have long recognised the potential non-linearity of the world. Keynes, for example, although he did not use the language of non-linear systems analysis, argued strongly that the effect on the economy of changes in interest rates depended crucially on the position in the economic cycle at which a change was introduced. In other words, for Keynes, the impact of a change in interest rates on the economic system as a whole was sensitive to the conditions in which it took place – sensitive to the values of the other key factors in the economy. In particular, as the economy began to move into recession, Keynes believed that reductions in interest rates could do little to prevent the slow-down in economic activity, because business confidence was collapsing very rapidly. But once confidence stabilised, albeit at very low levels at the bottom of the recession, reductions in interest rates could then 'be a great aid to recovery, and, probably, a necessary condition of it'.

The general approach in economics has assumed linearity as the norm, and the core model of economic theory, that of competitive equilibrium, still relies, for all its apparent mathematical sophistication, on the simple linear aggregation of individuals' behaviour.

We have met the general concepts of non-linear systems before in this book, but perhaps have not discussed them in such precise terms. The analytical approach of environmentalists, for example, is highly non-linear, taking into account the fact that the various factors which influence the environment affect each other in complex ways. And once the values of certain variables in the system move past critical threshold values, the behaviour of the system alters rapidly and fundamentally. This was the methodology adopted from the outset by the Limits to Growth studies in the early 1970s, which we discussed in Chapter 2, and which formed the basis for subsequent work on the environment.

The impact of, say, a further specified increase in global carbon dioxide emissions will vary dramatically depending upon the level from which the increase is being made. Sometimes, starting from certain levels of all the key factors in the system, the increase will have only a marginal impact. But from other sets of initial conditions, even a small change could lead to climatic change on a global scale. This, it should be said, is not mere theorising or speculation. As mentioned above, climatologists have discovered that the Earth's climate has changed in the past both more frequently and more rapidly than was previously thought.

Less explicitly analytical, but rich in descriptive detail, the work of economic historians such as Chandler discussed in Chapter 3 shows how the course of the economy over decades can be altered by a single set of decisions made at a particular point in time, such as the importance to the subsequent development of the American economy of the Sherman Act in 1890. The wave of mergers and acquisitions to which this led created large businesses of a size able to take full advantage of increasing returns to scale and scope in production, distribution, marketing and management techniques. And once the Americans had consolidated companies of this size – companies with the ability to operate globally – the large firms created by subsequent mergers and acquisitions among America's European competitors found American dominance hard to shift.

But perhaps the strongest manifestations of non-linearity of all the themes which run through this book are the two interconnected ideas that, first, there *is* such a thing as society; and second, that the behaviour of the economy as a whole *cannot* be deduced from the simple aggregation of its component parts. From the interaction of the myriad decisions taken at the micro-level by individuals and companies, complex patterns of behaviour emerge at the macro-level of the system as a whole. These patterns do not simply relate to the workings of the economy in isolation. They define the social norms, the social and cultural context in which the economy operates – concepts to which, as we saw in the early chapters, Adam Smith attached great importance.

CHAPTER 9

Profits, Growth and Economic Cycles

Three properties have been identified as essential to any model seeking to explain unemployment. Briefly, in the absence of shocks to the system, the model should be capable of settling into long periods of regular fluctuations. Second, the size of these regular fluctuations and the average level around which they fluctuate should be sensitive to the initial values of the system. And third, when the system receives a major shock, there should be no tendency for it to settle back into the regular behaviour which it exhibited previously. When it does eventually do so, after a period of irregular behaviour, a different pattern of regularity will be exhibited.

These key characteristics are observed in the long runs of data on American and British unemployment, and even in the shorter series of data on various European countries examined in Chapter 7. These empirical examples show that a non-linear approach is required in order to understand the dynamics of developed economies, rather than *a priori* theorising or the orthodox economic concepts of equilibrium and rationality.

Two further qualities are required of any model of the macro-economy, be it linear or non-linear. First, as we saw in Chapter 7, there is no fixed relationship between the rate of economic growth and employment and/or unemployment. In principle, any rate of growth is compatible with any rate of unemployment, and there is no presumption that higher rates of economic growth necessarily mean lower unemployment. Second – and this point is so obvious that it may be overlooked – developed economies grow over time. In Chapter 2 we discussed various definitions of growth, but even taking account of environmental factors (ignored in conventional economic statistics), in the long-term Western economies grow. So any macro-model must be able to generate growth in output over time.

A striking characteristic of non-linear analysis of data series with properties qualitatively similar to those of unemployment in developed countries, whether in physics, chemistry, biology, climatology or whatever, is that the essential dynamics of the phenomena being investigated can often be captured in a small number of well-chosen equations. Models with often only two or three equations can generate solution paths which describe the key underlying characteristics of the behaviour of systems which may be large and complicated. We have seen that when Lorenz discovered chaotic behaviour, he did so in a model of just three equations: with these, he was able to represent important features of the weather system of the whole world.

Of course, in simplifying so drastically, some information is set to one side. It is not possible to try to follow every single twist and turn in the data. But neither is it always desirable to do this. In economics, for example, each cycle in an economy, each period of boom and recession, will have its own particular features, which may never be repeated. The aim is not to try to capture every single event, but to represent the persistent features of developed economies, which govern their basic rhythms and fluctuations from cycle to cycle. The very process of simplification is a great strength of this approach, for it enables policy makers to focus on the essentials of the economic system.

The approach of constructing a small, non-linear model which approximates the fundamental, underlying behaviour of developed economies at the macro-level is in marked contrast to conventional models of the type widely used in governments and central banks around the world, as discussed in Chapter 5. Such models, typically large and cumbersome, containing hundreds of essentially linear equations, are used to generate both forecasts and policy advice for Western governments.

The track record of these models, as we saw, has been poor. But even putting this to one side, the whole scope of the models, despite their size, is seriously limited in terms of their economic content. Even if one could place any degree of confidence in them, by their very nature they are oriented to the short-term. They are constructed to attempt to explain the fluctuations in demand in the economy during the course of the economic cycle. Indeed, in practice their time horizon is limited to no more than two or three years. One consequence of this, for example, is that conventional macro-models associate change in the growth in demand with changes in employment and unemployment. In these models, higher growth creates more jobs and leads to lower unemployment. The precise, quantitative relationship varies from model to model, depending upon the particular linkages which are activated within the model, and on the strength of such connections once they are switched on. But regardless of the exact number of jobs which any particular model says is created by any given increase in growth, growth is needed to reduce unemployment.

This advice is seriously misleading for policy makers. During the course of any particular economic cycle, a faster rate of growth may well lead to the creation of more jobs; equally, jobs are lost as the economy slows down and moves into recession. But changes in the underlying rate of growth, around which the economy fluctuates during the course of cycles, may not have the same effect at all. Policies aimed at increasing the rate of growth may succeed, but they may not lead to higher employment and lower unemployment.

The non-linear approach will prove disappointing to those raised on a diet of the minutiae of policy prescriptions which flow from conventional macro-models, and which are a feature of government budget statements the world over, dominating much of the media debate between economists. There will not be the usual checklist of policies for beleaguered finance ministers bereft of ideas, of the kind to which they have become accustomed: 'Change taxes by x per cent, public spending by y per cent, interest rates by z per cent – and the economy will prosper.' This has become the narrow, and misguided, focus of economic debate.

There is a variety of mathematical specifications for small systems of equations which can generate patterns of behaviour of the kind we require. The model which is proposed here does not presume to be *the* general theory of how all advanced capitalist economies operate. It is, rather, indicative of the approach which is necessary in order to make intellectual progress in macro-economics.

One type of non-linear mathematical system holds out considerable promise, for it can be given an economic interpretation which makes good sense. Further, this interpretation not only restores the primacy which the early classical economists attached to understanding growth, as we saw in Chapter 1, but it also emphasises, as they did, the role of profits in sustaining growth. The economics of this system are very much in the spirit of the classical economists, who wrote at a time before their subject had ceased to be 'political economy' and became just plain 'economics', losing in the process its focus on the great economic issues of the day.

Applications of this mathematical system were first developed in the physical and biological sciences, and have subsequently been applied to many real world phenomena. In the 1920s, the system was introduced independently to the study of certain kinds of chemical reactions by Lotka, and to biology by Volterra, to examine, for example, movements in fish populations in the Atlantic. Volterra later expanded his earlier work into a book entitled *A Mathematical Theory of the Struggle for Life*. In academic literature the system is often known as the Lotka–Volterra system, or LV system as we shall call it for short. To understand the potential of the LV system, we need to have some concept of its mathematical basis. In biology, for example, it is used to analyse the fluctuations of populations of interdependent species over time. In its simplest form, this consists of two species. One species, the predator, lives by consuming the other, the prey. The two populations are linked symbiotically. More complicated systems, with many species which both prey on others and which themselves are sought out to be eaten, can readily be constructed.

But it is not just in the natural world that these interconnected fluctuations can be observed. For example, the mathematical relationship might be used as the basis for an initial analysis of the impact of an aggressive new competitor entering a market dominated for a long time by either a single company or an effective alliance of companies. The new entrant, using the biological analogy, can be seen as a predator, preying upon the sales and market shares of the existing firms.

More generally, a brilliant book published in 1976 by the American historian William McNeill seeks to explain some of the general movements in history, by reference to the interactions between predators and prey, in the effects of various viruses and diseases on human beings.* Although he does not use any mathematics explicitly, McNeill's book shows a sound grasp of the principles of the LV relationship.

A wide range of historical events can be attributed to the interaction of humans and disease, from the otherwise inexplicable Spanish conquest of the flourishing American civilisations, to the failure of the Chinese to develop the flood plain of the Yellow River for a thousand years after the civilisation of the Yangtze valley, despite the apparently far more favourable conditions which existed in the former area.

An important mathematical feature of the LV system is that, even in its simplest form, it is capable of generating the main characteristics which are observed in the movements of unemployment over time. Namely, it has a tendency to settle into stable fluctuations; the size and shape of these fluctuations are sensitive to the conditions from which the system starts; and, once shocked off a path of stable fluctuations, the LV system generates irregular behaviour, before settling into a new path of regular

*William McNeill, *Plagues and People*, New York: Doubleday, 1976.

cycles, distinct from its previous pattern of regularity.

The stylised behaviour over time of an LV system is plotted in Figure 14. The two variables in the system are linked together so that their fluctuations interact with each other. In biology, the two series could be sharks and small fishes, deer consuming a staple diet of moss, Arctic lynx feeding on snowshoe hares, to give just a few examples of prey–predator relationships. But it is important to emphasise that these examples are purely illustrative. The LV system is by no means confined to biology, and is a general way of modelling the behaviour of any two variables whose behaviour is linked in particular ways. For this reason, the variables in the chart are named anonymously, simply as Variable 1 and Variable 2.

FIGURE 14 Typical behaviour of a Lotka–Volterra
    system before and after a shock

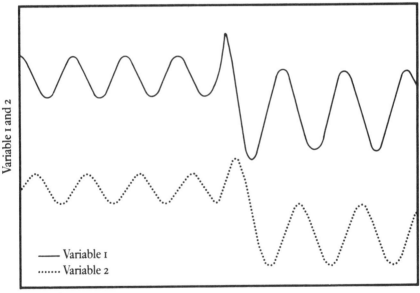

Time

Figure 14 shows initially a period of regular cycles in both the variables in the system. The systematic movements of the two factors, up and down, follow each other over time, so that when one is at a peak, the other is near to a low point in its cycle, and vice versa. A peak in one of the series does not occur at exactly the same time as a trough in the other, but they are close together. The chart then shows the impact of a shock to the system – such as might occur in economics when, for example, the price of oil is increased, as it was in 1973–4, – although it must be emphasised that the shock represented in the chart is purely illustrative and is not meant to depict the impact of any real event. Following the shock, there is a period of irregular behaviour, before the system settles into a new pattern of regular behaviour.

Another way of presenting this information is to use the technique of connected scatter plots, discussed in Chapter 7. There, we marked the points showing unemployment in any given year and its level in the previous year, and connected them sequentially over time. In Figure 15 we apply the same technique to the data used in Figure 14, this time identifying the points that show the values of both the variables in any given period, and then connecting the points over time.

FIGURE 15 Connected scatter plot of typical Lotka–Volterra
        system before and after a shock

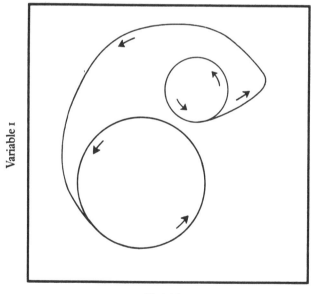

Variable 2

The periods of regular fluctuations shown in the first chart appear here in the form of ellipses. The precise shape of the ellipse will vary according to the particular specification of the system. It might be a neat ellipse in the shape of an American or rugby football. It might be squashed in one corner and wider at another. But whatever the exact shape, an ellipse emerges from the theoretical model. When this stylised system is shocked, the path traced by the line connecting the two variables in the chart moves off the original ellipse and winds round before becoming established in a new ellipse around different average levels of the two variables – around, to use the terminology introduced in Chapter 7, a new attractor point.

The position and length of the path describing the irregular period of behaviour of Figure 14 depends crucially on the position on the original ellipse at which the shock takes place. For purposes of illustration, we have taken rather a dramatic example. Although the two variables in the system eventually end up moving round an ellipse on which the average value of both of them is less than it was on the original ellipse, on the transition path between them they both rise in value before beginning to fall again and moving towards their new pattern of regular behaviour.*

The shock was designed deliberately to produce this result, in terms both of its nature and of the point of the cycle at which the shock is introduced, to illustrate how the consequences of shocks can easily be misread in systems whose behaviour can be approximated by non-linear models such as the LV system.

A policy maker receiving advice based on a linear model of the world – where such sensitivities to initial conditions never occur – would misinterpret the consequences of his or her policy, believing in the short-run that it had failed. And the 'short-run' might well be a period of several years, so that in practice a policy maker would be likely to abandon or even reverse the policy, despite the fact that in the long-run it was going to be successful.

LV models generate patterns of behaviour in their variables which exhibit the key features shown by unemployment in the developed economies. But there needs to be a minimum of two variables in an LV system, and the question arises as to the identity of the second variable. Figure 15 provides an important clue, for when plotted in this way with

*Of course, both the transition path to the new limit cycle of the data and the position of the new limit cycle itself will depend both on the nature of the shock posited, and on the precise specification of the equations in the system. The charts should be regarded as illustrative of the kind of behaviour which emerges from such systems, particularly from ones which are somewhat more sophisticated than the very basic LV system discussed in the text. (The chart assumes that the shock alters the position of the attractor point.)

unemployment, the second variable should trace out the shape of an ellipse around an attractor point.

Examining both British and American data, there are long periods in which recognisable ellipses exist between unemployment and the share of profits in national income,* exactly as the LV system requires. Of course, they are not the perfect ellipses of the stylised system, but the evidence demonstrates their existence quite clearly. The ellipses also shift position, to trace out paths around different attractor points, from time to time, but this property of the data is consistent with our view on how developed economies behave at the macro-level: the economy is moved to different solution paths by shocks.

There are good reasons for thinking that unemployment and profits should interact in this way. Suppose the economy is in an upswing. Growth is rapid, and the opportunity to make profits is good. Not only is there a strong demand for goods and services, enabling volume sales to be high, but in such trading conditions it is relatively easy to put up prices and increase profit margins. So the share of profits in national income rises.

But a growing economy stimulates demand for employment. The workforce, in all its differentiated splendour, whether white collar or blue collar, unionised or non-unionised, can see the opportunity to press for wage increases. As unemployment falls, wage demands intensify. The share of profits is squeezed, and in reaction to this companies begin to cut costs, by reducing inventories, postponing investment plans, and either laying off workers or 'letting them go' in the case of managerial grades of staff. As a result, the economy moves into a cyclical downturn. Unemployment is rising, and wage demands are moderated. Eventually, this enables the share of profits first of all to stabilise, and then to rise. Companies then begin, tentatively at first, to increase investment, take on

---

*As a matter of record, particularly over long periods of time, accurate data on profits are difficult to obtain. Data on wages and salaries are more reliable, and these are used to demonstrate the existence of the ellipses predicted by the LV model. Rises and falls in the share of wages in national income in any given year are not necessarily matched by an equal and opposite movement in profits. But over a period of years there is a strong tendency for this to be the case. So it is legitimate to use the more reliable data on wages as a share of national income rather than the theoretically correct but more uncertain data on profits when looking for the existence or otherwise of LV ellipses in actual historical data. Once again delving into the national accounts, wages plus profits do not, contrary to the perceptions of many theoretical economists, add up to national income, but they do constitute the bulk of it. Rental income and other minor categories make up the rest.

a few more people, and gradually the economy moves back into an up-turn once again.

Conventional economics pays little attention to this interplay between profits and unemployment as the key determinant of business cycles – an interplay which is observed in the empirical data. Instead, they use two approaches to explain the existence of such cycles. First, there are models which are built on the premises of the micro-theory of competitive equilibrium. In most such models, with individuals and companies maximising their self-interest and forming rational, correct expectations about the future, cycles can only be generated by the application of a series of random shocks to the model, for otherwise all markets clear.* In other words, we are asked to believe that the cycles which have been observed in every Western economy since the beginnings of industrialisation are due to the convenient existence of a series of random shocks, rather than to cycles being inherent in the behaviour of such economies.

In the macro-models discussed in Chapter 5, the existence of the business cycle is not based upon the foundations of micro-economic theory. Rather, it usually arises from the series of equations which were adapted in the post-war period from Keynes's *General Theory*, and through which Keynes's challenge to economic orthodoxy was sterilised into Keynesianism. In its simplest possible form, this model divides the total amount of spending in an economy in any given period into three categories: consumption by individuals; investment by companies; and 'the rest', comprising government spending, exports, imports and so on. Cycles can be generated in this model even if the 'rest' is assumed to grow at a steady pace, with no cycles at all.

The two behavioural relationships, the consumption function and the investment function, as they are known, are the fundamental equations in

---

*There are a few models of this genre which can generate cycles without the intervention of random shocks, but their rationales of cycles are hardly more appealing. For example, the French economist Jean-Michel Grandmont produced a theoretical model in 1985 in which cycles could be generated in a competitive economy in which everyone had perfect foresight. The key was to introduce different generations, the old and the young, into the model. Cycles appear because of a potential conflict between the real balance effect and the intertemporal substitution effect associated with real interest movements. But in this model the authorities can use a simple monetary rule to eliminate cycles completely, which makes one wonder why no monetary authority in the history of developed economies has ever implemented such a policy, even if only by chance. Of course, in an important sense, Grandmont's article is a deep criticism of the model of free-market, competitive equilibrium, for it takes all the assumptions of the model and shows that not only should governments intervene in the economy, but that their policies will, under certain assumptions, be highly successful.

almost all existing applied, large-scale macro-models. In practice, the specification of such equations, and their links to the rest of the model, are often complicated, and are the subject of much dispute between modellers. But the key to the existence of cycles in such models is that decisions to spend or invest in any particular period are not determined entirely by the values of variables in the same period, but depend as well on values which were taken in the past.* This in itself, although not obviously so to the non-mathematical reader, is sufficient to generate cycles, of a variety of forms. It might be helpful to think of this dependency on previous values of variables in the past – of income, say, in determining consumer spending – as magnifying the impact of changes. So that, for example, in a boom, incomes are rising and people spend more and reduce their savings. But eventually they end up spending rather more than the amount with which they feel comfortable, reduce their spending and start to rebuild their savings, so that the economy begins to slow down and to move into recession.

The consumption function has been the focus of an enormous amount of attention from model builders and econometricians, without any consensus emerging around the precise form it should take. Keynes himself, while acknowledging the potential importance of consumption in the economic cycle, placed more emphasis on investment as the prime source of fluctuations. His account of the reasons for the existence of cycles is, as we shall see shortly, complementary to rather than competitive with that of the LV system.

Keynes argued that expectations about the future level of sales and profits were important in determining the level of investment in any particular period. But unlike the rational expectations models of orthodox economics, Keynes did not grant companies the luxury of rational expectations and perfect foresight. He believed that people and companies often made mistakes in their expectations, especially during booms, when they always became more optimistic about the future than was justified by the evidence. But eventually they would realise their mistakes and confidence about the future would collapse, leading to lower investment, which would send the economy into recession.

With the experience of the 1980s and early 1990s fresh in our minds, Keynes's view of cycles strikes a chord. Far from having a perfect foresight, in America, Europe and Japan, at slightly different times, both

---

*In other words, a system of difference equations is set up.

people and companies did become much too optimistic about the future. Spending decisions were taken which seem absurd in the cold light of the 1990s, as the present state of the personal and commercial property markets in many countries amply testifies.

A more complete account of behaviour over the course of the economic cycle, around any given attractor point, would combine Keynes's theory of mistaken expectations with the approach of the basic LV system, in which cycles arise through behaviour in the labour market and the consequent fluctuations in actual, as opposed to expected, profits.

The two approaches are by no means mutually exclusive. In the LV model, for example, as the boom becomes stronger, wage demands intensify and the growth of profits begins to slow down. This actual slow-down in profits is a signal to companies to revise down their expectations of future profits à la Keynes, and in consequence to postpone investment plans. This in turn leads to further cut-backs in spending, and the economy moves into recession.

The LV approach should be thought of as the basic, underlying determinant of cycles, with Keynes's expectations being responsible for the magnitude of the cycle between the peak of the boom and the trough of the recession. Evidence in Chapter 7 shows that in the 1990s the European economies have settled into paths which generate considerable fluctuations around high average levels of unemployment. In the current circumstances, following the boom-and-bust syndrome of the past decade, people are especially uncertain about the future. And the more uncertain people are, the more prone they will be to react sharply to anything which causes them to revise their expectations. Hence large fluctuations in the course of economic cycles can be expected until nerves are settled and a less frenzied and uncertain atmosphere prevails.

The relationship between labour market behaviour and unemployment is an important one, to which we return in the final chapter, but first, we turn our attention to expanding the economic content of our LV model. As we saw in Chapter 7, a key empirical feature of developed economies is that the relationship between the rate of growth of any economy and the rate of unemployment is indeterminate: any given rate of growth is in principle compatible with any rate of unemployment. The simple LV model tells us that in theory a similar indeterminacy exists between the profit share and unemployment.

In Chapter 1, we noted that the great classical economists – Adam

Smith and Karl Marx, for example – gave a high priority to the study of the process of economic growth. They regarded the profitability of industry as a key determinant of growth, and economic theory in the first half of the nineteenth century devoted much of its energies to understanding whether the process of economic growth might eventually be halted by the emergence of an inappropriate distribution of national income between profits and wages.

The detailed work of economic historians such as Alfred Chandler, discussed in Chapter 3, highlights the importance of profits for the long-term success of individual companies. A high level of profits encourages investment, not just in machines, but in the company's workforce, in research and development, in new methods of working, in distribution and marketing networks and so on.

An explicit link was made between profits, investment and growth in a theoretical LV model by Richard Goodwin, a Cambridge economist, in a paper presented in 1965 at an economics conference in Rome. The paper was very short, only five sides in length, and was entitled 'A Growth Cycle'. Its content was entirely theoretical, and the author himself began the paper with the phrase, 'Presented here is a starkly schematized and hence *quite unrealistic* model of cycles in growth rates.'

Goodwin had an interest in applying non-linear systems to economics as long ago as the 1940s, and has continued in this to the present day. 'A Growth Cycle', although the most penetrating of all his work, is an article which is neglected in most courses on macro-economics, but history will surely reappraise it and accord it its proper recognition as a pioneer in theoretical non-linear macro-economics.*

Goodwin's original theoretical formulation assumed that all profits were invested, that they were invested in the domestic economy, and that investment was the sole determinant of the rate of growth of the economy. The former assumption is far too unrealistic, even for a theoretical model. For example, in the decades leading up to the First World War a large proportion of the profits of British industry was channelled abroad, with the United States being a prime location for the investment of such

---

*Goodwin's own interest in the LV system was that he believed it to be 'helpful to the understanding of the dynamical contradictions of capitalism'. In a later version of the paper, extended to all of six sides, he remarked that the symbiotic nature in the model of the relationship between industry and the workforce helped explain the 'pusillanimous nature of social democracy'. The paper was published originally in *Capitalism, Socialism and Economic Growth*, ed. C. H. Feinstein, Cambridge University Press, 1967.

funds, while for much of the twentieth century American industry invested heavily overseas, and the Japanese have done so more recently, with Britain and America being major recipients of Japanese investment in new factories.

But apart from the facts that profits may be used for investment abroad rather than in the domestic economy and that the level of investment in an economy, through an inflow of capital, may be higher than could be sustained by domestic profits alone, the proportion of profits which is invested may vary according to the underlying economic climate. For example, as more normal peace-time conditions were restored in the Western economies after the Second World War, there was an enormous backlog of demand for consumer products of almost any description. During the war itself, national resources on both sides had been switched compulsorily into servicing the war effort, away from the production of consumer goods. And particularly within Europe and Japan restrictions on consumption remained in force for several years after the war, as the shattered economies were guided back towards more normal conditions. In such conditions, there was a strong incentive to invest, given the pent-up demand of consumers, which had been restrained for a whole decade, almost guaranteeing that anything which was produced could be sold.

For these reasons, a model allowing investment to be a fixed proportion of profits, in any given period, is far more realistic than one requiring that all profits are always invested. What proportion of profits is invested in the domestic economy can be thought of as depending upon the state of long-term expectations about the prospects of that economy. In periods of regular patterns of behaviour, of regular cycles, such expectations will change slowly, if at all. But in response to shocks, to changed conditions, they could shift sharply.

The assumption that the rate of growth of an economy depends simply upon investment, provided that we define investment sufficiently widely, is not an unreasonable one, certainly as a first approximation. Increasingly, for example, investment is not seen simply in terms of plant and machinery, or even in terms of infrastructure such as transport facilities which support industry. Investment in people has become more and more important, and management gurus such as the American Tom Peters are now urging workers at all levels of companies to invest in themselves, through study at home if need be, in order to guarantee their own personal prosperity in the future.

There are promising signs in recent years that some economists are beginning to recognise the multifarious ways in which investment can increase the growth of the economy. Following the original work by Paul Roemer of the University of Rochester in 1986, the concept of 'endogenous growth' has received attention from applied economists. Although the importance of profits is not dealt with in this framework, the work represents a distinct advance on the previous efforts of economists to understand growth.

Essentially, the idea is that a virtuous circle can be created – that there are increasing returns to scale from investment. The more companies invest in, say, the training of their workforces, the greater the pool of skilled labour which is created for the use of the economy as a whole, and the greater the competitive pressure on other companies to ensure that their workforces are also properly trained. (There are, in the jargon, positive externalities of investment of this kind.) Thus the benefits of such investment are not just internal to the company which carries them out, but external, to the benefit of the economy as a whole.

The results of the work can hardly be said to add very much to the stock of knowledge which any intelligent business person has had for many years – namely, that investment in research and training is important to economic success – but for the discipline of economics, they represent a positive step.

Of course, investment by itself is not a guarantee of success. The work of Chandler, for example, shows the historical importance of management structures and skills, a finding reinforced by more recent work by researchers in business schools. But as an approximation, and bearing this qualification in mind, the assumption that the rate of growth of an economy at the macro-level depends upon investment is not unreasonable.

We are now in a position to draw together the various strands of our model, all of which are based on key features of the empirical data. We have noted that, over the course of the economic cycle, movements in growth and in unemployment are related, but that in the long-run the underlying relationship between them is indeterminate. This latter is a very important point which is simply not accounted for by orthodox economics, and which in consequence seriously misleads policy makers.

There is a similar relationship between profits and unemployment. During any particular economic cycle, movements in profits and unemployment are related, and these generate the pattern of regular fluctuations in unemployment which we observe for long periods in developed economies. But in the long-run, the relationship between them is indeterminate. The average level of investment is assumed in our model to be a fixed proportion of profits, and it is investment which determines the rate of growth of the economy.

The relationship between growth and profits is fixed, but since the relationship between profits and unemployment is not, the relationship between growth and unemployment cannot be fixed. So the LV model is able to account for a very important feature of the empirical data in developed economies, and one which is ignored by conventional macro-economics.

A great deal of public policy discussion on unemployment focuses on the need to increase growth in order to solve the problem. A variety of solutions is offered, both on the demand side of the economy in terms of the levels of public spending, rates of taxation and interest rates, and on the supply side, such as the belief that business in Europe is over-regulated and hence needs to be 'liberated' in order to fulfil its true growth potential.

In the short term, such policies may appear to work, in so far as they move the economy to a more favourable position on an ellipse moving around a given attractor point, of the kind represented in Figure 15. These, let us remember, are the stylised ellipses which emerge as the implications of our theoretical LV model. They are idealised represent-ations of the ellipses which actually exist in the empirical data. In practice, the ellipses which are traced around a given attractor point over the course of several cycles will all be different from one another. Even during periods of regular behaviour, some cycles may be shorter or longer than the average, or more or less intense in terms of the size of the fluctuations within them.

One of the reasons for the precise shape of any particular ellipse will be the mix of conventional economic policies which obtained during the course of that particular cycle. Such policies therefore still have a role, in that they can speed up the movement of the economy to a different point on the ellipse, or perhaps modify the size of the fluctuations which might otherwise have taken place.

But the real challenge facing policy makers, noted in Chapter 7, is not to accelerate movements on an ellipse around a given attractor point, or even to modify the shape of such an ellipse. Even if policies are success-ful in the short term in achieving these aims, the natural rhythms of the economy will eventually predominate, and unemployment will once again begin to rise during the course of the economic cycle.

The task is rather to alter the attractor point around which the ellipses move, so that permanent reductions in unemployment become possible. Without marked shifts in the position around which an economy moves over time, the average rate of unemployment over a period of years cannot be altered. For example, the charts in Chapter 7 which illustrate the current position of many European economies show that patterns of behaviour have developed which imply quite large fluctuations around very high average levels of unemployment. Without moving the attractor points of these ellipses in the charts, large, permanent reductions cannot be achieved.

This is not to say that policies directed at promoting growth should be abandoned. As we saw in Chapter 2, conventional economic measurements of growth need to be modified to take into account environmental and social factors. But, once this is done, growth can be beneficial, and contribute to an improvement in the human lot.

It is important to emphasise this point, for our intentions could easily be misunderstood. The fact that policy makers are currently misled into believing that higher growth will necessarily reduce unemployment does *not* mean that the pursuit of growth should cease to be a legitimate aim of public policy.

The underlying growth rate of the economy is determined by the rate of investment, which in turn depends upon the share of profits in national income. Economic policies to promote growth should therefore aim either to encourage a higher rate of investment for any given level of profitability, or to increase profits.

Governments have a range of policies for dealing with the former, from tax incentives for investment in new plant and machinery in industry, to policies designed to improve the quality of the labour force through training and education – in other words, to invest in people. Whether these policies are currently practised in many Western countries on a sufficient scale and/or are sufficiently well targeted to succeed in their aims is an open question. Nevertheless, most governments, and political parties in general, recognise the importance of having policies of this kind.

There is still often a confusion about what successful policies would achieve, with many policy makers believing that unemployment would fall. To emphasise again, maybe it would, and maybe it would not.

Increasing the growth rate does not necessarily reduce unemployment.

Far less attention is paid to the role of profits in determining growth. The neglect stems from the advice which policy makers receive from economists which, as we have seen, downgrades the importance of profitability *per se*. Yet achieving a higher rate of profit is at least as important a determinant of growth as promoting a higher level of investment out of a given level of profitability.

Of course, moving a step back from the level of approximation of our LV model, higher profits themselves do not always guarantee higher investment. An important issue at present, certainly in the Anglo-Saxon economies, as we noted in Chapter 3, is the extent to which short-term pressure from financial markets results in profits being paid out in the form of dividends rather than being reinvested in companies.

The classic goals of successful companies have been long-term profit and long-term growth – goals which were first established by American companies, which Japanese and German companies have retained to the present day, and which the rising economies of the Far East have certainly adopted. Policies designed to deal with the problem of short-termism in Britain and America will produce squeals of outrage from the financial community, on the grounds of interference with the sacred mechanism of the free market. This is the mechanism which, for example, conferred upon banks in both economies the right nearly to bankrupt themselves by catastrophic errors of judgment through speculating in the late 1980s, and then to hold industry to ransom through punitive interest rates in the early 1990s in order to rebuild their shattered balance sheets.

Such policies are quite straightforward to design. For example, any competent commercial lawyer could construct changes to company law which would make contested takeovers – an important feature of American and British financial markets, but almost unheard of in economies such as Japan and Germany – more difficult to carry out. In one sense, this would reduce the degree of competition in the economy, by making it more difficult for firms to be taken over on financial markets, and this is the argument which would be used. But as we saw in Chapter 4, the theory of competitive equilibrium, on which such arguments ultimately rest, has no real validity. As Keynes wrote almost sixty years ago, 'its teaching is misleading and disastrous if we attempt to apply it to the facts of experience'.

Of course, this does not mean that anti-competitive policies are always sensible. Each policy must be judged on its own specific merits, but it is not possible to appeal intellectually to the theory of competitive equilibrium for support in an argument. It is an empirical judgment as to whether the Anglo-Saxon economies would now be in stronger positions if the financial takeover madness of the 1980s, encouraged by financial deregulation, had not taken place, but in this particular instance it is a judgment which most people will make quite easily.

Regardless of the particular example under consideration, the profitability of industry is a target which should be far more prominent in public policy than it is at present, for raising profits is one way to achieve a higher rate of growth in the long run. And in the short run, higher profits do mean that less income is available to other sectors of the economy, and in particular to wage and salary earners, whose share of national income is by far the largest of any individual sector.

The model of the LV system is in many ways extremely simple. There is an equation to determine the growth of output, another for investment, and a third for real wage increases. (For interested readers, a mathematical description of the system is given in Appendix B.) Yet it is able to account for the key features of the behaviour of developed economies at the macro-level. Economies grow over time, and the LV model produces solutions in which growth takes place. Around any underlying growth rate, economies move in cycles, and the LV system generates such cycles. When a major shock takes place, such as the 1973–4 oil-price increases, the pattern of regular, cyclical behaviour is broken, and a period of irregular behaviour occurs, before economies settle into new, steady cycles. Again, LV models behave in this way. Finally, in practice higher economic growth does not necessarily, in the long-run, reduce unemployment, and LV models contain this effect.

The mathematical form is chosen deliberately in order for the theoretical model to be able to generate the key features of behaviour observed in the empirical data. And, importantly, the mathematical framework has a sensible economic interpretation. Each of the equations in the model, and the ways in which they interact, is justified at each stage by reference to economic evidence.

Instead of trying to derive a theory of macro-economic behaviour from beliefs about the behaviour of individuals and companies, we have treated the macro-economy as a system with its own behavioural properties, and have sought to construct a model to account for observed movements in the key variables. The process of analysis has not been driven by the *a priori* reasoning of conventional economic theory, but has been strongly guided by the data throughout.

The approach is very much in the spirit of the early classical economists, addressing issues of importance in contemporary political economy, and doing so analytically, but with constant reference to the evidence of the empirical data. In terms of its economic content, our model is in line with the thinking of the classicals, restoring profits and profitability to a central place in the understanding of developed macroeconomies, both in terms of growth itself and in terms of cycles around the growth path.

In catching up with the rest of the scientific world by using a non-linear methodology, the analysis discards the mechanical concept of equilibrium which pervades economics and which is responsible for so many of its shortcomings.

The basic LV system described above is a simplification of reality. And it has both mathematical and economic limitations. But it is capable of giving insights into the key determinants of growth and fluctuations in developed economies, and shows clearly that the direction of current efforts to reduce unemployment is quite misplaced.

CHAPTER 10

Economics Revisited

According to one's taste in conventional economic theology, policies in the 1990s designed to stimulate the level of demand in the economy, through for example increasing the level of public expenditure, either will or will not achieve their aim. The emphasis in the 1980s was very much weighted towards the monetarist perspective, which denies any long-term impact of such measures on the level of economic activity. But as we noted in Chapter 7, the election of President Clinton has led to a renewed interest among policy makers in managing the level of demand, albeit with a recognition that its scope is limited.

Those sympathetic to the efficacy of measures of this kind often look back with longing to the 1950s and 1960s, when it was widely believed that Keynesian policies of demand management not only worked, but were responsible for both the creation and the prolonged existence of full employment after the Second World War.

While demand management did have a role to play during this period of rapid growth and high employment, our LV model shows that other factors were even more important. Four points can be singled out. First, there was a high propensity for firms to invest out of profits. Second, the level of profits was felt by companies to justify the high level of investment. Third, behaviour in the labour market was underpinned by the prevailing social values. And, fourth, there was the effect of pure good fortune.

As noted in the previous chapter, when the Western economies, particularly those in Europe, emerged from the aftermath of the war and a period of strictly rationed consumption, there was an enormous pent-up demand for consumer products. Companies could carry out spending plans on investment, secure in the knowledge that ready markets existed for their products. Short-term demand management, tinkering with the temporary fluctuations in demand over the economic cycle, was in quantitative terms much less important than this massive, structural backlog of demand for consumer products.

The stable international economic framework which existed was important in underpinning the essential optimism of companies and of consumers. The post-war international monetary order, under the Bretton Woods system of fixed exchange rates discussed in Chapter 6, was an excellent example of the benefits of successful international co-operation. A stable environment encourages longer-term optimism and investment. But the role of chance, of the fortuitous circumstances in which the system began, should not be under-estimated.

By fortunate coincidence, the Western economies all emerged into normal peace-time economic activity in the early 1950s with low rates of inflation. There were differences in inflation rates across countries, but the fact that these were both small and around a very low average meant that undue pressure was not required in order to sustain the world monetary order of fixed exchange rates. Minor differences in inflation around a low absolute level could readily be accommodated within such a system.

No individual country, or group of countries, was therefore required to take on a burden of adjustment to bring its economy into line with the stronger performing economies, an adjustment which in the framework of orthodox economic policy would have involved measures designed to depress the economy and increase unemployment in order to reduce inflation. The experience of both the Gold Standard of the inter-war years and of the European ERM of the 1980s and early 1990s illustrates the problems which can be caused by international monetary agreements when some countries do have to make substantial adjustments.

The ERM had many of the characteristics of Bretton Woods, involving as it did the spirit of transnational co-operation and the framework of essentially fixed exchange rates between its member countries. The intentions of its supporters were wholly benign. Yet what was right for the world in the early 1950s was wrong for Western Europe in the 1980s. In the early 1980s economic conditions in the various Western European economies were far from convergence, as we saw in Chapter 6. Far more disparity between countries existed than had done thirty years previously, and prolonged periods of high interest rates proved necessary in many European countries to preserve the ERM framework, to the detriment of long-term confidence and expectations.

A second aspect of international co-operation, which contributed significantly to post-war prosperity, was the Marshall Plan, which involved extensive economic assistance to the war-shattered European continent from the powerful and intact economy of the United States. The plan was instituted by George Marshall when he was Secretary of

State in the Truman administration. Between 1948 and 1952 over $17 billion was given in aid to Western Europe, a truly enormous figure, equivalent to around $200 billion in today's terms. Recipients of the money were required to show their serious intent to co-operate rather than simply compete with each other, and it was during this period that the first steps were taken towards the eventual establishment of the European Community.

The Marshall Plan was undoubtedly the single most important factor which enabled the European economies to be launched on to a course of high growth. Without such assistance, short of dollars with which to finance its imports and with its capital stock of machinery, equipment and housing damaged by the war, Europe would undoubtedly have struggled for a number of years. The vision and generosity of America in these critical years brought enormous lasting benefits. But in an important sense, it was fortuitous that America at that time was willing to take on the task of helping European recovery, for such assistance would have been unlikely to have been forthcoming in the occasional isolationist spells of American history.

Against the background of a massive amount of aid in dollars to carry out restructuring in Europe, of a huge backlog of unmet consumer demand, and of international monetary stability, it is hardly surprising that the long-term expectations of companies were optimistic and that as a result investment was high. A virtuous circle was created in which consumers, too, became confident about the future, and continued to demand goods and services, which in turn justified further investment by industry.

Short-term management of the level of demand in an economy was very much a secondary factor when seen in this overall context. Economic cycles did exist in the 1950s and 1960s, but their amplitude, their movement from peak to trough, was very small compared to previous cycles in the historical experience of developed economies. As we argued in the previous chapter, if long-term expectations are optimistic, the cycle is likely to be weak, in contrast to the more uncertain conditions of the 1990s, in which people will react sharply to any change in their perceptions of longer-term prospects.

Behaviour in the labour market was important in sustaining the economic conditions of the 1950s and 1960s, in two ways. First, the workforce was content with the prosperity which was brought through economic growth, and did not engage in potentially debilitating struggles over the distribution of income between profits and wages. At the time, of course, in a number of countries, the workers were seen as being far from compliant. The 1950s British film *I'm All Right, Jack*, starring Peter Sellers, was a classic comedy, based on the theme of the intransigent and thoroughly unco-operative behaviour of trade unions. But whatever problems might have existed, the workforce did not attempt to erode profit margins permanently through their pay demands. As we saw in Chapter 6, such behaviour, and the resulting surge in inflation which would follow from it, was widely feared by economists in the 1940s as an adverse consequence of sustained full employment. But it did not happen, and companies were able to enjoy large profits, which justified the high levels of investment which they carried out.

The second point concerning labour market behaviour was that there genuinely was work for all. Groups in the workforce did not attempt to appropriate more and more of the proceeds of economic growth for themselves, as has happened in Europe in the past twenty years, thereby marginalising others into unemployment. We have seen that the LV model, reflecting reality in the developed economies, does not assume a relationship between the rate of economic growth and the rate of unemployment. For any given rate of growth, the average level of unemployment – the attractor point in our charts around which it moves – is indeterminate.

A perfectly feasible outcome for the Western economies in the postwar period would have involved a much higher average level of unemployment, with everything else remaining exactly the same: Marshall Plan, monetary stability, high investment, rapid growth. The sole difference would have been that those in employment would have become even better off than they did, at the expense of the unemployed. Even the rate of inflation would not necessarily have been affected, for we showed in Chapter 6 that the true relationship between inflation and unemployment involves the changes in these factors, and not their levels, so that a different positioning of the Phillips curve could have led to the same rates of inflation as were actually experienced.

It could be argued that, given the rapid rates of growth, there was a shortage of labour, and that this was the reason for full employment. Companies were desperate for workers, and would take on anyone willing to work. But as we saw in Chapter 7, different countries achieved quite different rates of growth with very similar rates of unemployment. Further, it was always open to those in employment to work longer hours in response to demand, thereby slowing down the process of the creation of new jobs.

A number of economies have preserved low levels of unemployment not just in the 1950s and 1960s, but after the 1973–4 oil shock until the present day. Japan, Austria, Norway, Switzerland and, until very recently, Sweden and Finland – all these countries have maintained for most of the post-war period very low levels of unemployment. And each in its particular way has exhibited a high degree of shared social values, of what may be termed social cohesion, a characteristic of almost all societies in which unemployment has remained low for long periods of time.

Like the elephant or the lobster, social cohesion is a difficult concept to define precisely, but, once seen, it is immediately recognisable. The social values in Western Europe after the war, for example, following a period of shared hardship and privation, were generally conducive to sharing the fruits of economic growth and to the preservation of high levels of employment. Of course, policy cannot march to the banging of an antique drum, and the decades immediately following the war represented a particular historical episode which no amount of nostalgia can restore.

But the countries which have continued to maintain low unemployment have maintained a sector of the economy which effectively functions as an employer of last resort, which absorbs the shocks which occur from time to time, and more generally makes employment available to the less skilled, the less qualified. There is, of course, a cost associated with this concept, but it is a cost which societies with a high degree of social cohesion have been willing to pay.

In Japan, this shock-absorber has been the domestic service sector. Japanese manufacturing, competing in world markets, is formidably efficient, but the domestic service sector – travel, restaurants, leisure activities and so on – employs far more people than comparable companies and industries elsewhere in the West. In September 1993, the *Financial Times* carried a back-page interview in which Gary Lineker, the former England soccer captain who went to play in Japan, was featured as the 'man of the week'. Asked about the main differences between soccer in Japan and soccer in Europe, Mr Lineker gave a very astute answer, in two parts. The first part, about aspects of the game itself, was immediately forgettable. The second part was not. The other main difference, he said, was that in Japan clubs employed far more people in their offices;

that was 'the way in which I suppose they keep unemployment down'. Similarly, in Japanese restaurants, for example, many people are employed to carry out what often seem to visitors to the country to be trivial or even pointless tasks. But whether it is soccer clubs, restaurants or whatever, the costs of all these people appear on the bill which is presented to the consumer of the services.*

The Japanese have been willing to pay for the cost of a low-productivity, private, domestic service industry. In the smaller European economies which have maintained low unemployment, the function of employer of last resort has been carried out by the public service sector, the costs of which appear less in the expense of private consumption than in high levels of taxation. Whether through high prices for private services or high taxes for public services, there is a cost of maintaining such sectors of an economy which is willingly accepted by countries with a high degree of social cohesion. In other words, the social values in these countries are such that everyone is granted a stake in society, and the opportunity to participate through employment in the gains of economic growth.

In both the Japanese and the Scandinavian cases, though by very different means, the electorates have been willing to pay for high employment, for social cohesion, by permitting sectors of the economy which by the standards of free-market individualism are inefficient.

The overall efficiency and performance of such economies has not been handicapped at all by paying the cost of their various types of social values. Japan, of course, has outstripped every other developed country in terms of growth, and the smaller European countries outside the European Community have generated growth rates at least equal to those within the EC. The power of markets has been harnessed to the wider benefit of society.

The idea of a strong, broadly shared, set of community values is compatible with a range of ideological positions. It can exist equally well under governments of the centre-right and of the centre-left. It is by no means an automatic recipe for high taxation and state interference.

The classical economists, for example, understood the potential power of market economies in practice, but they also understood the vital

---

*A friend of mine assures me that in one of the most exclusive restaurants in Tokyo a person is even employed with the sole function of reviving foreigners who have fainted when confronted with their bill.

significance of the moral climate in which economies operated. Adam Smith's message in particular has been grotesquely distorted over the past 200 years. As we saw in the first part of the book, the overall moral framework in which individuals acted was of enormous importance to him. The state had an important duty to promote and enhance such a framework, both intellectually and culturally. The idea, dear to Mrs Thatcher's heart, that there is 'no such thing as society' is quite alien to this view of the world.

In fact, one of the most effective manifestations of social cohesion is Christian Democracy in Europe, a tradition under siege from the relentless pressure of the value system of free-market economic theory, of the attempt to convert market economies into market societies, in which every transaction, every act of social intercourse, must take place within the nexus of cash and of self-interested individualism. Based upon the Catholic concept of All Souls, it is best symbolised by the word 'solidarity', a word which conveys a quite different meaning in most European languages than it does in English, where its overtones are of massed ranks of undifferentiated workers confronting the employer on the picket line. Christian Democratic solidarity represents a recognition of rights and obligations at all levels of society, something the landed gentry who ran the British Conservative Party for much of its history understood perfectly well. Above all, this tradition recognises that there is such a thing as society, and that human welfare is not maximised by the ruthless pursuit of individual self-interest.

Innovation, entrepreneurship and profits are still essential. Economic competition exists on a global scale, and economies must be equipped for it. But economic success can be achieved, and achieved more successfully, within a broader and more beneficial framework than that driven by the pure, individual rationality of the economics textbooks.

An alternative approach to Europe's unemployment problems is the American model of 'flexible' labour markets – or, in other words, the removal of as many restrictions as possible on the operation of free-market forces.

Over the post-war period as a whole, the United States economy appears to have had an attractor point for unemployment of around 6 per cent. There is considerable variation around this, but the American economy does not stay for very long at unemployment rates below 3 or 4 per cent, or above 8 or 9 per cent. This average level is low by current standards in most of Europe, but high compared to those of the 1950s and 1960s.

Many Europeans, while admiring the strength and power of the American economy, undoubtedly feel that the system of social values which prevails in the United States, manifested in the acute problems evident in the inner cities and the level of violent crime, for example, leaves much to be desired.

As we have seen, in Europe the current debate about employment centres on deregulation of labour markets and the reduction of the level of involvement by the state. But in many ways this is very much a second-order issue in terms of the flexibility of labour markets. By far the most effective way to bring about 'flexibility' – in the American sense – in the labour markets of Western Europe would be to open the borders to migration from Eastern Europe and North Africa. A constant supply of labour of this kind has been an important factor in the behaviour of the labour market in America.

The American system of social values and social relationships permits this kind of a solution. Within this framework, it may be hard to get unemployment down to very low levels, but equally the system for many decades now has prevented unemployment from rising to very high levels, even though an adverse consequence has been a rejection by many of the low wages which are on offer to the unskilled, and the choice of crime as a career instead.

In most of Western Europe, as we have seen, in the past two decades the proceeds of growth have been appropriated entirely by those in employment, to the exclusion of the unemployed. The collective con-sequences of the individual actions of those in employment set firm limits to the scope for reducing unemployment through conventional demand management techniques, or even through the more recently fashionable concepts of supply-side policies.

In such circumstances, conventional economic policies can at best move an economy around the ellipse which surrounds a given attractor point – in other words, they can alter the course of the economy over the cycle, while not affecting its average performance over the cycle as a whole. In contrast, a constant theme of this book has been the need to make the intellectual leap which grasps that behaviour at the macro-level of any system with any degree of complexity cannot be deduced by simply adding together the actions of its component parts.

Once this leap has been made, it is easier to appreciate the nature of the problem in Western Europe. Whatever the motives of individuals in employment, their behaviour in aggregate has meant that they form a cartel which excludes the unemployed from the benefits of economic growth.

So what can be done? One solution to the problem of high European unemployment, for example, is work-sharing. This could take the form of a shorter working week, or shorter working year in general, or specific arrangements to share jobs. More imaginatively still, it could even take the form of several years off work at certain points in the life-cycle, such as when one's children are young.

Provided that sufficient people already in employment were willing to accept the consequent greater leisure and lower pay – and after all, the patterns of employment envisaged by this proposal are very similar to those already adopted by many women in Western Europe – large numbers of the unemployed in Europe could be brought back into employment.

A substantial part of the labour force would still remain in 'conventional' full-time employment,* but existing female patterns of employment would extend across the labour force – to men as well, in other words – thus dramatically reducing unemployment.

This solution would require many people in employment to surrender income in exchange for leisure, and would entail a broad shift in social values. Keynes considered the same solution in the *General Theory*, arguing that: 'A point comes where every individual weighs the advantages of increased leisure against increased income. But at present the evidence is, I think, strong that the great majority of individuals would prefer increased income to increased leisure.' His only objection to the policy was that, at the levels of income which obtained in the 1930s, the solution was 'premature'. In the circumstances of the 1990s, at much higher average levels of real income, it is a policy whose time has come.

The existence and development of social norms are issues which have more typically been addressed by sociologists than by economists. Sociologists have always focused upon behaviour at the aggregate level, on analysing social norms and social conventions.

---

*The word 'conventional' is placed in inverted commas, because there is no unique definition of what constitutes full-time employment. It is a concept which, as we have seen, is changing all the time. In the living memory of many Europeans, it was regarded as normal that people should expect to work at least fifty hours a week for at least fifty weeks a year for at least fifty years.

The recognition that aggregate behaviour of systems can be qualitatively different to that implied by its individual components taken separately has been made by many other disciplines. Environmentalists emphasised from the outset the fundamental interdependencies and complex feedbacks which exist in the world's economy. Increasingly, the mathematical tools of non-linearity required to analyse such phenomena are applied in sciences such as biology, chemistry and physics, enabling deep new insights to be obtained. The implications for economic analysis are profound.

For all its apparent mathematical sophistication, the core model of theoretical economics, that of competitive general equilibrium, is premised upon an entirely faulty view of the modern world. Behavioural precepts derived from an autonomous, deterministic individual on a desert island, the idealised Rational Economic Man of economic theory, will not apply to human beings *en masse* in a large, modern economy.

The macro-behaviour of modern economies is a legitimate study in its own right, and the behaviour of such economies is most unlikely to be derived from the extrapolation of individual maximising behaviour to the aggregate scale.

In a complex non-linear system such as the macro-behaviour of modern economies, there are certain threshold values of the various factors in the system above or below which the behaviour of the system as a whole is transformed dramatically in a short space of time. For example, as we have seen, once the true, underlying relationship between inflation and unemployment is identified, the potential for such shifts can be seen as a fundamental part of the system. Similarly, the pattern of unemployment in Western economies over time consists of cyclical movements of near regularity, but whose pattern can be altered rapidly by shocks to the system.

The whole challenge of economic policy is to shift the attractor points around which economies move, and hence the whole solution path of the economy over time. This is so whether inflation or unemployment is the target of policy.

The traditional instruments of macro-economic policy, such as tax rates, public expenditure changes and so forth, are only a very narrow part of the spectrum of policies which need to be considered in order to achieve these radical shifts.

Keynes looked forward to the day when economists would have the same status as dentists – not, as this book might have seemed to suggest, in their capacity to engender fear in their patients, but rather as adjusters of minor problems in a well-ordered system.

Most conventional macro-economic policy falls into this category, of minor adjustments, although the temptation cannot be resisted to note that many of the economic policies of the 1980s seem to have had as much subtlety as the practice of extracting a tooth by tying it to a door handle and slamming the door shut.

A key feature of non-linear systems is that the behaviour of the system as a whole can be sensitive to variations in the overall environment. Over the course of time, the system possesses many potential solution paths. Any actual path which is observed, from the myriad potential paths which could have been followed, will not correspond, except by the purest of coincidences, to the one which would have been chosen by the globally optimal maximising behaviour of 'rational' individuals.

This potential sensitivity has yet another implication. The derivation of general laws for the control and benefit of the system, which are valid everywhere and at all times, becomes difficult if not impossible, thus negating the arrogant claim of the general equilibrium model of economics.

A change in one particular factor of importance at a certain time, given particular values for the other key factors, will have certain consequences. But the results may be quite different if the same change is made at another point in time, when slightly different values of other factors obtain. The particular history of the system, and the context in which the change is made, are of great importance.

Economic historians have long understood this proposition intuitively. The monumental work of Alfred Chandler, for example, points to the fact that the path which an economy follows can be very sensitive to a particular decision or set of decisions at a specific point in time. Once the economy has embarked upon this path, there is no tendency for it to revert to a natural equilibrium. The consequences of key decisions, whether for good or for ill, can persist for decades.

Recognition of economies as inherently non-linear systems enhances dramatically our potential to understand their behaviour. Yet, paradoxically, at the same time, it limits the degree of control to which we can ever aspire. Here we must ask ourselves, what kind of subject is economics?

Take the example of physics. A large body of theoretical knowledge exists as to how the world operates, validated not just in the laboratory, but through everyday applications. In this discipline, most data series available to scholars are pure, in the sense of being effectively free from measurement error. Typically, large numbers of observations on the phenomenon being investigated are available. And the experiment can be repeated, time after time if necessary.

In such a discipline, not only should the level of understanding of the data be high, but accurate predictions should be able to be made by any successful theory.

In contrast, the study of history is not expected to yield any framework in which successful predictions can be made. From time to time, schools of thought arise which claim this ability, but their record makes even economists seem like skilled clairvoyants.

The emphasis in history is on understanding and accounting for events after they have happened. A good physicist must rely on ex-ante prediction for his or her theory to be validated. A good historian relies on ex-post analysis.

Of the many difficulties faced by the historian but not by the physicist, three stand out. First, the data available to the historian contain errors, and are usually incomplete. The task, for example, of understanding Europe in the Dark Ages is handicapped severely by the fragmentary nature of the evidence. Second, human history has happened only once. It is not possible to unscramble events to see what really would have happened if Napoleon had won the battle of Waterloo, an essay challenge in which distinguished historians competed in the early years of this century. And third, human society, particularly in the political sphere, constitutes a non-linear system of unusual complexity, in some ways far more complex than the physical world. Large numbers of factors can be important at any point in time.

Economics might be thought to share many of the characteristics of history, but there do appear to be sufficient regularities in the data and a sufficiently small number of centrally important factors to enable systematic economic analysis and prediction to be important.

Rather than resembling history, economics is perhaps more akin to subjects such as palaeontology, astronomy and climatology. The data are incomplete, subject to error, and there is only one actual history available for study. Much of the work in these disciplines consists of careful collection and sifting of the data, building theories around the facts from the outset, rather than pursuing abstract theories on how a rational world ought to operate.

Despite the inherent difficulties of analysis, palaeontologists have discovered a truly fundamental law, the law of natural selection, which operates in the background of all biological situations. And the use of non-linear mathematical techniques, among other things, has decisively improved climatologists' understanding of the world's weather systems.

Another characteristic economics shares with these sciences is that from time to time external shocks are of crucial significance. Natural selection, for example, is the key determinant of biological events in normal conditions. But when the planet is struck by an enormous meteor, bringing destruction on a hemispherical or even global scale, survival of a species can simply be a matter of chance.

Shocks of this magnitude, by their very nature, are extremely hard if not impossible to predict. So there is inherent uncertainty in our ability to predict the future.

But by the rejection of the concepts of orthodox economics, of 'rational' behaviour in a mechanical, linear world of equilibrium, progress can begin to be made to a more powerful understanding of how economies behave, and, through this, to an improvement in human welfare.

This idea, that the human lot could be bettered through scientific analysis, motivated the great, classical political economists. It is also the idea which has motivated this book, and its illustrative use of the potential of non-linear systems analysis.

But perhaps the most important point of all, linked though it is to the underlying mathematics, must be stated in words, for it is a question of moral values. The concept, rampant in the free-market philosophy of the 1980s, that there is no such thing as society is one which, if it is allowed to persist, will prevent the creation of full employment regardless of the form which economic policy takes.

Behaviour of the system in aggregate cannot be deduced by simply summing up the behaviour of its individual component parts.

The promotion of the concept that the untrammelled, self-sufficient, competitive individual will maximise human welfare damages deeply the possibility of ever creating a truly affluent, cohesive society in which everyone can participate.

The historical tradition of Western political parties, other than those of the extreme right or left, recognises and understands the importance of this point. But it is a tradition which is being eroded by the idea that the operation of a market economy is incompatible with collective responsibilities. The name of Adam Smith is regularly invoked by those who subscribe to this latter concept.

But Adam Smith was a philosopher as well as an economist, famous in his time as much for his *Theory of Moral Sentiments* as for *The Wealth of Nations*. And as he understood so well, society *is* more than the sum of its individual parts.

Appendix A

Statistical analysis of the relationship between inflation and unemployment, 1952–92*

Essentially, in only one country out of the eleven examined in Figure 1 are both inflation and unemployment stationary series over the 1952–92 period, and, further, no co-integrating vector exists between them in the ten countries where this is not the case. The sole exception is the United States, but a regression of inflation on unemployment, in levels or logs, current or lagged, gives positive and often insignificant coefficient on unemployment.

In contrast, the change in inflation and the change in unemployment are stationary series. (All tests were carried out using the UROOT option in the TSP statistical package.)

Regressions of the change in inflation on the change in unemployment, 1953–92

All the regressions include a constant term. In each of them, the constant is a very long way from being statistically significantly different from zero, and hence is not reported.

The dependent variable in each of the regressions is the first difference of the log of the consumer price index. The explanatory variable is the first difference of the unemployment rate lagged one period in Germany, the Netherlands, Canada and the United States; the first difference of the log of the unemployment rate in Italy and Japan, and this latter variable lagged one period in Belgium, France, Sweden, Australia and the UK.

*The results are discussed in detail in my paper in *Unemployment in Europe*, Jonathan Michie and John Grieve-Smith (eds.), Academic Press, London, 1994.

Country	Coefficient and standard error on unemployment variable	$\bar{R}^2$	Q(3)
Germany	−0.009 (0.004)	0.085	5.93
France	−0.071 (0.039)	0.056	0.97
Italy	−0.061 (0.029)	0.084	0.88
Belgium	−0.024 (0.013)	0.064	5.00
Netherlands	−0.005 (0.003)	0.037	14.13
UK	−0.078 (0.017)	0.342	2.47
Sweden	−0.070 (0.016)	0.311	2.38
United States	−0.010 (0.002)	0.323	3.47
Japan	−0.159 (0.040)	0.271	1.16
Australia	−0.074 (0.018)	0.296	3.95
Canada	−0.009 (0.002)	0.389	1.44

Q(3) is the Box-Ljung test statistic of the null hypothesis of white-noise residuals from one through three lags, which has a chi-square distribution with three degrees of freedom.

All these equations except Italy and Australia satisfy a formal F-test for a structural break in each year from 1960 through 1982 and Japan just fails in 1975. There is a general tendency for the absolute value of the coefficient on the unemployment variable to be higher in the 1974–92 period than in the 1953–73 period, but not significantly so.

In the unrestricted form of these equations, in which inflation is regressed on inflation lagged, and current and lagged levels or logs of levels of unemployment, and/or the latter variables lagged one period, the hypothesis of no structural break in 1974 is decisively rejected for all countries. The sole exception is the United States, where the equation specified in this form is almost identical to the restricted equation reported above.

Appendix B

This appendix outlines briefly the mathematical specification of the LV model discussed in Chapter 9.

The following symbols are used:

α annual average rate of growth of labour productivity
β annual average rate of growth of labour supply
δ rate of depreciation of capital stock
μ proportion of profits invested
σ ratio of capital stock to output
θ responsiveness of real wage demands to unemployment

The basic system of differential equations is given by:

$$e'/e = \mu(1-w)/(\sigma - \delta - \alpha - \beta)$$
$$w'/w = \theta(e - e^*)$$
$$u = 1 - e$$

where e is employment as a proportion of the labour force, w is the share of wages in national output, and u is unemployment as a proportion of the labour force. The symbol ' indicates differentiation with respect to time, and e^* is the average rate of employment over the course of the cycle.

The equations do not determine the scale of time, and an appropriate scaling factor is required to obtain solutions measured in terms of years.

By way of example, values of the parameters which give an approximation of the British economy in the post-war period of full employment from 1948 to 1973 are as follows: $\alpha = 0.023$, $\beta = 0.007$, $\delta = 0.015$, $\mu = 0.486$, $\theta = 1.5$, $\sigma = 3.64 - 0.014*T$, $e^* = 0.989 - 0.00036*T$, where T is time measured in years from 1948 onwards, and where the time scaling factor = 3. The initial conditions in 1948 are e = 0.99 and w = 0.66.

Selected and Annotated Bibliography

The purpose of this section is not to set out every single academic article which either is or could have been cited in the text to support the points which are made. Rather, it is to provide a selection of the works which the interested reader might want to follow up in the first instance.

From Chapter 1, the book *Liar's Poker* by Michael Lewis (Coronet Books, 1990) is a very amusing inside account of how financial markets actually operate. Particularly given the pretensions of many of those who work in such markets, this book is highly recommended.

Readers interested in Adam Smith should read him in the original. A number of editions of *The Wealth of Nations* are available. Similarly, both David Ricardo and J. M. Keynes can be read directly in the original texts, namely and respectively, *The Principles of Political Economy and Taxation* and *The General Theory of Employment, Interest and Money*. Karl Marx is far more difficult to penetrate, and interested readers would be advised to read Chapter 1 of Angus Maddison's *Phases of Capitalist Development* (Oxford University Press, 1982) and the various references given there before even attempting to read Marx in the original. Maddison's book is interesting in its own right for the broad, quantitative sweep of economic history which it provides.

In terms of environmental analysis, the specific questions which arise in attempting to measure the impact of such factors on the rate of economic growth are well covered in the 1972 work by James Tobin and Bill Nordhaus ('Is Growth Obsolete?' in *Economic Growth*, National Bureau of Economic Research General Series, no. 96E, New York: Columbia University Press), and in the more recent book by Herman Daly and John Cobb, *For the Common Good* (Green Print, London, 1990).

The overall philosophy and analytical approach of the broader environmental perspective are set out very clearly in the original work of the Limits to Growth team, *The Limits to Growth* (Universe Books, New York, 1972) by Dennis and Donella Meadows, Jørgen Randers and William Behrens.

For an appreciation both of the potential usefulness of conventional economics in dealing with environmental questions and of its limitations, the book by Partha Dasgupta and Geoff Heal is recommended, although the non-mathematical reader will find it difficult (*Economic Theory and Exhaustible Resources*, Oxford University Press, 1979).

The academic literature on the theory of competitive equilibrium is not really accessible to the to the non-mathematical reader. A clear and succinct overview, with many further references, is given in the paper by Darrell Duffie and Hugo Sonnenschein, 'Arrow and General Equilibrium Theory' (*Journal of Economic Literature*, vol. XXVII, June 1989). The 1993 paper by Joaquim Silvestre in the same journal is also worth reading ('The Market Power Foundations of Macro-economic Policy', vol. XXXI, March 1993).

The paper by John von Neumann which established rigorously the existence of conditions for competitive equilibrium is available in English ('A Model of General Economic Equilibrium', *Review of Economic Studies*, vol. 13, 1945–6), this is, however, particularly challenging mathematically. Roy Radner's paper, 'Competitive Equilibrium under Uncertainty' (*Econometrica*, vol. 36, 1968) is perhaps the single most devastating technical critique of the concept of general equilibrium. Worth reading, too, are the papers by David Newbery and Joseph Stiglitz ('The Choice of Techniques and the Optimality of Market Equilibrium with Rational Expectations', *Journal of Political Economy*, vol. 90, 1982) and by Kelvin Lancaster and Richard Lipsey ('The General Theory of the Second Best', *Review of Economic Studies*, December 1956). All these papers require varying degrees of mathematical ability on the part of the reader.

The wide-ranging work of Alfred Chandler (*Scale and Scope: The Dynamics of Industrial Capitalism*, Harvard University Press, 1990) gives an account of economic development in America, Britain and Germany in the period 1880–1950. The wealth of evidence presented offers a deep criticism of the theory of the firm in orthodox economics.

A large amount of material is becoming available on the process of development in the Far East. The article by Rajendra Sisodia is an interesting description of the relative roles of the public sector and of free markets in the expansion of Singapore ('Singapore Invests in the Nation-Corporation', *Harvard Business Review*, May–June 1992).

Criticisms of the conspicuous consumption ethos of the 1980s are now widespread. Many of these, including the term 'conspicuous consumption' itself, were made in Thorsten Veblen's 1899 book *The Theory of the Leisure Class*, which is available in paperback editions.

The empirical performances of macro-economic forecasting groups around the world are summarised in the June 1993 edition of the OECD's regular publication *Economic Outlook*. A typical example of the range of differences which still exists in estimates of the impacts of various policy measures provided by conventional models is provided by K. B. Church et al., 'Comparative Properties of Models of the UK Economy' (*National Institute Economic Review*, London, August 1993).

The use of the methodological techniques of behavioural sciences to test the basic axioms of economic theory is, encouragingly, growing. One of the most damaging recent articles is by Graham Loomes, Chris Starmer and Robert

Sugden ('Observing Violations of Transitivity by Experimental Methods', *Econometrica*, vol. 59, 1991), which shows that individual preferences are not always internally consistent.

In terms of the relationship between inflation and unemployment, the original paper by Bill Phillips is worth reading, particularly for the care with which the data are examined, ('The Relationship Between Unemployment and the Rate of Change of Money Wages in the UK 1861–1957', *Economica*, vol. 25, 1958). The two other classics in this area are the paper by Paul Samuelson and Robert Solow ('Analytical Aspects of Anti-inflation Policy', *American Economic Review*, vol. L, no. 2, May 1960) and the attack on the concept of the Phillips curve made by Milton Friedman ('The Role of Monetary Policy', *American Economic Review*, vol. LVIII, 1968).

Interesting and non-technical accounts of complex systems are given in two books, both with the title *Complexity*. Both are recommended. The book by Mitchell Waldrop (Simon and Schuster, USA, 1992) deals more explicitly with some of the economic work in this area, whilst Roger Lewin's book (Phoenix, Orion Books, 1993) perhaps conveys more clearly the pervasive nature of the concept of complexity.

Much of the original work on complex systems was carried out by Ilya Prigogine, and his book with Gregoire Nicolis (*Exploring Complexity*, W. H. Freeman, New York, 1989) is highly recommended, although it might prove difficult for the non-mathematical reader.

Economists are beginning to show interest in the ideas of non-linear systems, and may find inspiration in, for example, the books of Howell Tong (*Non-linear Time Series: A Dynamical Systems Approach*, Oxford Scientific Publications, Clarendon Press, 1990) and J. D. Murray (*Mathematical Biology*, Springer-Verlag, Berlin, 1990). Neither of these books is suitable for the general reader.

Passages from *A Glasgow Gang Observed* and *Liar's Poker* are reprinted by kind permission of the publishers.

Index